MANAGING IN THE MIDDLE

ALA GUIDES FOR THE BUSY LIBRARIAN

MANAGING IN THE MIDDLE

THE LIBRARIAN'S HANDBOOK

EDITED BY ROBERT FARRELL AND
KENNETH SCHLESINGER

an imprint of the American Library Association

Chicago | 2013

ROBERT FARRELL has served as coordinator of information literacy and assessment at Lehman College, City University of New York, since 2008. He received his BA in philosophy from Columbia University in 1999, an MLS from SUNY Buffalo in 2002, and an additional MA from the CUNY Graduate Center in 2010. Over the past decade, Professor Farrell has worked in libraries at Columbia and CUNY, managing at various levels. His research interests include library management, the phenomenology of professional skill acquisition, and information-seeking behaviors as well as a variety of topics in philosophy.

KENNETH SCHLESINGER has been chief librarian at Lehman College, City University of New York, since 2007. Previously he was director of media services at LaGuardia Community College and also worked in the archival collections of Thirteen/WNET and Time Inc. Professor Schlesinger has an MLS in information and library science from Pratt Institute, an MFA in dramaturgy and dramatic criticism from Yale School of Drama, and a BA in dramatic art from University of California, Berkeley. His research and publication interests include library management, performing arts collections, digital preservation, and international libraries.

Extensive effort has gone into ensuring the reliability of the information in this book; however, the publisher makes no warranty, express or implied, with respect to the material contained herein.

ISBNs: 978-0-8389-1161-7 (paper); 978-0-8389-9637-9 (PDF); 978-0-8389-9638-6 (ePub); 978-0-8389-9639-3 (Kindle). For more information on digital formats, visit the ALA Store at alastore.ala.org and select eEditions.

Library of Congress Cataloging-in-Publication Data
Managing in the middle / edited by Robert Farrell and Kenneth Schlesinger.
   pages cm
 Includes bibliographical references and index.
 ISBN 978-0-8389-1161-7
1. Library administrators. 2. Communication in library administration. 3. Middle managers. I. Farrell, Robert (Professor) II. Schlesinger, Kenneth.
 Z682.4.A34M36 2013
 025.1—dc23   2012027380

Book design in Big Noodle, Museo Sans, and Classic Round typefaces.
Series cover design by Casey Bayer. Cover image ©leedsn/Shutterstock, Inc.

♾ This paper meets the requirements of ANSI/NISO Z39.48-1992 (Permanence of Paper).

Printed in the United States of America

17 16 15 14 13   5 4 3 2 1

ALA Editions purchases fund advocacy, awareness, and accreditation programs for library professionals worldwide.

PART I. MIDDLE MANAGEMENT 101

PART II. THE MIDDLE GROUND

ADVANCED SKILLS

PERFORMANCE MANAGEMENT

PROFESSIONAL CHALLENGES

PART III. EMPOWERMENT

LEADERSHIP

CAREER DEVELOPMENT

THE WORK OF THE MIDDLE MANAGER IN LIBRARIES AND OTHER INFORMATION ORGA-nizations is among the most challenging. Successful middle managers must be effective leaders and highly competent managers in order to handle competing expectations and demands. As they implement the directives set forth by senior management, middle managers must engage and inspire staff to perform to the best of their ability. They must be skilled in influencing others, both vertically (subordinate staff *and* senior management) and horizontally (peers across the library organization). The middle manager role is critical to the success of the library.

In addition to creating a work environment in which everyone is motivated to perform at the highest level, successful middle managers must also be able to prepare staff for new challenges that are certain to arise from the many changes occurring in the larger ecosystem in which libraries operate. These changes often prompt a rethinking of directives, a redesign of the work, and even new ideas for how staff should perform their work. The middle manager must recognize and embrace the need to learn and develop in the role.

Most individuals who are appointed or promoted to a middle management role have little or no experience in managerial work or leadership, especially in leading a diverse group of staff to perform day-to-day tasks and embrace new challenges. They must learn on the job. Luckily, most who assume this responsibility in today's libraries are eager to learn so they can become effective as soon as possible; they enter the middle manager role ready to work with staff and to ensure the best performance possible.

Often, the only resource available to help and guide the new middle manager is the person to whom the manager reports. There are many resources available on effective management and leadership—books, articles, tool kits, webinars, and websites—but there has not been a single resource of principles and practices for the middle manager in a library organization. *Managing in the Middle: The Librarian's Handbook* now fills that void.

This handbook is a compendium of articles contributed by a diverse group of authors, each of whom brings both strong knowledge of the topic and a wealth of practical ideas for effective practice. The articles include basic information about the traditional practice of management, best practices for managerial leadership, and interviews with middle managers and selected experts in the library field. *Managing in the Middle* also includes topics not usually found in resources on this role, such as social networking, avoiding procrastination, managing perceptions, and surviving layoffs.

This handbook is an essential resource for both the novice and the experienced middle manager. It provides guiding principles, best practices, and numerous practical tips for the effective execution of this critical role. High-level performance by the middle managers in our organizations is essential to our future. They lead and guide the staff, who in turn deliver the services so essential to our ability to make a difference for our customers. The editors and authors of this excellent volume have created a significant resource aimed at new and not-so-new middle managers for effective day-to-day practice and for ongoing professional development and personal success.

Maureen Sullivan
ALA President

C ONTEMPORARY MIDDLE MANAGEMENT HAS BEEN STEREOTYPED BY A VARIETY OF often competing historical characterizations. The "heroic" portrait of middle managers painted by authors such as Alfred Chandler has faded and given way to visions of the middle manager as organizational functionary, symbol of corporate "bloat" and "excess," or even buffoon—think of the character David Brent in the television show *The Office*. But the truth is that middle managers are more essential to organizational success now than at any time in the past (*Economist* 2011; Osterman 2009).

In his comprehensive study *The Truth about Middle Managers* (2009), Paul Osterman writes:

> As a group, middle managers are central, indeed crucial, to an organization's success. Middle managers perform much of the day-to-day work of the organization, but beyond this, they are much like general managers in that they are responsible for making many of the judgment calls and trade-offs that shape the . . . [organization's] success. They are also the key communications channel from senior management down through the ranks. They are committed to their work and, with their craft orientation, strive to perform at a high-level (170).

This is no less true in libraries than in other types of organizations. There are several excellent books written by individual authors that provide management advice for librarians (Gordon 2004) or focus on library middle managers (Mosley 2004, 2008). This handbook is different. We sought to "crowdsource" the collective wisdom of practicing library middle managers, experienced senior managers, and those who experience middle management firsthand—paralibrarians and others who are supervised—then compiled a collection of ideas that can be drawn or reflected on in a variety of situations.

Building on Osterman's insight into the "craft orientation" of today's middle managers, we adopt the view that middle management is a skill comprising skills. We believe that these competencies, which together embody the craft of middle management, are learnable. As the contributors to this book make clear, leadership, effective organization, sound communication practices—even emotional intelligence—are not inborn traits. They are habits of action and mind that any middle manager can learn.

And who better to learn from than those who have honed their skills on the frontlines of public and academic libraries?

The topics covered here are both timely and timeless, but many can be traced back to shifts in middle management theory and practice that occurred in the late 1980s and early 1990s. Maureen Sullivan's visionary work from that period on the future of library middle management in academic libraries might be read as almost an outline for many of the topics covered in this volume. Drawing on the management literature of the day, she calls for a "transformation of the middle manager's role" in research libraries (Sullivan 1992, 270).

The future library middle manager she describes will need to focus on "managing relationships" and become a "network facilitator of information," "translating goals into action." She will need to assume the role of "coach" and team builder "in which the manager is both a delegator and a doer, a strategist and an operator, and a long-range planner as well as an immediate implementer." She will need to be an "innovator or 'idea entrepreneur,'" as adept at "performance" management as she is at process improvement (1992, 270, 275, 277).

The case studies, practical guides, and personal reflections that constitute this book reflect the prescience of Sullivan's thinking and are grouped into three main sections:

- "Middle Management 101" provides insights into everyday practices of contemporary library middle management. In addition to chapters that focus on the basics of starting out in middle management, these contributors offer guidance on essential issues related to communication and emotional intelligence.

- The "Middle Ground" focuses on advanced middle management skills including project planning, productivity, performance management, and working with senior management.

- The final section, "Empowerment," provides guidance to middle managers looking to develop leadership in themselves and others. Topics include developing a leadership style, mentoring and team building, guidance on what to do if you or those you manage plateau, and how to handle "battlefield promotions" to senior management.

As Sally Decker Smith notes in her interview for this book, "All of us are smarter than any of us." This has been our guiding motto as we conceived, developed, and now share this work.

REFERENCES

Economist. 2011. "In Praise of David Brent." *Economist* 400 (8748): 56.

Gordon, Rachel Singer. 2004. *The Accidental Library Manager.* Medford, NJ: Information Today.

Mosley, Pixey Anne. 2004. *Transitioning from Librarian to Middle Manager.* Westport, CT: Libraries Unlimited.

———. 2008. *Staying Successful as a Middle Manager.* Westport, CT: Libraries Unlimited.

Osterman, Paul. 2009. *The Truth about Middle Managers: Who They Are, How They Work, Why They Matter.* Boston, MA: Harvard Business School Publishing.

Sullivan, Maureen. 1992. "The Changing Role of the Middle Manager in Research Libraries." *Library Trends* 41 (2): 269–281.

PART I

MIDDLE MANAGEMENT 101

1

IT'S A JOB, NOT A REWARD!

GAYLE HORNADAY

CONGRATULATIONS! YOU HAVE JUST BEEN HIRED AS A MIDDLE MANAGER, AND you're excited and happy to be moving into a new position. This is an important step in the advancement of your career and an early success that, you hope, will be one of many. But success is a continuing process, not an endpoint. You will constantly need to work on understanding your organization, your position, and what you need to do to be effective. You can be pretty sure that your new job is not a prize you've won for your last good deed, or for being so much "better" than the other candidates. Your past accomplishments simply demonstrate you may be capable of taking on the responsibilities of the new job description. Getting the job is only the first step of many tasks ahead of you.

Whether you have been at your library a long time or have just arrived to begin your new job, take time to develop a full understanding of your organization, both internally and externally. Make an active effort to gather information—don't just wait for bits and pieces to fall in your lap, though they often do. As a manager, you will need this knowledge to understand the library's various plans and priorities. Here is a checklist of information you should process:

Internal Information

- What are your staff members' demographics?

- Which branches, departments, and positions make up the library?

- What are the library's output statistics, such as circulation, collection size, program attendance?

- What is the general outline of the library's budget, and what is the budget for your area?

- What is the library's mission statement?

- What are the general plans for the next few years?

- How is communication managed?

- How are projects and new ideas implemented?
- Is the culture casual and easygoing, or more formal and structured?

External Information

- What is your user population's demographics?
- Is the library part of a larger organization (city, county, university, etc.)? Member of a consortium?
- How is the library funded?
- How is the library regarded in the community?
- What is your library's relationship with the state library or larger university system? With other neighboring libraries or educational institutions?
- What are the major challenges and opportunities of the local community served by the library?
- What obstacles exist to promoting the library and making it effective?
- What external roles does the library director or other staff have in the community?

Both your supervisor and your staff are likely to be willing resources in providing much of this information, but you should also use your own perceptions and observations as well as research skills. Don't rely on others to think of telling you everything you may need to know, and don't hesitate to seek out or ask about information you need.

Just as you study your library and its external environment, also look critically at how your position fits into the environment of the library. How does your department or branch (or other unit) help fulfill the library's mission? How does it contribute to achieving short- and long-term goals? How does your unit interact with other units in the library? As you get to know your workplace, try to develop insights about these points:

Internal to Your Unit

- Does staff have everything they need to perform well?

- How can you promote or improve morale?
- Do staff regularly participate in training and professional development opportunities?
- Do staff members have plans for individual growth and a career path?

External to Your Unit

- How does your unit help make other units successful?
- How does your unit contribute to library services?
- How do other units support yours?
- What is your staff's reputation?

At some point in learning about your new position, you may feel an urge to jump in and start making a difference. However, it's a good idea to think ahead to how your actions may affect the people and units you work with on a daily basis. Your management position doesn't give you license to act or make decisions without cultivating acceptance and support from both your supervisors and staff.

You may want to ask your supervisor to articulate some expectations for you and your unit, if this is not done soon after you begin your job. But not all supervisors are good at this, so you may need to interpret what you are told within the context you are developing. Are there specific goals you are expected to meet, or projects you will undertake in the near future?

One of the hazards of being "in the middle" is confusion about where your responsibilities begin and end. If you find yourself not understanding the scope of your duties, have a tactful discussion with your supervisor to clarify what your position should encompass. You can be sure your boss doesn't want to do your job. Like you, your supervisor is not perfect and has workplace insecurities and sore points like anyone else. Your boss will appreciate courtesy and support and, having received these, will be more likely to reciprocate.

An important step in assuming your supervisory role is to take time to speak individually with each of your staff members about their work situations. From staff's point of view, getting a new manager is a big change. It can create a lot of discomfort, even for, or maybe especially for, someone you have worked with for a long time. Find out what each person's concerns are about your unit, what changes each person may want, and what's important to each.

There may be obvious things you can do to improve your unit's operation, but one is to empower staff to find their own solutions as well. As a manager, it is not your obligation to solve everyone's problems at all times. Encourage staff to speak up about concerns, but also to suggest solutions to problems they perceive. And along with this, realize that you should be open to trying their suggestions as well as sympathetic to their concerns.

Part of your job will be to reconcile staff expectations with the whole picture in a way that supports productivity. As you become familiar with your staff and upper management, you may soon realize that various expectations of you are in conflict. For instance, staff wants you to allow complete scheduling freedom and flexibility, while administration requires that a specified level of staff be available every day. Negotiate and compromise. Most people are willing to give up something in return for their idea of a greater advantage. For example, a person may be willing to work several evenings in return for the weekend off. Don't make the mistake of trying to fill in every gap yourself or of being all things to all people. Be open about each side of the conflict. All concerned will be better able to compromise productively if they are aware of one another's expectations and needs. Make each side aware of conflicting expectations and be ready to offer realistic solutions.

One step toward reconciling expectations is to perpetuate dependable routines for communication, so staff members are well informed about issues that may affect them. Accurate information helps shape their expectations and wishes more realistically. Report to them about every management meeting, board meeting, or other informational event they may not have attended. This is not hard to do, but it can be time consuming and must be timely and consistent.

Significantly, communication must move both up and down. Your staff wants to know what management and administration are thinking about. Your supervisor and your peers want to know what is going on with your unit. This is not just a courtesy but a responsibility. If you neglect passing on information relevant to another person's performance, this omission soon becomes obvious and others lose trust in your ability to collaborate.

As a middle manager, you are probably working in an organization made up of several units similar to your own, managed by staff in positions analogous to yours. Realize that these units are interdependent, and your successful cooperation with others will increase the value of your contributions. As you assume new duties, you may find that others expect your unit to carry on as in the past, whether or not this is a good idea. Learn about these relationships and how the give-and-take works. If possible, find sustainable ways to make your unit more productive and helpful to others than in the past. Save money, help out when others are shorthanded, praise generously. Even small actions can result in better morale and greater efficiency.

Once you have assimilated a good understanding of your organization and particular unit, you will be better equipped to think about goals and improvement. Discuss possibilities for change with both your staff and your supervisor. While you are new to your position, you may be unaware of the history and full ramifications of even simple changes. It is not to your advantage to rush in with some "improvement" that was previously someone else's failure. Even so, it is your responsibility as a manager to show initiative in recognizing appropriate goals and improvements as well as to develop an ability to move forward to accomplish progress.

If you find yourself spending all your time responding to requests from staff and instructions from your supervisor, then you are managing passively rather than proactively. In this instance, you need to take a good hard look at your situation and try to get some insight about your role. Are these requests and instructions for actions you should already have initiated yourself? Have they oriented you to a new direction in which you need to continue? Or do you need to respond with reasoning about a different direction?

As a manager, you need to develop a plan. At some point in the process of training, acclimation, and fitting into your new role, you will recognize steps you can take to move forward with improvements and accomplishments. For example, you identify an area for improvement and have some ideas for changes. Or there is a project to be done and you have some innovative ideas on how to go about it. Early in your planning, start discussions with staff and supervisors about next steps you want to take. Follow the protocols of your organization to propose your idea and receive the go-ahead. Be ready to explain why your project is needed, how it will get done, and the outcomes it will have.

Does all of this sound like a lot to take on? Certainly, but it is important to remember that these are management tasks that you, as head of a unit, are designated to perform, with the actual work of the unit being done by staff. You may have some responsibility to take part in day-to-day duties, be familiar with procedures and functions, organize them, fill in when needed, and so on. Yet just as your supervisor doesn't want to do your job, you need to refrain from taking on jobs that really belong to others. If you are not satisfied with someone's performance or ability, then as a supervisor your task is to work with that individual to achieve productivity, not do the job yourself. If you are going to spend much of your time performing staff-level jobs, then your organization could save a lot of money by getting rid of your middle management position and adding a less expensive staff position. To be a successful manager, you should primarily perform at the highest level of your position, not the lowest.

To summarize, here are some major points to keep in mind:

Do

- Take time to learn about your community, organization, and unit.

- Talk with people around you to learn about their jobs and points of view.

- Recognize problems that need to be addressed.

- Make plans to solve problems and meet goals.

- Communicate regularly with your staff, peers, and supervisor.

- Ask questions when you need to.

- Cooperate and collaborate with other units in your organization.

- Allow staff to solve their own problems.

Don't

- Rush into changes without considering all the ramifications.

- Assume that your supervisory position gives you license to act without considering others.

- Think it is up to you to take care of everything. Others want ownership and recognition, too.

- Hoard information. Things are revealed, and when this happens staff will realize that you didn't communicate appropriately.

- Think you have to ensure everyone's perpetual happiness.

All this is a lot of work. You have to learn, research, make decisions, compromise, make mistakes. As a manager, you are required to give all the credit for success to your staff and blame yourself for mistakes. Do you ever wonder why you decided to enter management? Maybe it was because you wanted to be paid more, or because you thought you could exercise more control over things. Now you're finding out that it is not that much money, and you don't have much control over anything. You spend a lot of time talking and listening and often feel like you haven't accomplished anything at the end of the day.

Nevertheless, as time goes on, you will see evidence that you are helpful and productive. People will depend on you, they will bring problems to you and consult you about plans and projects. Staff will use information and communications from you to think independently and respond to situations. As you see this happen, you will realize that you are successfully fulfilling a function in operations, and that people respect you and your staff. At some point, your unit will complete a successful project, and you will see that improvements are having the desired effect, and others also think so. The professional respect of your colleagues and your growing confidence in your abilities are your well-deserved rewards.

2

STEPPING RIGHT INTO THE MIDDLE OF . . .

ANNE C. BARNHART

STARTED MY CURRENT POSITION AS HEAD OF INSTRUCTIONAL SERVICES (IS) IN October 2009. The IS division encompasses reference, instruction, the liaison program, and government documents. Including myself, there are seven librarians and one support staff member in the division. Unbeknownst to me when I began, I had stepped right into the middle of, well . . . a lot. I started in October, the middle of a semester, and found myself in a department mired in some long-running personality conflicts. As fate would have it, as a result of these conflicts I found myself also serving as intermediary between IS and senior administration.

In this chapter I discuss some of the conflicts and what I did to try to resolve them. I describe two specific steps I took to create departmental unity, the consequences of these actions, and where I hope to take things in the future. Further, I show that by empowering a division a new middle manager can create a strong group dynamic and inspire members to become reengaged with their jobs and the larger organization. Some of these ideas might not work in other institutions. Heck, some of them might not even work in mine, but I just haven't figured that out yet.

I began to get a sense of the organizational culture even before joining the library during the interview process. The search committee was made up of people I was to supervise. My future direct supervisor (the associate dean) and the dean of libraries both met with me during the interview, but the majority of my interactions were with the eight-member IS division. They had been tasked with finding their own boss.

When I started, I soon began to discover the extent to which the department, without a dedicated head for several years, had become fractured. Division members felt disenfranchised and underrepresented in larger library decisions. They were distrustful of the library administration (which they referred to as a "cabal") and did not believe they had a voice at the table. Yet, at the same time and despite their distrust of administrators (of which I was now one), I sensed that they were willing to give me a chance.

DISCOVERING SOURCES OF DISUNITY

I met with each division member individually and requested them all to tell me about their position, what they liked or disliked, the library atmosphere, campus culture, and what they believed I might do to improve things. I also asked each member about their professional goals and aspirations and was surprised by how much they opened up to me from the very beginning. Encouraged by their show of confidence, I was determined to try to heal the department as quickly as I could.

Division members also expressed feeling rudderless and in need of a mission statement and objectives, so they would know they were working toward common goals. Further, I observed that, although individuals were willing to speak openly in private, they tended to shut down in meetings, which I attributed to a lack of mutual trust. There was seemingly a culture of defeatism in the group, illustrated, for example, by the perception that projects started or suggested by division members had been promptly shot down by the administration.

What I found confusing was that many of the purportedly squelched projects were nearly identical to suggestions the dean had requested I pursue as division head. Since both sides seemed sincere in their intentions and interpretations, I began to suspect a serious problem in translation.

EARNING TRUST:
GROUP GOAL SETTING AS TEAM BUILDING

To best win my division's trust, I opted to address their concerns using an approach of resolving issues together as a group. Ideally, I sought to build a division that felt cohesive and empowered. I asked each member to provide some goals. Of the twenty-nine suggestions submitted—accounting for redundancies—I identified twelve distinct goals. Once again, I found that goals identified by individuals in my department largely paralleled suggestions the administration had previously presented, again underscoring the disconnect between the administration and the division.

We scheduled a division meeting and faculty requested it be held in another building, so they could speak more freely without worry of being overheard, misunderstood, or taken out of context. I prepared for this meeting by bringing a giant notepad and writing each of the twelve goals on its own oversize sheet of paper. As a group we annotated each goal, noting what it meant, what it implied, whether or not it was within the jurisdiction of our division, and, in light of an impending library renovation, if now was the time to take it on.

Obviously, twelve goals were still too many, so we needed to prioritize further. I gave each person three stickers to paste, one each, on sheets with the goals corresponding to their top three selections. We tallied votes and used these results to determine our immediate course of action.

The top three areas of focus were our credit-bearing library skills course, LIBR1101 (7 votes); marketing the IS division (6 votes); and drafting an IS mission statement (6 votes). With the exception of the mission statement, our prioritized goals echoed what the administration had asked me to focus on: marketing our services and improving our instructional program. In the short term, this was fortunate for me, for it was relatively simple to please both constituent groups simultaneously. The long-term complication would be to figure out why there was such a severe communication gap.

MOVING TOWARD UNITY:
SCORING A QUICK GROUP VICTORY AND
DEFINING WORK ROLES

Our next division meeting focused on immediate versus longer-term goals. I wanted the division to have an early success, one that would allow us to start marketing some of our services right away. Although there were some perfectionist tendencies within the group, perhaps due to anxiety about senior administration approval and support, we reached consensus on a marketing postcard to be handed out to visiting prospective students. I told my department we did not have to create a perfect ad campaign, just one simple item to hand out. Staff worked together to design a postcard for a scheduled prospective student day. Our first success.

Before moving toward our larger goal of creating a mission statement, we needed to define how the division would function going forward and what each member's responsibilities would be in the new structure. To do this, we would have to deal with the strife and contention surrounding divisional workload and duties that had been developing for years.

The IS division is responsible for our instructional program (credit-bearing and instructor requests), reference services (desk, e-mail, and online chat), and liaison program, all of which I oversee. To some degree, all librarians are involved in reference, liaison work, and instruction, regardless of rank or position. (This actually means that I coordinate librarians who do not necessarily report to me and, in some cases, are actually above me on the organizational chart). Not all librarians enjoy these responsibilities, and some are simply not comfortable working directly with students. Consequently, I quickly learned from the IS division that many felt overburdened by the amount of teaching they did in comparison to their non-IS faculty colleagues.

Our liaison program coordinates the activities of all librarians. Each librarian, even the dean and associate dean, are liaisons to academic departments. Liaisons, in theory, are responsible for collection development of their departments, discipline-specific library instruction, and being the face of the library for these academic units. These duties require a certain personality type. Ideally, a liaison is outgoing, interested in the subject area, and enjoys teaching.

The reality was that no one was monitoring the liaison program, and this meant that librarians who were less inclined to reach out simply didn't. Departments across campus had widely varied relationships to the library, depending on the personality of the liaison librarian. There was also a significant disincentive for liaisons to do outreach to their departments, which could mean additional work for them. More visible librarians are typically going to receive more instruction requests from department faculty. Library liaisons who are not comfortable teaching had no motivation to offer services they would then have to provide.

We discussed this phenomenon at length in IS meetings. As head of the division responsible for overseeing the liaison program, I wanted to see greater equity across departments. IS librarians were concerned that this would result in doing more teaching work for non-IS librarians. In theory, senior administration agreed that all librarians should teach. In practice, this was difficult to enforce. And was "enforcing" really in the best interest of our students?

One could argue that librarians should be required to teach since, after all, instruction is mentioned to each candidate (at least in passing) during the interview. So what if that interview was five years ago and that librarian had yet to teach a single session? Some librarians, in fact, seemed to not comprehend what being a liaison meant. One librarian declared, "I know that at any time my phone could ring and the [liaison] department could call to ask for a session. It hasn't happened yet, but when it does I will gladly teach the class." That same librarian, when queried, said she had done no outreach to the department, had never been to a department meeting, and had not offered to do any library sessions.

I needed to change the culture. I needed to support librarians who were interested in teaching but uncomfortable doing so. I also had to make sure all departments on campus had equal access to library instruction regardless of the interest of their assigned liaison. And I had to accomplish this without making IS librarians pick up the slack.

How could I encourage non-IS librarians to accept more teaching assignments and simultaneously ease the burden of IS librarians? I needed to increase the liaison work of non-IS librarians in order to free up some IS librarian time to cover more requested one-shots. Realistically, changing the liaison program was going to take more work before it became easier. I knew IS librarians would have to do even more before they would see what their non-IS colleagues were taking on. And I had to get buy-in from people who did not report directly to me. Addressing teaching load concerns took more time, and summer 2010 was the target.

In addition to teaching one-shots, our university has a credit-bearing library skills course, LIBR1101. Each IS librarian teaches multiple sections of this course (face-to-face and online sections) each semester. It is rewarding and fantastic that the library has a credit-bearing course that fulfills one of the general education core requirements. Nevertheless, it is also time intensive, and many IS librarians (even relatively recent hires) were feeling burned out. Though this may seem distinct from the liaison problem, I believed the overlap of the teaching workload intertwined these two issues and required a multifaceted solution.

After observing my colleagues' strengths and surveying their interests, I created a new model for our liaison program. It consists of a team-based approach with an IS librarian as leader of each team (divided as the university divides its separate colleges: Business, Education, Humanities, Nursing, Sciences, Social Sciences). Each team was allowed to divide up different responsibilities however it wanted.

In theory, this meant that a librarian who represents a humanities department but does not want to teach could offer to maintain (weed) the collections of librarians who do more teaching. This approach allowed IS librarians to mentor their colleagues and help them become more comfortable with teaching. I first presented this idea to IS librarians and gave them a chance to modify the plan. They were enthusiastic about it because it gave them some authority in an area where they feel knowledgeable. Designating them team leaders empowered them to decide how work would be distributed.

HINDRANCES TO UNITY

To be honest, this pilot has not created as much divisional unity as I had hoped. Unfortunately, we began it at the same time the library was starting a major building renovation. We had underestimated how disruptive construction would be. For the duration of the construction, we lost our library classroom, which complicated efforts for securing library instruction space across campus. This situation discouraged librarians from doing any major outreach campaigns as well. I, too, scaled back what I was offering to departments because I did not want to extend more than I would be able to deliver.

In hindsight, I believe I left too much to the discretion of team leaders and did not provide enough guidance. As a division, we can reevaluate this summer when construction is finished and design a more structured Pilot 2.0 for the upcoming academic year. Although this model needs a lot of improvement, the immediate result is that it gave librarians in my division a chance to take ownership of their jobs instead of feeling overwhelmed by the amount of work.

MOVING CLOSER TO UNITY

Once we addressed and clearly outlined the division's workload concerns, despite the persisting issues we achieved enough unity to draft a mission statement collectively that clearly articulates our vision. We were also positioned to create a work plan outlining what we want to accomplish in the next academic year and have even started a strategic plan.

I learned from the liaison pilot project that each librarian appreciates having an area of responsibility, so they know their focus. In our annual evaluations, we are rewriting job descriptions to include both a fixed part (what all IS librarians do) and a flexible area of focus that mirrors the individual's professional goals for that year. In this respect, achieving their clearly stated goals is part of their job, and there will be no communication gap between expectations and performance.

Our division still is not completely united, but we are getting there. We have the opportunity to add two new librarians to our team. We have met to discuss what we want and what we do not want. In the process, I need to make certain we do not fall into the morale trap of developing a fortress-like "us vs. them" mentality with the rest of the library.

With this in mind, I purchased copies of Robert I. Sutton's *The No Asshole Rule: Building a Civilized Workplace and Surviving One That Isn't* (2010) for everyone in the division plus the non-IS librarian who will be on our search committee. Together we are reading this book to help determine what kind of workplace we want and what kind of colleagues we want to be for each other.

Moreover, I'm bringing in an outside facilitator through our employee assistance program to lead a discussion of the reading. We also must resolve whether we want to give copies of the same book to new hires. We don't want to turn them off, but neither do we want them to feel excluded if we reference a book they have not read.

The search committee is also reading selections from Gavin de Becker's *The Gift of Fear* (1997) to help choose good colleagues. On a whim, I also bought copies of *The No Asshole Rule* for everyone on the administrative team. I was hesitant to distribute them in an administrative meeting, but I mentioned it to the dean first and she was supportive. We have not yet met to discuss our "assigned reading," but by giving the same book to my division and the administration I hope to create a shared experience to help bridge that communication gap.

REFERENCES

de Becker, Gavin. 1997. *The Gift of Fear and Other Survival Signals That Protect Us from Violence.* New York: Little, Brown.

Sutton, Robert I. 2010. *The No Asshole Rule: Building a Civilized Workplace and Surviving One That Isn't.* New York: Business Plus.

3

TESTING THE WATERS

Creative Role Playing for Management Success

AMANDA LEA FOLK

The explorer, like the learner, does not know what terrain and adventures his journey holds in store for him. He has yet to discover mountains, deserts, and water holes and to suffer fever, starvation, and other hardships. Finally, when the explorer returns from his journey, he will have a hard-won knowledge of the country he has traversed. Then, and only then, can he produce a map of the region.

—Jonas Soltes, on John Dewey's
philosophy of the learner

I T HAS BEEN SAID THAT MANAGEMENT, LIKE LEADERSHIP, IS BOTH AN ART AND A science. However, those of us who desire to become managers and leaders are not necessarily natural artists or scientists. Does this mean that those of us who have not been blessed with innate management or leadership skills cannot be successful as managers? I say no. Managerial and leadership skills are learned, developed, and honed through both education and experience. Indeed, Linda A. Hill, a faculty member at Harvard Business School, agrees: "What we know for sure is that managers are mostly made, not born" (Hill 2004, 122).

Since this is the case, it is imperative that middle managers, like the explorer mentioned in the epigraph, learn the organizational terrain. Top-level managers must be willing to mentor their middle managers so they develop management and leadership skills needed for success in their current positions and beyond.

But what if we don't receive guidance or feedback from our superiors? How are we supposed to learn from our experiences and become effective managers? In such situations, to hone their management skills middle managers need to create "provisional selves" actively and treat different administrative issues as "case studies" by conducting a form of role playing. "Action learning [e.g., case studies or role playing] is effective for managers as it is what they do: develop solutions to complex problems, implement them, and then evaluate" (Holland 2008, 40).

MAKING THE MOST OF THE MIDDLE: CASE STUDIES, ROLE PLAYING, PROVISIONAL SELVES

One of the benefits of being in a middle management position is that it can help you determine if you would ultimately like to become a top-level manager. Before we enter formal management positions, many of us have had only a glimpse of what it truly means to be a manager. It is possible we have idealized visions of management positions, and we don't always see the grunt work and politics involved in being a top-level manager, or a middle manager at that. Although the pay is often higher, it is certainly not a glamorous position.

When you become a middle manager, you have officially entered the realm of management, and you will be privy to issues that involve change management, conflict management, and human resource or personnel issues. As a middle manager, you are able to decide if you enjoy working through these types of issues, or if they completely drain you, before you take the plunge into top-level management.

It is entirely possible that once you do get to experience the life of a manager, even at the middle management level, you'll decide you are not cut out for a career in top-level management. Perhaps you find dealing with administrative or management issues mind numbing. Perhaps being a manager is not at all what you expected. That's okay. You've gotten your feet wet as a manager and decided that the water isn't as nice as you expected before you took the ultimate plunge. In any case, even if you do decide middle management is the perfect fit for you, you still need to address refining your managerial skills. A great way to do this is to treat different situations as case studies and place yourself in a role-playing position.

Why should middle managers do this? As S. Manikutty notes, it's when people are at "the lower middle management" level that "the quest for an answer to the question, 'Who am I?' [as a professional] arises" (2005, 60). It is the point in our career where we truly need to decide what our management styles are and where we would like our career paths to take us. Being a middle manager allows us to create a "provisional self," from which we can observe decisions top-level managers are making.

Herminia Ibarra describes the experimentation with provisional selves as "trials for possible but not yet fully elaborated professional identities" (1999, 764). By creating a provisional self, we can take real-world cases from our own organizations and place ourselves in the top-level managers' shoes to analyze different situations that arise. Creating case studies and playing the role of top-level manager with a provisional self is one way to use your middle management position to hone your management skills. When a difficult decision must be made or a difficult issue arises, particularly a personnel issue, I like to do just this. Here are the steps I take to create a case study and role-play:

- On a piece of paper (or in your head), write down all the information you have about the situation you are analyzing, including what happened and who was involved. (*Note:* you might want to use fictional names, or be sure to shred this document.)

- Next, analyze how the situation was handled. Do you agree with the outcome?

- Think about how you might have handled this situation. Is it different from the real-life experience?

- In what other ways could this situation have been handled? What are the pros and cons of each method?

- What was the outcome of the real-life situation? Was it the best possible outcome?

- Analyze the way you would have handled the situation and other possible methods, and determine what the potential outcomes for those would have been.

- Based on the real and potential outcomes, which methods would have been ideal?

If you, as a middle manager, decide to create a provisional self and role-play, you will truly be able to explore your management style. Role playing is a great complement to creating a provisional self, for it allows you to "apply [your] knowledge . . . in a risk-free situation . . . and reflect on [your] own work experience and its impact on [your behavior] after the role play" (Griggs 2005, 60). By observing and reflecting on the management styles of your superiors and understanding the effect those styles have on library staff, you can pick and choose management elements that best suit you and your personality. Moreover, using case studies, provisional selves, and role playing helps create confidence in yourself and your decisions, which your colleagues will respect.

Daniel Vasella, former chairman and CEO of Novartis, says, "I learned from every supervisor I had—through positive and negative examples" (Wademan 2005, 37). When you are a middle manager, every day can be a learning experience. Make sure you take advantage of these opportunities.

REFERENCES

Griggs, Karen. 2005. "A Role Play for Revising Style and Applying Management Theories." *Business Communication Quarterly* 68 (2): 60–65.

Hill, Linda A. 2004. "New Manager Development for the 21st Century." *Academy of Management Executive* 18 (3): 121–126.

Holland, Peter. 2008. "Teaching Advanced Human Resource Management and Employment Relations to a Diverse Graduate Student Population: A Call Centre Action Learning Approach." *Employment Relations Record* 8 (2): 35–47.

Ibarra, Herminia. 1999. "Provisional Selves: Experimenting with Image and Identity in Professional Adaptation." *Administrative Science Quarterly* 44 (4): 764–791.

Manikutty, S. 2005. "Manager as a Trainer, a Coach, and a Mentor." *Vikalpa: The Journal for Decision Makers* 30 (2): 57–64.

Wademan, Daisy. 2005. "The Best Advice I Ever Got." *Harvard Business Review* 83(1): 35–44.

4

LEARNING THE ROPES

LIS and Professional Training Are Not Enough

AMANDA LEA FOLK

L IS EDUCATION IS SIMPLY NOT ENOUGH TO CREATE STRONG MANAGERS AND leaders. In their study of LIS online syllabi and job requirements, Kayvan Kousha and Mahshid Abdoli found a significant gap between management education and expectations: "There were remarkable gaps for about 30% of subject areas such as 'management of libraries,' 'interpersonal communication' . . . suggesting that these subjects did not appear to have much representation or weight in the many LIS programs, but they were requested as the essential qualifications by the LIS employers" (Kousha and Abdoli 2008, 1).

In his dissertation "Educational Preparation of Entry-Level Professional Librarians Employed by Florida Research Libraries," Agmad Elgohary presented similar findings. He reports that "competencies under management . . . categories were not sufficiently acquired by entry-level research librarians. In particular, library schools did not equip their graduates with seven out of nine (78%) required management and marketing competencies" (Elgohary 2003, 93). In this study, the deficient competencies included outcome evaluation, community analysis, performance measurement, network management, marketing planning and techniques, and preparing a budget (2003, 64). Furthermore, only 54 percent of the forty-eight ALA-accredited LIS programs require their students to take a management course for completion of the graduate program, and an even smaller number, less than 19 percent, require an internship or experiential learning opportunity (Mackenzie and Smith 2009, 135–136).

Although these findings may appear troubling, we need to remember that LIS programs are serving their customers, who primarily seek skills necessary to secure their first, entry-level position in the profession. Jenifer Grady writes, "LIS education is intended to prepare graduates for professional roles and responsibilities related to functional areas of responsibility, including reference, instruction, cataloging, and information systems" (2009, 233). Moreover, while attending an LIS program, library students are often not thinking about what type of position they will have in five or ten years. The management theories taught in LIS programs give students a glimpse of what might come down the road, but it is simply not enough to prepare students to be effective managers the minute they have their degree. This should not be viewed as a flaw or shortcoming in an LIS education. Rather, we must recognize that most librarians must receive some kind of on-the-job training to supplement the theoretical foundations provided in LIS programs in order to become effective managers.

The idea that managerial and leadership skills cannot be taught solely in the classroom extends beyond LIS programs. Linda A. Hill writes, "When designing our new required leadership course at Harvard [Business School], we took seriously the notion that we could not teach the MBAs to manage—they had to teach themselves" (2004, 122), because "unapplied knowledge is knowledge shorn of its meaning" (Whitehead 1947, 219). Indeed, this idea extends beyond faculty in the ivory tower. Successful corporations around the world have implemented programs in which senior managers mentor and coach junior and middle managers so that these up-and-coming leaders cultivate the skills necessary for success in senior management.

In 2005, Christine D. Hegstad and Rose Mary Wentling published the findings of their study, which investigated formal mentoring programs that have been implemented in seventeen Fortune 500 companies. They state that "these business organizations are likely to be ahead of the competition in various aspects, including the development of their human resources," as well as hoping to "increase employee retention and satisfaction" (Hegstad and Wentling 2005, 467–468). Certainly, this mentoring is particularly important for middle managers, who are now viewed as the "work horses of the world" and "can be counted on to get the job done" (Janto 2004, 5). Because of the nature of the position, top-level managers give a lot of responsibility to middle managers within their organizations. "Middle managers are the linking pin that takes the visions of upper management and fuses [them] with the pragmatic needs of the workforce. The middle manager becomes the arbitrator of conflicting corporate objectives and worker needs" (Skrabec 2001, 21).

Librarians who are middle managers have opportunities to take continuing education courses or workshops in management through professional associations at all levels (local, regional, state, and national). In addition, many of these associations offer mentoring opportunities for their members. However, a 1992 study published in *College and Research Libraries* demonstrated that middle managers are not always required to participate in these opportunities, although they are often encouraged to do so. "Eleven (16%) CDHs [cataloging department heads] and 9 (13%) RDHs [reference department heads] indicated that ongoing management training was required of them" (Wittenbach, Bordeianu, and Wycisk 1992, 326).

Even if middle managers voluntarily participate in continuing management education opportunities, is it enough to make them successful? These opportunities serve as an extension of the theory learned in library school, allowing professionals to brush up on management theories. But they don't give middle managers the hands-on experience to hone their managerial skills, particularly regarding personnel management.

There are exceptions to this, of course. Continuing education and professional opportunities dealing with the more concrete aspects of management—such as budget planning, strategic planning, or business planning—do give participants hands-on experience.

One example of a successful mentoring opportunity offered by a professional association is ALA's Emerging Leaders program. The benefit of this program is that it allows professionals in early stages of their careers to gain hands-on, practical experience as members of ALA. In other words, theory is put into practice.

Still, it would be difficult—if not impossible—to offer this type of professional development opportunity for personnel or human resource management, for such managers must learn and grow from experience gained by observing and handling situations within their own organizations.

REFERENCES

Elgohary, Agmad A. 2003. "Educational Preparation of Entry-Level Professional Librarians Employed by Florida Research Libraries." PhD diss., Florida State University.

Grady, Jenifer. 2009. "Answering the Calls of 'What's Next' and 'Library Workers Cannot Live by Love Alone' through Certification and Salary Research." *Library Trends* 58 (2): 229–245.

Hegstad, Christine D., and Rose Mary Wentling. 2005. "Organizational Antecedents and Moderators That Impact on the Effectiveness of Exemplary Formal Mentoring Programs in Fortune 500 Companies in the United States." *Human Resource Development International* 8 (4): 467–487.

Hill, Linda A. 2004. "New Manager Development for the 21st Century." *Academy of Management Executive* 18 (3): 121–126.

Janto, Joyce Manna. 2004. "Redemption: Reflections of a Life in Middle Management." *Trends in Law Library Management and Technology* 15 (1): 5–8.

Kousha, Kayvan, and Mahshid Abdoli. 2008. "Subject Analysis of Online Syllabi in Library and Information Science: Do Academic LIS Programs Match with Job Requirements?" Paper presented at the World Library and Information Congress: 74th IFLA General Conference and Council, Québec, Canada, August.

Mackenzie, Maureen, and James P. Smith. 2009. "Management Education for Library Directors: Are Graduate Library Programs Providing Future Library Directors with the Skills and Knowledge They Will Need?" *Journal of Education for Library and Information Science* 50 (3): 129–142.

Skrabec, Quentin R., Jr. 2001. "The Lost Grail of Middle Management." *Industrial Management* 43 (3): 19–22.

Whitehead, Alfred North. 1947. *Essays in Science and Philosophy*. New York: Philosophical Library.

Wittenbach, Stefanie A., Sever M. Bordeianu, and Kristine Wycisk. 1992. "Management Preparation and Training of Department Heads in ARL Libraries." *College and Research Libraries* 53 (4): 319–330.

5

IS AN MBA A GOOD CHOICE FOR MIDDLE MANAGEMENT LIBRARIANS?

ELIZABETH O'BRIEN

I HAVE HAD SIX YEARS TO CONTEMPLATE WHETHER LIBRARIANS ARE A GOOD match for an MBA program, and whether there is value in the degree for middle managers in academic and public libraries. I entered my "B-school," the Schulich School of Business at York University (Toronto, Ontario) with wide-eyed innocence, curiosity, and reverence for a subject area about which I knew little. I was promoted to my first management position when I received my B-school acceptance and felt the timing inspired. What better way to learn how to manage than to take courses like managerial accounting, operations management, and strategic planning? After enrolling, I took a leap of faith that this degree would be helpful for my current position—not in twenty years as a future executive, but in my current middle management position as coordinator of circulation.

In this chapter, I share my six-year journey of completing an MBA, on a part-time basis, while being a library middle manager and raising my young family. Many times during my stint in business school, I questioned the value of this degree for my profession. Now one year post-graduation, I've concluded that the MBA program is a valuable asset for library middle managers. It has provided me with a solid foundation of management principles and techniques, applicable to any organizational context, which I can draw on throughout the stages of my career.

In the following I cover lessons learned in subjects such as team dynamics, change management, and strategic planning, as well as their applicability to the library middle manager. I also include a checklist of tips for librarians considering the MBA program. And finally, for those not interested or unable to pursue an MBA but who want training in management topics, I mention a few other sources of professional development and training opportunities.

LESSONS LEARNED: OVERVIEW OF MANAGEMENT SKILLS

All managers face similar responsibilities regardless of sector or industry—people and financial management are two common areas. Prior to becoming a manager, I had no formal training in managing either. I recall taking a course in library school on management, but it was too brief and too long ago to help me in my new gig managing a team of eight unionized employees.

I faced a common challenge. New graduates in their first job out of library school rarely have management responsibilities. After a few years into their careers, they may be promoted into management but rarely have the training in how to manage human resources and finances. I was no exception. The MBA, however, provides a solid foundation in managerial issues. Most two-year MBA programs dedicate the first semesters to core courses (finance, human resources, marketing, and accounting). The final semesters provide opportunities for students to specialize in electives. Both my core and elective courses helped shape and enrich my management experience. I now have more self-confidence in managing others because I know that my decisions are grounded in solid management theory and best practices.

Strategic Planning

My time in business school helped me develop an appreciation and enthusiasm for strategy. Prior to my degree, my knowledge of the subject was extremely limited. I knew about SWOT analysis (strengths, weaknesses, opportunities, and threats), one tool often used in strategic planning, but I had never gone through the process. My MBA program provided me with not just a course on planning but the opportunity to conduct an eight-month intensive strategic planning process for an organization. My key takeaway from this experience, which I applied to my current position and our recent strategic plan, was to focus on what my organization does uniquely (or better) than anyone else in order to develop plans that support and emphasize those strengths. Although I am a middle manager, my knowledge of this area facilitated my leadership in my library's strategic planning process.

Team Development

Group work is key to most MBA programs—even online MBAs require virtual group projects. In contrast to my LIS program, nearly all my MBA courses had a large team-based component. At first I cringed at the group projects, but slowly I came to realize the value of these out-of-class experiences. My group work experiences gave me instances to apply the theory I had just learned in class about team-based development known as Tuckman's "Forming, Storming, Norming, Performing" (Tuckman 1965). This model proposes that, over time, groups go through a typical pattern or stages of development characterized by conflict, followed by cohesion, ultimately leading to effective performance.

I also became versed in negotiation and conflict resolution through group projects. Working closely with others

helped me respect the multiple perspectives around the table and taught me how to be an active listener. I utilized all these skills in my early days as a middle manager and continue to benefit from them today.

Change Management

Change within organizations is a constant, especially with advances in technology. Supporting employees to handle change effectively is one of the most critical skills managers need. I was able to take a twelve-week B-school course on change management that set forth a broadly structured approach to address change holistically. It was peppered with practical exercises and frameworks that I eventually used when my organization experienced change.

One of the most valuable perspectives I learned from managing change in the workplace was acknowledging the need for employees to grieve a change. Even if a change is positively received or would yield many benefits, it is critical to recognize the end of one phase to allow easier transitions to the new state. Elisabeth Kübler-Ross's (1969) "Five Stages of Grief" framework (denial, anger, bargaining, depression, and acceptance), a psychological model used in many fields, is taught in business school as a useful model for helping employees manage organizational change.

Project Management

An elective course in project management helped me develop what has become one of the most valuable skill sets I now bring to my organization. Project management trained me how to take a large, complex project and divide it into smaller, doable tasks through tools like the Work Breakdown Structure (for details, see Lewis 2002, chap. 4). Libraries often have many new initiatives developed as special projects, and applying a disciplined approach to managing these can go a long way toward project success. Managing projects is a great leadership challenge for the middle manager, for it provides the chance to manage a large number of employees, often entailing high-profile exposure to senior management. Project management could be seen as a testing ground for middle managers to determine their suitability for executive positions.

HOW CAN AN MBA IMPACT MY CAREER?

Perspective

MBA programs train students to think in ways particularly useful for library managers. A large component of

B-school is learning how to see a situation from a different perspective. This critical foundation skill, called reframing, is tested repeatedly as the program progresses. In its simplicity, reframing helps you examine problems from multiple perspectives. For example, the benefit of a strategic perspective is that you learn how to apply several different tools to assess the direction a library is going. Moreover, you are equipped to identify long-term costs and benefits of potential directions, as opposed to addressing immediate needs. In class, this typically occurred through case studies and discussions, which helped enrich my experience and forced me to think beyond my own boundaries.

The benefit of an operational view—that is, the view of daily actions and their effects—is that it helps you understand how to improve the efficiency and effectiveness of many tasks that occur in a library. Taking a systems perspective, where interconnections and dependencies are considered, helped me participate in an operational review of two key processes in our library. I was able to diagram these processes into workflow charts, then implement changes to make them more efficient.

Differentiation

Librarians with an MBA degree are uncommon. Many librarians have two master's degrees, but the MBA/MLIS combination is still rare in my experience. Kent State University's joint MLS/MBA is one of the exceptions. In competitive job markets, unique training or degrees help resumes attract attention. A librarian colleague I interviewed confirmed that it was her MBA that helped her stand out against other internal applicants and secure an upper management position at an academic library.

Even though I still continue in a middle manager position, I have no doubt that this degree has advanced my career. I have been given assignments to lead complex projects of strategic significance to my organization. Prior to entering the degree program, I didn't believe I had the leadership qualities required for executive management. Now, if the invitation arises to move into senior management, I am confident that the degree coupled with my professional experience has provided me the tools and self-assurance to accept these challenges.

MAKING YOUR DECISION

Is an MBA right for you? Consider the following:

The program is intensive. Although not particularly difficult, B-school coursework is demanding (though I did struggle with mathematics in my finance class). There is a lot of required reading and

meetings with group members outside class time. You may find the endurance and persistence necessary to complete the degree over six years difficult to muster, as it was for me. The program will take a toll on you personally and consequently on the people around you.

Programs vary in duration and intensity. Many institutions offer part-time programs, which are great for those who wish to distribute work over several years. There are also intensive, fast-track programs that can be completed in a calendar year. And there are executive MBA programs, which are good options for seasoned managers. The length of some programs may be reduced by previous work experience or educational background.

Librarians can be viewed as different. I was the only librarian in my program. Most MBA students have backgrounds in finance, technology, engineering, or science, though this is changing. Starting out, I worried that I would not be able to contribute to discussions or group projects competitively with my colleagues. I believe some had similar concerns about my skill set. Nevertheless, my research and analytical skills, honed through my LIS degree, proved to be a huge asset to all my group projects. I found assignments completed with groups were some of my most rewarding experiences.

High cost. The degree can be expensive, upwards of $60,000. Employers in any sector today, as compared to the past, rarely pay for their staff to pursue MBA degrees. One avenue to consider taking is an online MBA, which can be more affordable. But in addition to financial costs there can also be high tradeoffs to one's personal life and relationships.

Specialized MBA programs. Many B-schools offer MBAs with specific concentrations. My alma mater, York University, has a wealth of electives. I was particularly drawn to their specialization in non-profit management and leadership, and this influenced my choice of schools. In the final semesters of my program I took four elective courses specializing in the nonprofit sector. I found these extremely valuable, as all my prior experience has been in this area.

If it is not realistic for you to pursue an MBA, there are many other paths for management training that do not involve a degree. Continuing education programs from library schools and associations provide a broad selection of courses suitable for librarian middle managers. Further, a wide variety of courses are available through many of the same institutions that offer MBA programs as well as community colleges and online. I recommend reviewing the offerings of each school to get an overall view. The alternatives may not provide the same full benefits of an MBA, but they will better position you to meet new challenges in a changing future.

REFERENCES

Kübler-Ross, Elisabeth. 1969. *On Death and Dying.* New York: Macmillan.

Lewis, James P. 2002. *Fundamentals of Project Management: Developing Core Competencies to Help Outperform the Competition.* New York: AMACOM.

Tuckman, Bruce W. 1965. "Developmental Sequence in Small Groups." *Psychological Bulletin* 63 (6): 384–399.

6

EXPERTISE, INFLUENCE, AND MAGICAL THINKING

Interviews with Middle Managers

MELISSA LANING AND NEAL NIXON

WHAT ARE THE CHARACTERISTICS AND PRACTICES OF A GOOD MIDDLE MANager? How do middle managers get things done in their organizations? What are the rewards? One of the best ways to learn about becoming an effective new manager is listening to the advice of others who have already achieved success in the position. As librarians, we naturally look to the literature for information and inspiration related to our professional lives. The careful searcher will discover a variety of enlightening first-person narratives, often from relatively new middle managers (e.g., *Library Personnel News* 2000; Schachter 2006; Sowards 1999).

Another interesting and useful approach to learning about middle management is to review a case study from a different type of organization (Lubans 2004). Articles that look at the topic through a historical, analytical framework can also help practitioners achieve perspective on their roles and responsibilities (Bailey 1987; Sullivan 1992).

We chose to build on the advice found in these personal narratives by asking a group of colleagues who are currently in middle management positions to share counsel and observations from their own experience. We conducted one-on-one interviews with seven librarians at a university and community college library in a medium-sized city in the southeastern United States. The focus of these conversations was on the perceptions middle managers had of their roles. To facilitate these conversations, we developed a uniform list of questions designed to elicit responses about the nature and practice of middle management. The questions are included in the appendix to this chapter.

Interviewees ranged from relatively new library managers to those who have served in a management position for more than twenty years. The group was also diverse in terms of functional area, gender, and race. This article summarizes the common themes that emerged from those conversations in hopes of providing more insights on the successful practice of middle management in libraries.

MIDDLE MANAGEMENT MATTERS

Common themes quickly emerged from these conversations with middle managers. One that predominates is the role of the position in the library organization. All interviewees identified responsibility for a discrete functional area of the library as the primary reason they identify themselves as middle managers. There were additional references to reporting lines both upward and downward, but the conversations made it clear that middle managers believe the primary work of their area is stewardship of their respective departments and supervision of their staffs. As a group, they clearly believe that goals of library administration could not be accomplished without them.

In addition, demonstrated expertise and a willingness to dig in and actually do the work of the unit are key personal traits and success factors for the majority. For the most part, individuals in our study are librarians first and managers second. They conveyed that a deep understanding of the work being performed in their areas is a primary source of authority inside their units and with upper administration. Their comments suggest that respect from their staff and ability to achieve departmental goals are more closely related to their skills as librarian practitioners than to their skills as managers. In essence, if you know the work, people will listen. For many of them, staying actively involved in the daily work of their departments appears to be the way longer-term middle managers keep themselves refreshed and engaged in their positions. One of the most frequent points of advice our respondents had for long-term managers is to stay on top of changes in the field in order to remain effective leaders.

Communication skills are the second most important attribute identified by our interviewees in their roles as middle managers. The examples they provided of good communication relate to implementing administrative directives or work-related training, but providing information upward was mentioned during multiple interviews. Advocacy was often expressed as actively petitioning for unit initiatives or personnel. Listening was frequently mentioned when the critical nature of communication was discussed.

Another important theme that emerged was in response to a question about the organizational power of the middle manager. The majority of those interviewed expressed the view that they have influence within the broader organization but little formal authority. Not surprisingly, the lack of authority our interviewees experience in these positions is occasionally a source of frustration for them, but not always. More than once, we heard that having the buck stop somewhere else in the organization is a perceived benefit of the middle management role. They have an opportunity to influence decision making without full responsibility for the outcome, providing a safety net of sorts and a chance to learn important lessons about organizational culture.

When and how interviewees garner and use their influence was one of the more intriguing aspects of the discussions. There was consensus that relationship building is the primary method for expanding organizational influence (also referred to as personal power). However, interviewees expressed distinct differences about which relationships are most important to build. For some, influence derives from the top and upward relationships are primary. For others, relationships with peers are equally, if not more, important. Regardless of how influence is achieved, our interviewees viewed the capacity to affect decisions as validation of their own abilities, as well as for those who report to them.

A final observation several interviewees made about power/influence concerns "magical thinking." Managers sense that others in the organization believe they have more control over policies and decisions than they actually do. They commented that, for those outside middle management, power/influence is tied to their position in the organization rather than to an individual. As a consequence, staff expectations of what a middle manager can actually achieve are frequently much greater than what middle managers themselves feel can be delivered, which can be a source of frustration for everyone involved. The more senior practitioners in our group discussed managing such expectations as an important aspect of the job.

A final theme that emerged from our conversations is that, for the majority, middle management is a destination position, not necessarily a stepping stone to a higher spot in the organization. They take pride in their position and achievements. For the most part, middle managers like the work they're doing and speak of it as "real" work. To our surprise, few interviewees saw their current positions as a career path to senior management.

THE GOOD NEWS ABOUT MIDDLE MANAGEMENT

Interviewees expressed a great deal of satisfaction with their positions. They consider themselves experts in their respective areas. Middle management allows them to be recognized for their expertise, and they use their knowledge and skills to effect positive change. The changes middle managers implement are usually in the form of process improvement, but they can also be related to policy or organizational change.

Our subjects like working with others to achieve a common goal. They see tangible results as more easily achievable within the scope of their own department than in the larger organization. Extrapolating from these comments, this sense of achievement and a belief that it is not often present in senior management positions are primary reasons middle managers do not universally desire or seek advancement.

These middle managers have the advantage of being able to see a direct relationship between their efforts and results. Mentoring and empowering others in direct reporting relationships are some of the greatest rewards of middle management positions. For example, several mentioned great satisfaction in watching paraprofessional staff they had mentored decide to enter an MLS program and move on to professional library positions.

THE BAD NEWS ABOUT MIDDLE MANAGEMENT

The occasional need to implement decisions they didn't make or don't support is the primary negative aspect of the job. This was often expressed as a feeling of powerlessness. Having said that, it was universally understood that it is their job to implement these decisions and convince staff to support them. It is also important to note that middle managers are less dissatisfied about implementing decisions they don't like when they know they have been granted some degree of input.

Middle management spends a great deal of time putting out fires and resolving personnel conflicts within their own areas. This is stressful and frequently not very satisfying, because certain issues never seem fully resolved. In general, middle managers like to get things done and believe their efforts matter, but sometimes this is just not possible, no matter how skillful they are. Another downside of the constant need to respond to small irritations is that it takes away time from self-reflection and professional development.

Several indicated they had to learn too many lessons on the job and that, in retrospect, they wish they had received prior training in management specific to middle management responsibilities. Though many agree that additional training would have been helpful, most are unable to identify what would have been the most appropriate source of training.

ADVICE TO MIDDLE MANAGERS

We asked what advice they would give to new or experienced middle managers. With only one exception, the advice to both groups was the same.

Number one on the list was to know as much as possible about the work performed by each member of the department. Being an experienced and skillful manager of people is necessary, but not sufficient. Knowing your area was repeatedly stressed as the most important indicator of good middle management. This means being able to perform each job in the department, though this level of knowledge was not endorsed by everyone. A corollary to this advice from the majority was that stepping in and doing departmental staff work from time to time is important to demonstrate continuing expertise and solidarity with those on the front lines.

Number two was that, although functional expertise is primary, middle managers must also enjoy the art of management, or they run the risk of becoming micromanagers. If middle managers don't embrace leadership, they may concentrate their energies on monitoring processes and people instead of on necessary planning and decision making. In addition, they share responsibilities and take pleasure in using their position to empower others.

The third item was to maintain good working relationships with peers. Most see this as essential for exerting influence and getting work done in our highly interconnected library organizations. Beyond the work-related advantages of these relationships, they provide a professional and personal network of support. For many, these networks somewhat compensate for lack of formal management training.

Number four was to ask for help whenever necessary. Because middle managers are so frequently focused on their own departments, they can become isolated and forget that peers, mentors, and professional associates are more than willing to share their own knowledge and provide useful insights into a pressing local problem.

Interviewees provided some additional recommendations for long-term middle managers related to the need for continuous learning. Regardless of how long they had served in a middle management position, they identified complacency as a potential occupational hazard. They expressed that overcoming complacency is their own responsibility. Keeping current with trends in the profession was considered the best way to accomplish this. Curiosity was identified as a valuable aspect for middle managers.

CONCLUSIONS

Our interviewees provided great insights into the job of library middle management, how they get things done, and what they like about their jobs. Through participation in these conversations, the authors reached their own conclusions about middle management and have some advice for senior library administration:

Effective middle managers are key to implementing leadership vision and strategic initiatives through their attention to the ongoing operations of the organization. Select them wisely and nurture them through mentoring and appropriate training. Middle managers like to be given the authority to be the "masters of their own domains," but they do not necessarily find it empowering to be placed in the position of having to negotiate on behalf of the library with administrators in higher level positions.

Last, middle managers want senior administrators to provide clear direction, preferably after consultation. Without strong leadership from senior management, middle managers find it much more difficult to be effective and experience the rewards they hope to achieve in their positions.

((()))

The authors express sincere thanks to colleagues who thoughtfully responded to these questions and provided us with so many valuable perspectives into their roles as middle managers.

REFERENCES

Bailey, Martha J. 1987. "Middle Managers in Libraries/Information Services." *Library Administration and Management* 1 (4): 139–142.

Library Personnel News. 2000. "Carrying Out Orders When You're in the Middle." *Library Personnel News* 13 (3/4): 4.

Lubans, John, Jr. 2004. "Leading from the Middle." *Library Administration and Management* 18 (4): 205–207.

Schachter, Debbie. 2006. "Stuck in the Middle (Management)." *Information Outlook* 10 (11): 8–9.

Sowards, Steven W. 1999. "Observations of a First-Year Middle Manager." *College and Research Libraries News* 60 (7): 523.

Sullivan, Maureen. 1992. "The Changing Role of the Middle Manager in Research Libraries." *Library Trends* 41 (2): 269–281.

APPENDIX: INTERVIEW QUESTIONS

1. Do you consider yourself a middle manager (MM)? Why or why not?

2. What is the role of the MM in your organization? What are some positive and negative aspects of MM? What are some of the surprises?

3. How much power would you say MMs have in your organization? Do they use it effectively?

4. What are the traits and practices of a successful MM?

5. Can you think of an example of successful MM from your own experience or from your organization? Why was it successful?

6. What are common mistakes that MMs make?

7. Can you think of a MM experience that did not end successfully? Why was it unsuccessful?

8. What advice would you give to a new MM?

9. What advice would you give to someone who has been in a MM position for a long period of time?

7

BUSINESS BOOKS FOR THE LIBRARY MIDDLE MANAGER

An Annotated Bibliography

JOE C. CLARK

THIS ANNOTATED BIBLIOGRAPHY LISTS BOOKS THAT OFFER PRACTICAL APPROACHES to everyday issues encountered by library middle managers, from conducting performance evaluations to addressing difficult situations. It is divided into six categories relevant to most middle managers: general management, leadership, conflict management and consensus building, performance assessment, coaching and motivation, and interviewing and recruitment. Tags indicate major topics in each book. This bibliography is concise—titles were selected by user ratings, reviews, price (usually less than $25), and availability at bookstores and libraries.

With hundreds of books on general management and specific management topics, I begin with several series, franchises, and publishers that I find worth exploring.

SERIES, FRANCHISES, AND PUBLISHERS OF NOTE

The One-Minute Manager franchise, by Kenneth Blanchard and various coauthors, has sold millions of books. The original work, first published in 1981, stresses three things: one-minute goals, one-minute praisings, and one-minute reprimands. Most of the following books serve as companions to this original volume. Topics include team building, negotiation, leadership, and work/life balance.

The For Dummies series by Wiley has been available for twenty years and offers titles on just about any topic imaginable. Several management titles provide information for both new and experienced middle managers. Topics of interest to middle managers include communicating effectively, leadership, coaching, motivating employees, conflict resolution, managing teams, performance appraisals, and successful time management.

McGraw-Hill's Perfect Phrases series supplies managers with hundreds of phrases to use in specific situations. Each title usually offers some insights on addressing the situation. Subjects include performance reviews, handling conflict, difficult situations, motivating and rewarding employees, documenting performance problems, communicating change, and setting performance goals. If you encounter difficulties making your words effective, you should find this series useful.

Perfect Phrases for Managers and Supervisors, **2nd ed.,** by Merly Runion, provides verbiage similar to that found in several books in the Perfect Phrases series referenced above. It includes phrases for delegating, setting goals, coaching and empowering employees, conducting performance reviews, and addressing behavior problems. Runion begins with chapters on workforce demographics and communication as well as the dynamics of communication.

American Management Association (AMACOM; www .amanet.org) publishes dozens of books, many of which library middle managers will find useful. Subject areas include leadership, business writing, customer service, project management, time management, and training.

The Briefcase Books series by McGraw-Hill offers a variety of topics for middle managers. With similar icons to Wiley's For Dummies series, they are easy to use and provide practical advice. Topics include project management, communicating effectively, interviewing techniques, mentoring, and performance management.

The Harvard Business School Press Pocket Mentor series presents solutions for middle managers in a reader-friendly format. Though only some are relevant to library middle managers, each title presents self-tests, tools, and examples to master skills. Areas covered include leading teams, managing projects, providing feedback, leading people, becoming a new manager, persuading people, managing stress, and giving presentations.

GENERAL MANAGEMENT

Grimme, Don, and Sheryl Grimme. *The New Manager's Tool Kit: 21 Things You Need to Know to Hit the Ground Running.* New York: American Management Association, 2009.

Twenty-one tools are examined in this book's six parts: Leading People, Different Strokes, Leader Effectiveness, Optimizing Contributions, Personal and Interpersonal Effectiveness, and Eliminating Conflict. The tools address how to keep employees happy, life/work balance, active listening, dealing with difficult people, and preventing workplace harassment and violence. It

is full of tips, worksheets, applications, and tables. This information is of value to both new and initiated library managers. A resource guide lists websites, books, and articles for further study.

Tags: Leadership, Communication, Coaching, Team Building, Work-Life Balance, Conflict Management

Hill, Linda A. *Becoming a Manager: How New Managers Master the Challenges of Leadership.* Boston: Harvard Business School Press, 2003.

Written specifically for new managers, individuals considering management, or those who train new managers, this book examines the process of becoming a manager. Hill analyzes the experiences of nineteen new managers and offers valuable insights on the transition to becoming a manager. Unlike most titles in the bibliography, this work is over 300 pages and therefore not suitable for quick reference

Tags: Manager Roles, Coaching, Team Building, Lifelong Learning, Communication

Hunsaker, Phil, and Tony Alessandra. *The New Art of Managing People: Person-to-Person Skills, Guidelines, and Techniques Every Manager Needs to Guide, Direct, and Motivate the Team.* Rev. ed. New York: Free Press, 2008.

Based on the philosophy that employees work best when their managers encourage optimum personality expression, the authors present ways to understand and relate to different types of people. Interactive communication skills assist the knowledgeable supervisor with solving problems in an open and honest environment. Filled with diagrams, figures, and bulleted lists, this book should help any manager work more effectively with employees.

Tags: Manager Roles, Performance Appraisals, Ethics, Diversity, Learning Styles, Decision Making, Communication, Team Building, Conflict Management, Leadership

Parkinson, Robert, and Gary Grossman. *Becoming a Successful Manager: Powerful Tools for Making a Smooth Transition to Managing a Team.* New York: McGraw-Hill, 2010.

Although the title suggests that this book is for new managers, it offers information that will prove useful for the experienced as well. The focus is on building a strong team that can solve problems and enjoys good communication. Short chapters address topics in a concise manner and provide "discovery lessons" and "questions to consider" to reinforce points. The appendix summarizes the entire work in bulleted lists.

Tags: Manager Roles, Communication, Coaching, Hiring, Performance Appraisals, Delegating, Conflict Management, Conducting Meetings

Tracy, Diane. *The First Book of Common-Sense Management: How to Overcome Managerial Madness by Finding the Simple Keys to Success.* New York: William Morrow and Company, 1990.

Geared toward new managers, this book offers basic information in small quantities. Most pages make one point, usually reinforcing a theme (e.g., "a leader is . . ."), or as part of a list (e.g., the principles of learning have eleven points, each on its own page). Tracy, who is president of her own management consulting firm, uses a Zen-like approach for this book, dispensing advice in a succinct and minimalist manner.

Tags: Manager Roles, Leadership, Teamwork, Conflict Management, Hiring, Interviewing, Performance Appraisals, Communication

Tulgan, Bruce. *It's Okay to Be the Boss: The Step-by-Step Guide to Becoming the Manager Your Employees Need.* New York: Harper Collins, 2007.

Tulgan presents a straightforward approach to being a manager, including setting expectations, coaching, monitoring performance, and intervening when needed. He dispels what he considers the seven top management myths (which include being fair by treating everyone the same, and that "hands off" is the way to avoid confrontations with employees). In the final chapter, Tulgan provides steps to implement management practices outlined in the book.

Tags: Leadership, Communication, Performance Appraisals

LEADERSHIP

Brown, W. Steven. *13 Fatal Errors Managers Make and How You Can Avoid Them.* New York: Berkley Books, 1987.

Geared specifically for profit-driven businesses, this book still supplies plenty of advice relevant to library middle managers who supervise others. The errors Brown presents include treating everyone the same way, focusing on problems rather than objectives, failing to develop people, and recognizing only top performers. An "evasive action plan" for avoiding each error appears at the end of each chapter, and charts and action contracts help reinforce concepts.

Tags: Leadership, Coaching

Kotter, John P. *Leading Change.* Boston: Harvard Business School Press, 1996.

Although this book is targeted to both middle and upper management, library middle managers implementing change should find many valuable strategies. Kotter describes an eight-stage process for leading change: (1) establishing a sense of urgency, (2) creating the guiding coalition, (3) developing a vision and strategy, (4) communicating the change vision, (5) empowering employees for broad-based action, (6) generating short-term wins, (7) consolidating gains and producing more change, and (8) anchoring new approaches in the culture. The author stresses lifelong learning through mental habits such as risk taking, self-reflection, and being open to new ideas.

Tags: Leadership, Communication

Ponder, Randall D. *Leadership Made Easy.* Entrepreneur Press, 2005.

Ponder, a consultant on leadership development, divides this work into four parts. Part One, "Understanding Leadership," examines the importance of a leader as well as leadership style and attitudes. Part Two focuses on technical and analytical skills such as managing priorities and projects, problem solving, and training. Part Three centers on relationship skills including communication, teamwork, motivation, conflict resolution, and coaching. Ponder then discusses strategic abilities (vision, strategy, and change), which he considers upper-management skills, in Part Four. This book should be useful for any library middle manager.

Tags: Leadership, Conflict Management, Project Management, Training, Communication, Team Building, Diversity, Coaching

Wagner, Rodd, and James K. Harter. *12: The Elements of Great Managing.* New York: Gallup Press, 2006.

This book is based on empirical research by the Gallup Organization. It addresses twelve elements of work life, which served as the basis for the 1999 best seller *First, Break All the Rules.* This sequel centers on meeting needs of employees while addressing the needs of the organization. The twelve elements required by the engaged employee include knowing what is expected, recognition for work well done, knowing someone cares about you as a person, being encouraged to develop professionally, and knowledge that your opinion counts. Having an understanding of the twelve needs will help any library middle manager better supervise employees.

Tags: Leadership, Communication

CONFLICT MANAGEMENT AND CONSENSUS BUILDING

Bell, Arthur H., and Dayle M. Smith. *Winning with Difficult People.* 3rd ed. Hauppauge, NY: Barrons, 2004.

The authors provide techniques for coping with the twelve difficult personality types, which include "the backstabber," "the busybody," "the short fuse," and "the liar." They also address active listening, writing to difficult people, and strategies for dealing with specific types of challenging situations. A personality trait assessment allows readers to determine their predispositions and how they can predict behavior with other personalities. Easy to read, with plenty of good tactics for handling demanding bosses, employees, and patrons.

Tags: Communication, Leadership, Conflict Management

Bolton, Robert. *People Skills: How to Assert Yourself, Listen to Others, and Resolve Conflicts.* New York: Simon and Schuster, 1979.

Bolton focuses on five skills critical to developing interpersonal relationships: listening, assertiveness, conflict resolution, collaborative problem solving, and skill selection, which enables one to determine which communication skill is most appropriate to a given situation. He also examines twelve barriers to communication. This work is thorough and well written.

Tags: Communication, Conflict Management

Dressler, Larry. *Consensus through Conversation: How to Achieve High-Commitment Decisions.* San Francisco: Berrett-Koehler, 2006.

Understanding how to build consensus will help any middle manager get buy-in from high-level administrators or put together a successful team. Dressler skillfully defines consensus, analyzes what is necessary to create it, and explains how to work with disagreement and traps that can undermine the process. Ten tips for better consensus meetings, such as setting clear ground rules, distinguishing "must" from "want" criteria, and putting the discussion in a fishbowl, are covered. This book is a must for middle managers making changes or having issues with buy-in on any level.

Tags: Conflict Management, Communication

Grote, Dick. *Discipline without Punishment: The Proven Strategy That Turns Problem Employees into Superior Performers.* 2nd ed. New York: American Management Association, 2006.

This approach does not provide traditional warnings, reprimands, and suspensions; rather, it focuses on personal responsibility without punishment. Though some aspects are beyond the scope of a middle manager, such as a paid day-off (which Grote calls "Decision Making Leave"), some steps and approaches should help middle managers resolve employee performance issues.

Tags: Conflict Management, Performance Assessment, Communication

Kusy, Mitchell E., and Elizabeth L. Holloway. *Toxic Workplace! Managing Toxic Personalities and Their Systems of Power.* San Francisco: Jossey-Bass, 2009.

This book, the result of a two-year study, is in two parts. The first concentrates on understanding toxic people and environments, and the second discusses the Toxic Organization Change System Model. Addressing toxicity at the organizational, team, and individual levels, the authors examine strategies to move beyond a toxic workplace. Though material on toxicity at the organizational level is beyond the purview of middle managers, it is informative and worth knowing. The final chapter explores nine myths regarding toxic employees, including that toxic behavior is a solo act and toxic people know exactly what they are doing. Two appendixes provide the researcher with methods and responses from the author's national survey.

Tags: Leadership, Team Building, Coaching, Performance Appraisals, Communication, Conflict Management

Maravelas, Anna. *How to Reduce Workplace Conflict and Stress: How Leaders and Their Employees Can Protect Their Sanity and Productivity from Tension and Turf Wars.* Franklin Lakes, NJ: Career Press, 2005.

Helping with stressful situations both at work and in life, Maravelas discusses how to handle conflict and end workplace blame and mistrust. She details the cost of irritability and contempt in the workplace, then proceeds to list steps to replace negative energy with energy-sustaining activities. Maravelas also looks at possible causes of workplace stress, addressing tense issues, five reasons to ditch hostility, and how to create a culture of appreciation. Numerous examples, exercises, diagrams, and quotes reinforce her message. This work is suitable for all middle managers.

Tags: Communication, Conflict Management

Stone, Douglass, Bruce Patton, and Sheila Heen. *Difficult Conversations: How to Discuss What Matters Most.* New York: Viking, 2010.

Difficult conversations abound when working with people, and middle managers generally have more than their fair share. These authors teach at the Harvard Negotiation Project and discuss several approaches to such conversations, including decoding their structure and complexity, as well as the emotional and identity issues at stake. The book concludes with a five-step checklist for difficult situations which, if followed, should take stress out of such encounters.

Tags: Communication, Conflict Resolution

PERFORMANCE ASSESSMENT

Arthur, Diane. *The First-Time Manager's Guide to Performance Appraisals.* New York: American Management Association, 2008.

This book focuses on all aspects of performance appraisal including overview, preparation, writing advice, face-to-face meetings, and how to handle difficult situations. Throughout each chapter, tips concisely summarize the material (the complete list of tips appears as an appendix). Though geared specifically to first-time managers, the information should prove helpful to any middle manager who approaches performance appraisals with anxiety.

Tags: Performance Appraisals, Communication

Falcone, Paul. *2600 Phrases for Effective Performance Reviews: Ready-to-Use Words and Phrases That Really Get Results.* New York: American Management Association, 2005.

Similar in format to the Perfect Phrases books, the first half of this work (80+ pages) is what one might expect: phrases for core performance competencies. The second half consists of performance evaluation phrases for specific jobs, which is less useful to library middle managers. Appendices include lists of high-impact verbs and adverbs and a common five-point grading scale.

Tags: Performance Appraisals

Green, Marnie E. *Painless Performance Evaluations: A Practical Approach to Managing Day-to-Day Employee Performance.* Upper Saddle River, NJ: Pearson Prentice Hall, 2006.

Beginning with an explanation of why performance management is even necessary, Green walks the reader through the entire performance evaluation process: setting goals, documenting fairly and legally, addressing performance issues, rating, writing up evaluations, conducting the evaluation session, and encouraging employees to participate in the process. The book is easy to use, with summaries and self-tests at the end of chapters. Green suggests that readers pick and choose concepts that work for them in developing their personal approach to the evaluation process.

Tags: Performance Appraisals, Communication

Neal, James, Jr. *Effective Phrases for Performance Appraisals: A Guide to Successful Evaluations.* Perrysburg, OH: Neal Publications, 2006.

The majority of this work consists of effective phrases in thirty-three categories, such as planning, motivation, and writing skills. The remainder presents two-word phrases, helpful adjectives and verbs, terms for performance rankings and time frequency, and a useful five-page chapter on guidelines for successful evaluations. Although the author presents only positive phrases that reflect superior performance, they can be modified for negative performance situations. Recommended for any middle manager who struggles to find words for performance appraisals.

Tags: Performance Appraisal

COACHING AND MOTIVATION

Chandler, Steve, and Scott Richardson. *100 Ways to Motivate Others: How Great Leaders Can Produce Insane Results without Driving People Crazy.* Rev. ed. Franklin Lakes, NJ: Career Press, 2008.

Each of the one hundred motivational strategies are self-contained as short numbered chapters, allowing one to integrate techniques at a selected pace. Chapters provide examples and quotes, and a variety of topics are covered, including "Do the Worst First," "Give Up Being Right," "Always Show Them," and "Motivate by Doing."

Tags: Leadership, Team Building, Coaching

Ford, Lynda. *Transform Your Workplace: 52 Proven Strategies to Motivate, Energize, and Kick Productivity Up to the Next Level.* New York: McGraw-Hill, 2005.

This book by professional consultant Ford offers fifty-two short chapters complete with bullet points, exercises, and tables. She uses the FAST acronym (focused, action-oriented, simple, and timely) for these strategies and suggests incorporating one concept a week.

Tags: Leadership, Coaching

Grensing-Pophal, Lin. *Motivating Today's Employees.* 2nd ed. Bellingham, WA: Self-Council Press, 2002.

This edition is divided into three parts: the basics of motivation; the first line of influence; and programs, policies, and practices. The first section examines motivational theory, common fallacies, and what motivates employees. Properly getting new employees on board, in conjunction with communication and coaching, are covered in the second section. The third provides more of a human resources/upper management perspective on how an organization can offer perks that keep employees motivated. Grensing-Pophal has plenty of straightforward advice for middle managers.

Tags: Motivation, Coaching, Communication, Human Resources

Johnson, W. Brad, and Charles R. Ridley. *The Elements of Mentoring.* Rev. ed. New York: Palgrave Macmillan, 2008.

Quickly becoming a classic, this work examines sixty-five elements of effective mentoring. These center around six themes: what outstanding mentors do; traits of great mentors; arranging the mentor-mentee relationship; knowing oneself as a mentor; what to do when things go wrong; and welcoming change and closure. Each element is considered in a short chapter, which is summarized in a bulleted "Key Components" list. A list of scholarly references is provided for those seeking further study.

Tags: Coaching, Communication

Murphy, Mark. *Hundred Percenters: Challenge Your Employees to Give It Their All, and They'll Give You Even More.* New York: McGraw-Hill, 2010.

The premise of this work is that most employees do not give 100 percent. Murphy discusses methods for increasing productivity and challenging your employees. These include goal setting, accountability with constructive feedback, positive reinforcement, the roles of demotivation and motivation, and how to handle employees with bad attitudes.

Tags: Communication, Coaching, Employee Recognition

Ventrice, Cindy. *Make Their Day! Employee Recognition That Works: Proven Ways to Boost Morale, Productivity, and Profits.* 2nd ed. San Francisco: Berrett-Koehler, 2009.

This edition focuses on techniques to make your employees feel valued, which in turn results in higher morale and productivity. Topics include elements and types of recognition, motivating employees, creating a respectful work environment, and how to best recognize someone. Real-world examples, action lists, and tips abound, offering many useful takeaways.

Tags: Coaching, Leadership

NTERVIEWING AND RECRUITING

Falcone, Paul. *96 Great Interview Questions to Ask before You Hire.* 2nd ed. New York: American Management Association, 2009.

This book's three parts address interview questions; selecting and securing candidates; and issues in interviewing, reference checking, and recruitment. Though some of this information may not apply to middle managers, Falcone addresses what is legal (and illegal) to ask, conducting successful telephone interviews, and getting real information from references. Regarding traditional interview questions, he discusses why each question should be asked, how to analyze responses, what constitutes a good answer, and what red flags to look for.

Tags: Recruitment, Interviewing

Hoevemeyer, Victoria A. *High-Impact Interview Questions: 701 Behavior-Based Questions to Find the Right Person for Every Job.* New York: American Management Association, 2006.

Behavior-based interview questions elicit accurate examples of a candidate's behavior and experiences, which provide insight on future conduct. Hoevemeyer begins by examining various types of interview questions, then explains how to utilize behavior-based questions to select the candidate best suited for your organization. Most of this work is sample questions grouped by category, plus information on other hiring aspects such as telephone screening, creating an interview guide, assembling interviewer data, and using established competencies in performance management and training. The author also provides a short list of resources.

Tags: Recruitment, Interviewing

Podmoroff, Dianna. *501+ Great Interview Questions for Employers and the Best Answers for Prospective Employees.* Ocala, FL: Atlantic Publishing Group, 2005.

In addition to the 501+ interview questions, Podmoroff discusses how to set the proper tone during the beginning of an interview as well as building interview questions with follow-up questions (probes). For a question or group of similar questions, an analysis is provided from the interviewer's perspective. Most chapters focus on questions related to a specific area, such as motivation, decision making, teamwork, and creativity. One chapter offers skill-based behavioral questions, and the final chapter lists competencies along with a definition for each.

Tags: Recruitment, Interviewing

Thompson, Carolyn B. *Interviewing Techniques for Managers*. New York: McGraw-Hill, 2002.

Rather than focus on the job interview, this book presents techniques for interviewing in a variety of contexts, such as discussing projects with a colleague or gaining needed information from a frustrated patron. Based on behavioral interviewing, this work should allow all middle managers to improve communication skills.

This is one of McGraw-Hill's Briefcase Books and presents the content in an easy-to-read fashion with sidebars and icons to reinforce key points.

Tags: Communication, Interviewing

Yates, Martin. *Hiring the Best: A Manager's Guide to Effective Interviewing and Recruiting*. 5th ed. Avon, MA: Adams Media, 2006.

Although this book is geared for the business environment, Yates covers all aspects of hiring, including determining one's needs, how to read a resume, telephone interviews, the art and science of the interview, and legal protocols when interviewing. He lists interview questions along with what they are designed to reveal and follow-ups for obtaining additional information. The fifth edition has a list of reference websites that provide additional information on a host of subjects.

Tags: Interviewing, Recruiting

8

RETHINKING INTERPERSONAL COMMUNICATION FOR MANAGERS

MARIE L. RADFORD

ONE OF THE FASCINATING CHARACTERISTICS OF HUMAN COMMUNICATION IS that it is something people do every day in all kinds of different contexts: at work and at home, among family, in friendships and romantic relationships, even when buying something from the store. Communication is an integral skill for middle managers who face communication situations with superiors and subordinates on a daily basis. One way of viewing a manager's work is as a series of communication encounters with individuals or small groups/teams (with occasional public speaking to larger groups).

In work and in life, communication is ubiquitous and commonplace. Yet it is also complex and difficult to understand and master. This seeming contradiction can make the manager's role frustrating: if communication is so common and supposedly easy, why is communication in the workplace so difficult and stressful?

Communication scholars have spent decades studying the dynamics of communication. They have attempted to describe and understand what makes communication effective and ineffective and how a person's communication skills might be improved. One problem these scholars have identified is that people have certain ideas about communication that make change difficult. Because individuals grow up communicating in a certain way, they tend to believe that their communication style is a natural part of their personalities, a fixed part of them and who they are. Many also believe intuitively that communication is a simple linear process of one person transmitting thoughts to another, and that good communication is "achieved" when the receiver has in mind the same idea the speaker intended.

Although communication scholars have largely abandoned these views for more interactive, relational, and constructivist approaches, many people see these linear and transmission views of communication as simply common sense. Getting beyond these linear conceptions to the realization that meaning is negotiated and co-constructed, rather than just merely transferred from one person to another, is vital to understanding what happens when people communicate. This realization can also enable managers to adapt their behavior accordingly, so that communication is more effective for everyone concerned.

Library management textbooks typically present a best practices approach to communication and reinforce linear and transmission conceptions of communication (e.g., Stueart and Moran 2007). They provide lists of "what to do" and "what not to do" to communicate effectively, which usually means that communication encounters for managers are presented as goal-directed events, where the manager enters into a conversation or meets with a group in order to forward a particular goal (e.g., to inquire about progress on a project; to request information, feedback, or action). However, this best practices approach with a focus on goals has limitations that stem from the complex and relational nature of human interaction.

One useful framework is to consider communication in terms of the relational needs of people rather than simply transmitting messages to achieve goals (e.g., Radford 1999; Radford and Connaway 2010; Ross, Nilsen, and Radford 2009). This approach is taken from seminal work by Watzlawick, Beavin, and Jackson (1967), who asserted that every message has two dimensions, the content (the "what" or information to be communicated) and the relational (the "how" message is to be taken, based on the relationship of the participants). When middle managers communicate with subordinates, it is important for them to realize that others have relational, interpersonal needs in addition to content or information needs. For example, consider the following fairly common interaction in public and academic libraries.

SCENARIO 1
OVERDUE FINE DILEMMA

The scene: A library user is at the circulation desk. When she tries to check out an item, the circulation assistant finds that the user has an overdue fine. The library's procedure is to not allow checkouts until the fine is paid if the fine is over $10.00.

Circulation assistant: "I'm sorry, but you must pay the $10.50 fine you owe before you can check out this item."

Library user: "I don't have any money on me today, can I pay next time I come in? I really need this item for a deadline I'm working on."

Circulation assistant: "I'm not able to let you do that, but you can talk to the department head, who is in her office, if you like."

Library user: "O.K, that would be good. Thanks."

Circulation assistant goes and gets the department head, who is in the middle of doing a report and is annoyed at being interrupted. The department head unhappily gets up and goes with the assistant to the circulation desk.

Department head: (speaking loudly to the circulation assistant in front of the library user) "Why are you bothering me with this type of thing? It's only 50 cents over the $10 limit. Go ahead and do the override, and don't ever bother me again with this type of problem—you already know what to do, just do it!" Storms back to office and shuts the door.

Circulation assistant: Turns red, looks down, and does the checkout. Is upset for the rest of the day.

Library user: Turns red, accepts book, mumbles "thanks," and walks away, feeling upset.

This exchange between the department head and the circulation assistant would be considered an example of poor managerial communication, but why is it seen this way? We can look at the interaction from both content and relational perspectives. On the content level, what the manager has to say to the circulation assistant is certainly clear. She has told the assistant he is empowered to make these decisions on his own, both in this case and in future cases. The user has gotten what she wants, the checkout of the needed item. At the level of content, the interaction can be considered effective and successful.

On the relational level, however, the manager has made several mistakes. First of all, she has shamed and embarrassed the assistant and library user by shouting and being condescending. Second, she has not thought about what long-term effects this interaction might have on the relationship between herself and the assistant, or on the library user's view of the library. Third, she has humiliated the assistant in public, in front of the library user and, indeed, anyone else who might have been near the circulation desk, whether other users or staff, or even possibly upper management.

From a relational point of view, this incident will not be quickly forgotten by the circulation assistant, even if the manager chooses to later apologize. The library user was also shamed by this encounter and could have a long-term association with these negative feelings when visiting the library in the future (see Chelton 1997).

The takeaway from this scenario is to consider the relational dimension of communication in all communication situations. Even though content was successfully communicated, relational damage has been done that is likely to be irreparable. Trust has also been compromised. A more empathetic approach in which the manager takes the relational aspect into account could involve two very different conversations, the first in the manager's office (scenario 2) and the second at the circulation desk (scenario 3).

SCENARIO 2
IN THE DEPARTMENT HEAD'S OFFICE

Same as scenario 1, taken from when the circulation assistant goes and talks to the department head, who is in the middle of doing a report and is annoyed at being interrupted.

Department head: (Stays seated in her office. Listens to what the assistant has to say and replies in a pleasant voice) "I'm glad you brought this to my attention. I'm tied up here with this report. What do you think? Would it be possible for you to go ahead and do the override for the user, then ask her to come in and pay the fine soon?"

Library assistant: "Yes, that sounds good."

Department head: "Okay, then, good. I'd also like you to know, by the way, that the next time this happens you don't have to ask me. I trust you to use your own judgment. I'm sure you'll know what to do. Thanks."

SCENARIO 3
AT THE CIRCULATION DESK

Same as scenario 1: Circulation assistant goes and gets the department head, who is in the middle of doing a report and is annoyed at being interrupted. The department head gets up and goes with the assistant to the circulation desk.

Department head: (Greets library user with a smile) "Hello. Chris here has told me about your fine. Although our policy is not to allow borrowing if you have more than $10 in fines, as Chris has said, in this case since you are only 50 cents over we are willing to do the checkout, if you agree to come in soon to pay the fine. I think this will be okay with Chris." Turns to Chris and nicely asks: "What do you think?"

Circulation assistant: "Yes, sounds fine." Chris checks out the item and gives eye contact and a pleasant nod to the library user.

Library user: "Thanks so much. I'll stop by soon. I really appreciate it."

Soon afterward, the department head calls the assistant into the office and says: "I'm so glad you brought that overdue fine situation to my attention. By the way, the next time this happens, I want you to know you don't have to ask me. I trust you to use your own judgment, I'm sure you'll know what to do. Thanks."

((()))

The conversation in scenario 2 reveals sensitivity to the importance of both the content and relational dimensions of communication and the cocreation of meaning. The department head allows the assistant to feel like he did the right thing and is empowered to make decisions in the future. The scenario 3 conversation is also positive since it reaffirms the assistant's self-esteem in front of the library user by including Chris in the decision to allow the override. The assistant will feel good about the incident and will also know what to do in similar situations in the future. The manager has worked to save the subordinate's face and to involve him in the decision making. In addition, the subordinate has been thanked and praised, which allows him to feel valued.

The relational approach to communication is also consistent with having an assertive communication style. In scenario 1 we saw an example of negative, aggressive communication, whereas scenarios 2 and 3 are more in line with positive, assertive communication. Managers who are assertive clearly state what they want, but they do so in a manner that pays attention to others' content and relational needs. "Assertive people hold themselves and others accountable, especially to speak up. . . . they believe they and others have the responsibility to ask for what they need" (CareerTrack 1994, 10). Some of the behaviors of the assertive communicator are (1) making a direct request; (2) using declarative "I" statements; (3) remaining calm if needing to confront, describing unacceptable behavior and giving expectations for future behavior; (4) engaging in collaboration and compromise; and (5) expecting accountability, holding the other person responsible while asking for what is wanted. These behaviors (except for 3, as there is no confrontation in this case) are exemplified in scenarios 2 and 3.

The relational perspective is also applicable to interpersonal communication with upper management. The power differential sometimes makes middle managers feel that they are not empowered in decision making, but, again, it is important to establish good relationships through frequent dialogue and to strive to understand the other person's perspective and framework for how they interpret events and communication encounters.

CONCLUSIONS

Our communication prowess as middle managers is certainly vital to our success. But rather than depend on static recommendations to "be clear" or to "be direct," middle managers must develop a heightened sense of intuition, based on previous experience and on relationships they have developed with each person over time. This heightened sense allows managers to consider alternatives, to see situations from the another person's perspective, and to decide how best to approach people with a request, for example, or when it might be an opportune moment to do so.

Common sense and experience tell us that mistakes are inevitable, but such mistakes are valuable since they present significant learning opportunities. Success in resolving these mistakes, misunderstandings, or problems with others also leads to increased confidence in one's ability to assess a situation and take appropriate action.

Given a new awareness of how this "affect dimension" is present and impacts our ability to be effective managers, incremental improvement can be made as we learn from our experience and trial-and-error. Seeing how our communication style affects others and making positive changes may take some self-reflection and may involve asking others for feedback. Whether they interact with subordinates or superiors, or peers for that matter, savvy managers take responsibility for their communication behaviors and actions and also think in terms of the effects of their communication choices. It is a personal choice to work toward accomplishing organizational goals while maintaining positive relationships with everyone and presenting a positive role model.

REFERENCES

CareerTrack. 1994. *Assertive Communication Skills for Professionals.* Boulder, CO: CareerTrack.

Chelton, M. K. 1997. "The 'Overdue Kid:' A Face-to-Face Library Service Encounter as Ritual Interaction." *Library and Information Science Research* 19 (4): 387–399.

Radford, Marie L. 1999. *The Reference Encounter: Interpersonal Communication in the Academic Library.* Chicago: Association of College and Research Libraries.

Radford, Marie L., and L. S. Connaway. 2010. "Getting Better All the Time: Improving Communication and Accuracy in Virtual Reference." In *Reference Renaissance: Current and Future Trends,* ed. Marie L. Radford and R. D. Lankes, 39–54. New York: Neal-Schuman.

Ross, Catherine Sheldrick, Kirsti Nilsen, and Marie L. Radford. 2009. *Conducting the Reference Interview.* 2nd ed. New York: Neal-Schuman.

Stueart, R. D., and B. B. Moran. 2007. *Library and Information Center Management,* 7th ed. Englewood, CO: Libraries Unlimited.

Watzlawick, P., J. H. Beavin, and D. D. Jackson. 1967. *Pragmatics of Human Communication.* New York: Norton.

9

THE MIDDLE IN THE MIDDLE

Maintaining Your Sanity while Mediating Conflict

AMANDA LEA FOLK

> Change means movement. Movement means friction. Only in the frictionless vacuum of a nonexistent abstract world can movement or change occur without that abrasive friction of conflict.
>
> —Saul Alinsky, *Rules for Radicals*

ARE YOU A DEVIL OR ANGEL?" JOYCE MANNA JANTO, DEPUTY DIRECTOR OF THE Law Library at University of Richmond, asks herself in an article that reflects upon her life as a middle manager (Janto 2004, 5). Somewhat surprisingly, this question is not directed toward how her own management style is perceived; rather, she is addressing the overall shift in the perception of middle management from the 1980s to the present. The term *middle management* used to be associated with laziness, greed, and corporate bloat—or as a "devil." However, Janto argues that this perception is changing, not just in the corporate world but in libraries: "Now middle managers are seen, maybe not as angels, but as the work horses of the world. Not flashy, not exciting, but we can be counted on to get the job done" (2004, 5).

Because of the nature of a middle management position, we try to balance requests from both our superiors and our subordinates while attempting to complete daily tasks. This requires us to act as a go-between for these parties, serving as a mediator or negotiator. This difficult position can sometimes make us feel as if we are devils, even when we are trying to be angels.

In his classic article about middle managers, Hugo Uyterhoeven (1989, 137) wrote that middle managers "act as subordinate, equal, and superior: upward, they relate to their bosses as subordinates—they take orders; downward, they relate to their teams as superiors—they give orders; laterally, they often relate to peers in the organization as equals." Looking at this description, we see that one of the positive aspects of being a middle manager is that we have a unique perspective on our library; we know a lot of what is happening on the administrative side, but we also are involved in the day-to-day tasks that enable the library to function. This means that we usually know what's in the pipeline, but we also know the intricacies of workflows and how our staff operates daily.

Such knowledge and perspective at times can be quite frustrating for middle managers. Staff members often feel more comfortable coming to us to make requests for change or to air grievances, and administrators rely on us to hand down and enact directives that may not be popular. This can make us feel we are stuck between a rock and a hard place—the middle in the middle. Being in this position, we are expected by our colleagues to mediate or negotiate conflicts between various parties. But what exactly does it mean to be a mediator or negotiator?

During the Renaissance, the term *mediator* could have been (almost) synonymous with the phrase *middle manager*. At that time, a mediator was simply "a go-between; a messenger, agent." Over time, though, the definition of *mediator* has become a bit more nuanced, meaning "a person who intervenes between two parties, especially for the purpose of effecting reconciliation; an intercessor; a person who brings about an agreement, treaty, etc., or settles a dispute by mediation" (OED Online).

Typically it is assumed that, when a person is acting as a mediator, he or she is a disinterested third party. Although this is sometimes true of middle managers, it is not often the case. Instead, we become more a negotiator, or "a person who discusses a problem with the aim of achieving agreement between different people or groups of people" (Ivanovic 2006, 176). A negotiator usually represents one of the parties in the negotiation and is not a disinterested third party. As middle managers we often have a stake, albeit sometimes only a minor one, in the decision being handed down or in the conflict we are attempting to resolve. Because of this, we walk a fine line between being a mediator and being a negotiator, sometimes acting as a combination of both.

What's a middle manager to do when placed in the middle of conflict? Literature about library middle managers in the role of mediator or advocate is lacking to date. One can find many great articles and books about conflict and change management in libraries, but middle managers are in a unique position since they are not top-level managers with full authority (Uyterhoeven 1989). Here are my seven recommendations for middle managers who are acting as mediators, trying to keep all sides as happy as possible, and attempting to maintain a modicum of sanity at the same time.

Can you hear me now? Good!—The art of listening. If you're acting as a mediator or negotiator, chances are tensions are already running high. These tensions create a veritable breeding ground for misinterpretation and misunderstanding, even among groups who otherwise communicate well, which is why it is imperative that middle managers hone their communication skills. In many of these situations, one of the best communication skills you can apply, which is often forgotten, is simply listening

to what is being said. Not only does this help you truly understand the situation you are trying to mediate, it also shows respect toward those who are speaking.

In his book *The Power of a Positive No,* William Ury (2007, 85) writes, "Perhaps the simplest way to show respect is to listen with positive attention. . . . Listen for what underlying interests and needs may be driving them." Middle managers can demonstrate that they are listening by asking questions and restating, in their own words, what was just said. If your colleagues know you are listening to them and understand their arguments, you will continue to build trust and respect, which is important for a negotiating middle manager.

No one responds well to arrogance, and everyone wants to be heard. This point goes hand-in-hand with listening carefully and earning the trust and respect of your colleagues. Many middle managers, particularly those who are new or young, fear that asking for input or opinions demonstrates a weakness in their decision-making or leadership skills (Schachter 2008, 44). Don't fall into this trap. This could make you appear arrogant or condescending, even if that was not the intention.

Everyone has a valuable opinion or idea, no matter their rank in the hierarchy. A manager might think he has thought through a decision thoroughly, but he could be presented with an alternative perspective by a staff member that could alter it for the better. Remember, "How you see the world depends on where you sit" (Fisher, Ury, and Patton 1991, 23). "The expression of various opinions and approaches may lead to innovation and change, which can help the organization achieve its goals in new and better ways" (Kathman and Kathman 1990, 146).

A middle manager is the person to present directives from the administration to staff, some of which are unpopular. Gathering staff input, when possible, is one way to help eliminate opposition and make staff comfortable with changes being implemented (Schachter 2008). It also helps them believe that, by routinely making contributions to their library, they are considered valued members of the team, which boosts morale. Finally, gathering staff input allows you to put yourself in their shoes and truly understand their side of an issue or conflict. Fisher and colleagues (1991, 23) write, "The ability to see the situation as the other side sees it, as difficult as it may be, is one of the most important skills a negotiator can possess."

Honesty is the best policy, and sometimes "no" is the best answer. If you are a middle manager, it is not uncommon for staff members to ask you to appeal to administrators on their behalf. It is up to you to decide how to handle each situation. If you think the request is unreasonable or simply not feasible, you need to be honest and up front with staff. You should be armed with reasons why this is the case—perhaps it's the budget, or the timing is simply wrong. Further, if you plan to take action on a request, you need to articulate what you think is a sensible time line, so staff know how you will handle this situation. This allows you to work at your own pace without being asked about something constantly, which is frustrating and can cause burnout.

Although it is not always appropriate, or even possible, to say no to our superiors, we sometimes need to do just that by being honest about the circumstances "on the ground." For example, the administration informs you it would like to make changes in your staff members' job descriptions, but you know this will cause strife and discord within your department. You need to be honest about the reaction staff will have, why they will have that reaction, and how that reaction might affect morale and productivity. Determine the sources of and reasons for the changes in order to work out a compromise between your staff and the administration. If the changes are still implemented, you will at least know you've gone to bat for them.

Know the difference between a want and a need. Being the one who brings staff members' grievances or appeals for change to upper management can put you in a difficult position. One way to help make this a bit easier is to determine whether the request being made is a want or a need. We often want more than we actually need. As a middle manager, you don't want upper management to perceive you as constantly coming to them with requests. It is up to you to do your homework and be fully prepared when you visit them on behalf of your staff.

Let's say you supervise the workflow of a technical services department. Several catalogers come to you requesting that another part-time person be hired to help address some of the workload. You know that, at this time, the library's budget is tight, but not strained. In these circumstances, extra expenditure requests are highly discouraged. This is when you need to apply your library research skills to a management situation. You need to speak candidly to staff, conducting a reference interview of sorts to determine if time management or workflow indeed is the issue, or if there truly is a backlog with which staff cannot keep up. If the issue is time management or workflow, thus making the request a "want," you might work with staff to create more efficient processes to resolve their frustrations.

If, on the other hand, your staff is working at maximum efficiency and the backlog is growing, your department may need that extra person to supplement existing workflow. Just make sure you have all your numbers and evidence that indicate this is a need when you make an appeal to upper management, so you can be an effective negotiator.

Understand and respect different personality types. This attitude should include generational differences, cultural differences, and differences in communication styles. Such diversity helps us progress as an organization, but it can be a hindrance if it generates too much conflict. As a negotiator or mediator, you encounter many different personalities and communication styles—some that make your life easier and others that do not. Even if an employee's communication style drives you to your wit's end, it is best for both you and your staff not to alienate this employee, which would cause friction in the department. Keep in mind that such employees are not "trying to be difficult, but they need different or more information than you do. They're not intending to be rude" (Jourdain 2004, 23).

Remember, diversity is what helps the organization grow and change. The different perspectives and experiences each staff member brings to the table help the organization make informed decisions. Also, keep in mind that there are some traits you simply cannot change; rather, you need to develop coping strategies. You should develop different strategies for different employees, depending on their strengths and weaknesses.

Kathy Jourdain, a facilitator coach and consultant argues, "The good news about communication styles is that we all have the ability to develop flexibility in our styles. The greater flexibility we have, the more skilled we usually are at handling possible and actual conflicts" (2004, 25). This flexibility includes understanding how we, as mediators or negotiators, can attempt to prevent potential misunderstandings between different parties and effectively convey messages between them.

Remember that, fundamentally, we are all human beings. Although it is always preferable to separate one's work life from one's personal life, it is not always possible. Administrators and staff alike go through difficulties outside work, such as illness or grieving the loss of a loved one, which may affect their attitudes or performance at work. When this happens, it can be particularly hard to work out an agreement between conflicting parties, since these negative emotions can escalate existing conflicts. Former Ecuadorian president Jamil Mahuad reminds negotiators "that most negotiations are fundamentally about human relationships" and to remain empathetic during negotiations (Hackley 2004, 4). "Empathy allows the supervisor to approach in a supportive manner that will help the person express his or her concern and then return to the task at hand" (Montgomery and Cook 2005, 158).

Emotional intelligence, which includes being empathetic, is an important skill for a middle manager, particularly one mediating or negotiating conflict, to possess. Daniel Goleman, father of the emotional intelligence trend, believes that "people with these competencies [emotional intelligence] are adept at inducing desirable responses in others through handling difficult and tense situations with diplomacy and tact, spotting potential conflict, bringing disagreement into the open, and helping to de-escalate them, encouraging debate and discussion and orchestrating a win-win solution" (Schreier 2002, 100–101).

Pay attention to trends, but create a style that works for you and your colleagues. It seems like almost every day a new, "hot" management book is published. Though it is important to stay abreast of current management trends, ultimately you need to create a management style that is effective and comfortable for you and your colleagues. Be flexible with your style and realize that you need to change as your library and its staff change. Just as you need to be honest about what you expect from your staff and superiors, it is critical to understand what they need from you as a manager, especially when serving as a mediator or negotiator. Finally, keep in mind that your job as a middle manager occasionally requires you to be in some difficult and frustrating positions. You need to do the best you can with the tools readily available to you.

REFERENCES

Fisher, Roger, William Ury, and Bruce Patton. 1991. *Getting to Yes: Negotiating Agreement without Giving In*. New York: Penguin Books.

Hackley, Susan. 2004. "First, Empathize with Your Adversary." *Negotiation*, April, 3–4.

Ivanovic, A. 2006. *Dictionary of Human Resources and Personnel Management*. 3rd ed. London: A&C Black.

Janto, Joyce Manna. 2004. "Redemption: Reflections of a Life in Middle Management." *Trends in Law Library Management and Technology* 15 (1): 5–8.

Jourdain, Kathy. 2004. "Communication Styles and Conflict." *Journal for Quality and Participation* 27 (2): 23–25.

Kathman, Jane McGurn, and Michael D. Kathman. 1990. "Conflict Management in the Academic Library." *Journal of Academic Librarianship* 16 (3): 145–149.

Montgomery, Jack G., and Eleanor I. Cook. 2005. *Conflict Management for Libraries: Strategies for a Positive, Productive Workplace*. Chicago: American Library Association.

Schachter, Debbie. 2008. "Learn to Embrace Opposition for Improved Decision Making." *Information Outlook* 12 (10): 44–45.

Schreier, Lori S. 2002. "Emotional Intelligence and Mediation Training." *Conflict Resolution Quarterly* 20 (1): 99–119.

Ury, William. 2007. *The Power of a Positive No: How to Say No and Still Get to Yes*. New York: Bantam Books.

Uyterhoeven, Hugo. 1989. "General Managers in the Middle." *Harvard Business Review* 67 (5): 136–145.

10

HORIZONTAL COMMUNICATION

Social Networking in the Middle

NANCY J. KRESS

A S INTERMEDIARIES BETWEEN THE VERTICAL AND HORIZONTAL INTERSECTION of the organization, middle managers have the essential function of promoting communication that improves effectiveness. Instead of following vertical lines of communication—top-down, formal reporting lines—which stifle communication and cooperation across organizational boundaries, the middle manager as knowledge facilitator can coordinate an adaptive network of lateral exchanges between individuals and groups (Blumentritt and Hardie 2000, 41). Horizontal communication channels are more effective because individuals can leverage the expertise of those in other areas of the organization (Borgatti and Cross 2003, 433). Facilitating horizontal communication, middle managers can increase organizational effectiveness by connecting disparate people with mutually beneficial knowledge and skills, empowering employees, and creating a trusting environment to promote information sharing.

It is unrealistic to expect staff to be able to solve every problem on the basis of their accumulated knowledge, experience, and skills. Providing employees with the opportunity to develop personal networks promotes connectivity in the organization. Middle managers can develop their employees' ability to acquire information from elsewhere in the institution by creating efficient horizontal communication systems of the people involved in various aspects of the organization's work. In this chapter I present a model for middle managers to put these concepts into practice, describing how to target opportunities to initiate, develop, and maintain employees' social networks.

COMMUNICATION IN LIBRARIES

Most libraries can be characterized as a bureaucracy. The flow of communication is vertical, which centralizes control of information, so those at the top know what is going on. This system is most effective when management adheres to the chain of command. Instructions move down, information moves up (Simpson 1959, 189–190).

In 1979, Beverly Lynch wrote about the nature of library organizations, drawing on the work of Max Weber, a German sociologist whose analysis of bureaucracy is still central to the study of organizations. Lynch paraphrases Weber to describe bureaucracy as "characterized by a hierarchy of office, careful specification of office functions, recruitment on the basis of merit, promotion according to merit and performance, and a coherent system of discipline and control." She continues: "Libraries will remain bureaucratic in form . . . not in the red tape or pettiness of officials, but in the attempt of the library to control its environment" (Lynch 1979, 260, 267).

Almost thirty years later, little has changed. In 2007, Wood and colleagues wrote in *Beyond Survival: Managing Academic Libraries in Transition* that "virtually all organizational development experts—even those whose main focus is teams—acknowledge the validity and enduring value of the hierarchy" (Wood, Miller, and Knapp 2007, 42). The organizational chart prescribes formal relationships between staff and their supervisors. This restricts communication, since employees' primary sources of information are each other and their manager. Cooperation and collaboration between departments can be elusive when organizations are structured along functional and hierarchical lines, creating information monopolies.

But information technology has brought quantum changes to how librarians work and communicate. Library work has become more complex and knowledge intense as the purpose of libraries has shifted from providing books to providing information. Library work has increasingly become knowledge work, distinguished by recording, creating, and refining information and representations of information. Technologies such as e-mail and other forms of electronic communication have replaced phone and written correspondence as primary channels of communication (O'Kane, Hargie, and Tourish 2004, 75). Increases in speed and ease of access should coordinate information dissemination throughout the library, but the passing of information between people doesn't equal communication.

Knowledge work requires a different kind of communication, in which staff need more information from each other than from their supervisor. Excessive divisionalization creates critical gaps that prohibit cross-functional knowledge transfer. Slow, bureaucratic command-and-control communication models need to be replaced by models that integrate the exchange of information horizontally across functions.

Horizontal communication is described as the flow of information among peers at similar levels and across functional areas. The information staff need to perform day-to-day work comes not from senior management but rather from departments, groups, and individuals laterally within the organization. The old command-and-control style of management stifles cooperation across organizational boundaries necessary for meeting goals. Horizontal communication is less formal and structured than both downward communication and upward communication.

A benefit of horizontal communication is information sharing that facilitates group cooperation across all levels of the organization. These links across divisions are necessary to disseminate knowledge that facilitates problem solving and task coordination between departments and teams. When staff have a mutual understanding of what is needed to meet organizational goals, spontaneous flow of communication can cross throughout the organization (Massie 1960, 88). Many decisions can readily be made by staff without conscious attention from management.

In theory, we expect library employees to find information needed to inform their decisions through formal channels such as databases, the Internet, and data repositories. But in reality, employees tend to turn to informal channels, because of "information overload" or sparse information flow from formal channels such as academic journals. Although the amount of information on many practical topics has grown to prodigious proportions, these information repositories are underused because employees prefer to turn to colleagues for information (Cross and Parker 2004, 11).

Therefore, it is important to recognize that informal communication often supplants formal communication and occurs as part of social relationships (Bryson 1997, 277–278). People need information to do their work, and they prefer to get it from people they know, respect, and trust. Middle managers coordinate parts of the organization, positioned between the priorities of administrators and the realities of operational capabilities. By facilitating connections between people that would otherwise never communicate with each other, middle managers can promote and develop connectivity.

Libraries are dependent on the middle manager to act as intermediary of the communication network, as the central figure involved in one-on-one exchanges with individuals within and outside their department. A new role for middle managers is that of knowledge facilitator, by bringing employees together to share knowledge and create communication links in the organization (Blumentritt and Hardie 2000, 41).

LEVERAGING SOCIAL NETWORKS TO IMPROVE COMMUNICATION

Social networks are formally defined as relatively stable patterns of information exchange, which develop when individuals and groups of people communicate on a regular basis (Graber 2003, 93). Organizations also contain networks, although more purposefully and consciously designed. The middle manager can span communication gaps in these networks by directly connecting individuals, no matter where they exist on the organizational chart. Hierarchy tends to divide information flow along functional lines, which makes communication inefficient and less manageable.

Collaborative technology and e-mail are important for information sharing in libraries, but not sufficient to establish consistent channels of communication. Managers who offload communication onto technology are missing a key reality: people prefer to interact with one another in person (Hargie and Tourish 2004, 249). Two examples of how middle managers can facilitate development of horizontal networks are by improving the composition of networks and by influencing the degree of trust in new relationships.

Library middle managers can increase and enhance the flow of information by promoting new contacts across functional and hierarchical boundaries. Employees are often unable to initiate contact on their own, because hierarchy dictates that information must pass through the chain of command. Middle managers have relationships with a wide range of staff throughout multiple levels of the organization and are able to create new interactions between organizationally separated employees. Managers should seek to create new patterns of communication to fit the information requirements of their employees, from those in mutually relevant situations.

To assess which relationships will benefit from this investment, find out which staff in other areas of the library have potentially important information those who directly report to you may at some point need. Provide employees with the means to develop their personal networks by directly introducing people who would otherwise never communicate with each other.

Other dimensions of network composition to consider are sources of information and quality of information. Staff higher up can be critical to making decisions, staff at the same level are good for specific information for similar work issues, and staff at lower levels may have the technical ability to solve routine problems (Cross, Abrams, and Parker 2004, 155). Tailor selection of individuals to the relevance of the task to be performed. Involve people on the periphery only when a newcomer will add a beneficial perspective.

As the links multiply, the flow of communication changes from top-down to cross-functional exchanges. These interactions create more flexibility in the institution as middle managers add, restructure, or change connections between individuals. Over time, the efficient operation of the library can become highly dependent on these information conduits. The multiple steps required to navigate the hierarchy are eliminated, which creates shorter paths for staff to coordinate completion of tasks.

Interpersonal trust is necessary to maintain cohesive social networks. When trust does not exist, people are reluctant to collaborate or share information. In an organization characterized by a strong hierarchy, people recognize that knowledge is power, which results in a tendency for some to withhold information. Another way trust breaks down is when staff are afraid to appear ignorant. On a practical level, no one can know everything, and there is a perception in libraries that everyone is expected to be an expert.

Two types of actions that build trust in networks are competence and benevolence (Cross and Parker 2004, 99). Competence focuses on employees' awareness of each other's expertise and trusting the quality of information. Benevolence focuses on exposing one's lack of knowledge to another. Managers can overcome these issues foremost by being honest about not having all the answers themselves. Expertise inspires trust, but so does admitting the limits of one's knowledge.

Middle managers have a host of connections with differing areas of expertise and can help staff determine the competence and reputation of others as sources for information. Staff often seek information only within their unit, for they are reluctant to disclose lack of knowledge to those they don't know. As a central figure in the various networks that link the organization, the middle manager acts as a catalyst to open up channels that promote effective information sharing.

REFERENCES

Blumentritt, Rolf, and Neil Hardie. 2000. "The Role of Middle Management in the Knowledge-Focused Service Organization." *Journal of Business Strategies* 17 (1): 37–48.

Borgatti, Stephen P., and Rob Cross. 2003. "A Relational View of Information Seeking and Learning in Social Networks." *Management Science* 49 (4): 432–445.

Bryson, Jo. 1997. *Managing Information Services: An Integrated Approach.* Brookfield, VT: Gower.

Cross, Rob, Lisa Abrams, and Andrew Parker. 2004. "A Relational View of Learning: How Who You Know Affects What You Know." In *Creating a Learning Culture: Strategy, Technology, and Practice,* ed. Marcia L. Conner and James G. Clawson, 152–168. Cambridge, UK: Cambridge University Press.

Cross, Rob, and Andrew Parker. 2004. *The Hidden Power of Social Networks: Understanding How Work Really Gets Done in Organizations.* Boston: Harvard Business School Press.

Graber, Doris A. 2003. *The Power of Communication: Managing Information in Public Organizations.* Washington, DC: CQ Press.

Hargie, Owen, and Dennis Tourish. 2004. "How Are We Doing? Measuring and Monitoring Organizational Communication." in *Key Issues in Organizational Communication,* ed. Dennis Tourish and Owen Hargie, 234–251. New York: Routledge.

Lynch, Beverly. 1979. "Libraries as Bureaucracies." *Library Trends* 27 (3): 259–267.

Massie, Joseph L. 1960. "Automatic Horizontal Communication in Management." *Journal of the Academy of Management* 3 (2): 87–91.

O'Kane, Paula, Owen Hargie, and Dennis Tourish. 2004. "Communication without Frontiers: The Impact of Technology upon Organizations." In *Key Issues in Organizational Communication*, ed. Dennis Tourish and Owen Hargie, 74–95. New York: Routledge.

Simpson, Richard L. 1959. "Vertical and Horizontal Communication in Formal Organizations." *Administrative Science Quarterly* 4 (2): 188–196.

Wood, Elizabeth J., Rush Miller, and Amy Knapp. 2007. *Beyond Survival: Managing Academic Libraries in Transition*. Westport, CT: Libraries Unlimited.

11

FEELING GOOD IN THE MIDDLE

Emotional Intelligence at Work

ROBERT FARRELL

EMOTIONS AT WORK ARE GREAT WHEN THEY'RE GREAT. TEAM SPIRIT, ENTHU-siasm, the excitement of new challenges, the feeling of accomplishment and pride in successes—these emotions make the job worth having (Goleman 1998). But being both authority and subordinate, library middle managers often find themselves in tricky, emotionally fraught situations of various kinds. Take the following scenarios:

- As public services coordinator, you oversee the circulation department. A team you have assigned to complete part of a mission-critical, multiteam project has produced a result at variance with your direction, setting other teams back weeks.

- As head of reference in a medium-sized public library, you assign peer colleagues equal time at the reference desk. The majority of your peers view this as fair, but two don't and resist these assignments, causing workload imbalances for other staff.

- You've shown you accomplish things in your middle management position. Upper management now sees you as the go-to person when new projects or committees arise—even ones outside your direct responsibilities. Your plate, once full, is now overflowing.

Emotions in the workplace come into play whenever people have strong concerns or are personally invested in a situation. What we care about, want, desire, and think best shape our dispositions and thus our internal and external reactions to events and circumstances. Each of us brings these concerns to the workplace. When we're in tune, things click. But our personal concerns often differ from others'. When our wants and cares conflict, our priorities, attentiveness—and ultimately our actions—are at odds with others, causing negative emotions. These give rise to "crucial situations" (Patterson et al. 2004), and we are presented with a choice: react in habitual, unreflective ways, based on an emotionally distorted sense of reality, and get taken on an emotional ride; or act with awareness, sensitivity, and insight into ourselves and others and guide crucial situations to positive resolutions.

Consider the first scenario. Many managers reactively bulldoze their way to short-term solutions under such circumstances. It is easy to feel anger at a team that has botched a clearly laid-out job. The typical reaction—after upbraiding them—is to force or threaten them to redo their work as quickly as possible. A blind reactor might also try to take it upon himself, or handpick another team to fix the problem, potentially adding stress to his own life and running the risk of burning out others.

In the second and third scenarios, most managers don't go into bulldozer mode. The blind reaction is usually to muddle through and hope things change. At best, we find workarounds in order to avoid confrontation or—as might be done in the second scenario—we refer problems to a higher authority. At worst, short-term emotions lead to long-term resentments that result in heated blow-ups between normally reasonable people or a general feeling of misery and distrust in the workplace.

Rather than bulldoze or simmer, the best strategy for long-term success and well-being is to get smart about emotions. Few people are born or raised to be smart about emotions, but fortunately "the ability to monitor one's own and others' feelings and emotions, to discriminate among them and to use that information to guide one's thinking and actions"—what has come to be called *emotional intelligence*—is a learnable skill set (Cherniss et al. 1998; Salovey and Mayer 1990, 189). What follows is a brief overview of strategies to help you act and thrive—not merely react and survive—in crucial situations.

COMPONENTS OF EMOTIONAL INTELLIGENCE

Research into emotional intelligence has exploded since the concept first arrived on the scene in the early 1990s and many definitions and capacities have been determined as characteristics of it. "Self-regulation," the ability to maintain "zeal" and "personal motivation" at work, and understanding how emotions are caused and function are but a few (Goleman 1998; Oatley 2004). But there are two core components middle managers should develop first:

- Emotional self-awareness—being able to recognize when and what one is feeling or likely to feel in crucial situations.

- Situational sensitivity to others' emotions in crucial situations.

Emotional Self-Awareness

Emotional self-awareness is the ability to recognize what you are feeling in a particular situation or how you feel in general, and how those dispositions affect your per-

ception of others and (re)actions to a given situation. Acquiring self-awareness allows us to shift from passively reacting to things based on immediate, self-generated emotions to mediating emotionally determined impulses. It gives us the freedom to reflect and thereby intelligently choose our words and actions.

There is no shortcut to developing emotional self-awareness. It requires a major time investment and can be difficult. But it ultimately and importantly allows one to "minimize automatic, habitual, or impulsive reactions" when interacting with others (Brown, Ryan, and Creswell 2007, 223).

How does one do it? There are many techniques, but in recent years psychologists have begun to turn to Eastern philosophical traditions, particularly Buddhism, to provide methods for developing various forms of self-awareness including emotional self-awareness. Practices that develop what Buddhists call *mindfulness* and *meta-attention* have been recognized as particularly helpful. Mindfulness, the capacity to engage in "sustained, voluntary attention continuously focused on a familiar object," is typically cultivated through meditation or meditation-like sessions with the breath as the object of focus (Wallace and Shapiro 2006).

It is argued by proponents of mindfulness that such attention can then be applied to one's own mental state, allowing one to monitor it (meta-attention), thereby leading to a more insightful and direct awareness of one's emotions as they arise. By bringing such awareness into everyday life—by becoming "mindful"—one eventually learns to recognize and check emotional impulses that may distort one's perceptions of a situation, cloud one's judgment, or color one's verbal exchanges.

But becoming emotionally self-aware requires more than attention to feelings during crucial situations. You also have to know beforehand what you emotionally react to and why—how your emotions, usually unconsciously, influence your actions. Self-knowledge is required. What in yourself allows that person in the workplace to push your buttons? Why is it that, when people do some particular thing at work, you feel like exploding? When and why do you cross certain lines you shouldn't, and why do you not speak up when you should? In crucial situations, it is not the other person who's doing something to you. Your own emotional disposition and reactions are taking you on a ride.

Situational Sensitivity

There is a simple word for situational sensitivity to other people's emotions: *empathy*—knowing where someone is coming from, and understanding the immediate and larger situational and dispositional context of their behaviors

(Patterson et al. 2004). However, getting an accurate sense of others' emotional states is no simple thing, especially in heated situations when our attention is usually focused on ourselves and not those with whom we are interacting. We stay inside our heads and are apt to tell ourselves one-sided "ugly stories" about others to explain their behavior, one of the main barriers to empathy. Situational sensitivity allows us to "tell the rest of the story" and see the situation and others with more objectivity and empathy (Patterson et al. 2004).

It is very likely that there are people at work you are not really interested in knowing any more than you have to. These are probably the people you have the most difficulty with and about whose behaviors you have ready-made explanations. It is important to get past any habitual reactions you may have developed with such people if you are to improve your relationship. The most natural way to do this is to talk informally with difficult coworkers on a regular basis. Simple things such as being approachable and encouraging people to visit your office to chat, literally keeping your door open at work as much as possible, help you develop a deeper awareness of others' situations, which increases empathy over the long term.

This can, of course, be done well or poorly. But if you take a genuine interest in people you work with and get to know a bit about their lives, their values, and how they see the world, that knowledge will serve as background for contextualizing their behaviors.

Emotional Expression

If this natural approach doesn't work—and sometimes it doesn't—you need to find other ways to "get out of your head" and start seeing people in their deeper context. One way is to develop techniques to clearly see what's right in front of you. Peoples' external behaviors, facial expressions, gestures, and tones of voice—whether deliberately or unconsciously produced—can serve as helpful clues to what someone is feeling. Getting a "read" on people—being sensitive to what they are feeling in a particular moment—is an art, not a science—and it is difficult to learn. But there are methods for developing this ability.

Perhaps one of the most useful books in this area is Paul Ekman's *Emotions Revealed.* In addition to chapters on emotional awareness and triggers, Ekman outlines key facial expressions and other signals characteristic of a wide range of emotions. Recognizing emotions in others, he argues, can provide "information you can benefit from in determining how you are going to respond" to an employee "now or later" (Ekman 2007, 107).

Reading such a book won't let you see into peoples' souls. But the method does provide a way to shift your focus from yourself and your feelings to those of your colleagues in crucial situations.

TYPES

Developing expressional and gestural recognition is a micro-level approach to increasing situational sensitivity. A second, more macro-level approach is to turn to typological personality matrices to shift the focus from oneself to another. Personality matrices are schemes that allow you to classify people as a "kind" or "type" of person. They help you compose a complete picture of someone's strengths, weaknesses, and general tendencies.

Many of the most useful and most popular matrices have arisen out of the Jungian, Myers-Briggs psychological tradition. Among books of this kind, three stand out: *Type Talk* (Kroeger and Thuesen 1989) and its successor, *Type Talk at Work* (Kroeger, Thuesen, and Rutledge 2002), and *Please Understand Me II* (Keirsey 1998). You may be familiar with the eight core "personality preferences," or behavioral tendencies, posited by the theory:

- Sensing vs. Intuitive with respect to gathering information

- Thinking vs. Feeling with respect to making decisions

- Extroverted vs. Introverted with respect to finding motivation and energy

- Judging vs. Perceiving with respect to planning and executing actions.

From these eight behavioral preferences, a matrix of sixteen "personality types" is generated, each of which is described and analyzed in the course of the books. The purpose of the system is to help you identify different type tendencies in your colleagues and thereby better understand, communicate, and work with them. By so doing, one begins to see that different types approach the world in different ways. Conflict results from misunderstanding the needs and capabilities of others.

Let's take our third scenario above as an example. People who rise to the top tend to be extroverts who like to take on every challenge and see them to completion. Perhaps you are this way, too, and meet each new task with an excited "bring it on" attitude. But perhaps you are happier undertaking concentrated efforts that require time and privacy.

How do you communicate with your boss who has a different approach and relationship to work? How do you get him to understand where you're coming from? Type theory gives you a neutral and productive way to look at your differences, think about solutions, find compromises, determine directions for growth, and avoid misunderstandings that lead to resentments or blow-ups.

Whether you buy into this system or any other system is not important. The theorists themselves point out that "typewatching" is not a science and warn against using type theory to pigeonhole people. People are a mix of types, they say, but tend toward one or another in varying situations. But, like any matrix, it can be a useful heuristic when you are working with different personalities.

CONCLUSIONS

How would an emotionally intelligent library middle manager act in our scenarios? Unfortunately, there are no rules about what to do in every emotional situation. But we can consider questions an emotionally intelligent person might ask in these situations. For the first scenario alone, one might ask:

- When putting together the team, did I consider the styles and personalities of the team members? Were they the best combination of people for the job, or did I doom them to failure?

- Why didn't team members approach me during the process? Are there fears, distrust, or other emotional barriers between us? Do I make people feel embarrassed or insecure about asking me for direction or clarification?

- When things go wrong, do I tend to ask for information to "complete the story," or do I interpret events based on my anger, frustration, or disappointment? What should I do in this situation?

- How can my next steps build team spirit and repair broken trust, not set the stage for resentment and later emotional flare-ups?

- Can I speak to the team now, or do I usually need a day or two to collect myself before addressing emotion-causing issues?

It takes a fair amount of self-awareness and situational sensitivity to ask even these rudimentary questions when emotions are high. But in the asking, one puts that needed distance between oneself and one's reactions, the first step toward feeling good in the middle.

REFERENCES

Brown, Kirk Warren, Richard M. Ryan, and J. David Creswell. 2007. "Mindfulness: Theoretical Foundations and Evidence for Its Salutary Effects." *Psychological Inquiry* 18 (4): 211–237.

Cherniss, Cary, et al. 1998. *Bringing Emotional Intelligence to the Workplace: A Technical Report.* Piscataway, NJ: Consortium for Research on Emotional Intelligence in Organizations, www.eiconsortium.org/pdf/technical_report.pdf.

Ekman, Paul. 2007. *Emotions Revealed: Recognizing Faces and Feelings to Improve Communication and Emotional Life.* New York: St. Martin's Griffin.

Goleman, Daniel. 1998. "What Makes a Leader?" *Harvard Business Review* 76 (6): 93–102.

Keirsey, David. 1998. *Please Understand Me II: Temperament, Character, Intelligence.* Del Mar, CA: Prometheus Nemesis.

Kroeger, Otto, and Janet M. Thuesen. 1989. *Type Talk: The 16 Personality Types That Determine How We Live, Love, and Work.* New York: Dell.

Kroeger, Otto, Janet M. Thuesen, and Hile Rutledge. 2002. *Type Talk at Work: How 16 Personality Types Determine Your Success on the Job.* New York: Dell.

Oatley, Keith. 2004. *Emotions: A Brief History.* Oxford, UK: Blackwell.

Patterson, Kerry, et. al. 2004. *Crucial Confrontations: Tools for Talking about Violated Expectations and Broken Promises.* New York: McGraw-Hill.

Salovey, Peter, and John D. Mayer. 1990. "Emotional Intelligence." *Imagination, Cognition and Personality* 9 (3): 185–211.

Wallace, B. Alan, and Shauna L. Shapiro. 2006. "Mental Balance and Well-Being: Building Bridges between Buddhism and Western Psychology." *American Psychologist* 61 (7): 690–701.

12

TOP COMMUNICATION RULES FOR EFFECTIVE LIBRARY MANAGEMENT

LOUIS HOWLEY, KATHRYN BOCK PLUNKETT,
AND NICOLE SUMP-CRETHAR

WHAT IS THE ESSENTIAL SKILL LIBRARY MIDDLE MANAGERS NEED TO BE EFFEC-
tive? As members of the Mountain Plains Library Association's (MPLA) Communications Committee, we believe communication is at the heart of middle
management success. According to the American Management Association, 90 percent of all problems in an organization are the direct result of poor communication.
Estimates of the costs of poor communication in organizations have ranged as high
as $100 billion a year. As Susan Stewart states it, "The three most important factors
in effective library leadership are: Communication, Communication, Communication"
(1991, 55–63).

But what do everyday library staff and professionals think? To answer that question,
we sent an e-mail survey to members of the twelve-state MPLA region. Responses were
received from fifty-six members. The survey consisted of one question: "What is the No. 1
communication rule all library supervisors should follow?"

Responses revealed a variety of communication practices and other related behaviors essential for motivating staff and building trust. According to our survey, these are
the top communication rules for effective library management:

- Listen and respond.

- Communicate and keep staff informed.

- Be positive, respectful, and fair.

- Be a role model and model desired behaviors.

Common sense? Yes. Common practice? Many of the suggestions provided by our
respondents clearly arose in reaction to poor management communication, suggesting
that managers have much to learn from those they manage. Our chapter seeks to give
voice to those on the front lines.

LISTEN AND RESPOND

Many of the most concise answers to the survey were that supervisors simply need to listen. Respondents usually offered little expansion on the listening requirement. But many were emphatic about the need: "I would recommend that all supervisors LISTEN!" Others emphasized their statements with multiple exclamation points. Clearly, listening is vital to the employee-manager relationship. But how can managers accomplish this?

Several survey participants expanded on their initial statements, one mentioning that listeners need to be attentive and seek understanding. This implies more active listening. Supervisors who listen by embodying this ideal also ask employees questions and respond to them and their concerns, even if the response is simply acknowledgment.

Another respondent emphasized how critical true listening by managers is to communication. For example, managers who truly listen do not simply wait for the employee to finish speaking and then go on to the next topic. Instead, a manager should view communication as a reciprocal activity of listening and responding.

A third highlighted the need for managers to seek feedback after listening and help create a workplace culture that encourages feedback. According to this participant, people should feel safe to share their insights.

Many comments regarding listening related directly to the theme of "respect," another key component of our survey results addressed below. One person reproached managers who send e-mails or communiqués when listening should be the primary activity. Employees don't expect automatic agreement from managers in every context, another explained. Instead, they expect managers to listen and carefully consider employee concerns.

Although the admonition to listen seems straightforward, clearly listening alone is not enough for a good manager. Employees expect reciprocity, consideration, and understanding as outcomes from listening. The work of actively listening would be well worth the effort of a conscientious leader, in the opinion of these survey participants.

COMMUNICATE AND KEEP STAFF INFORMED

Participants who listed sharing information as their number one rule for supervisors conveyed a variety of points on the subject. One respondent's urging that managers simply "Tell everyone the same thing" was echoed by others. The theme that the information shared should be shared in the same way and in the same amount to everyone in the workplace was also common. Keeping rumors and misinformation to a minimum recurred as reasons for this warning.

Our results demonstrated that employees are aware that managers are sometimes prevented from sharing everything they know, but they also expect honesty and frank communication about things supervisors can share. One suggestion offered for such circumstances was, "Just to say, 'I have information I am not permitted to share with you at this time, but rest assured that as soon as I can, I will.'"

Certainly, opinions regarding the amount of information shared vary among participants. One person argues that a supervisor cannot share too much information since some points may apply to one person and not another. This person believes information often has to be "yanked" out of supervisors.

Regular information sharing was cited as the best way to avoid confusion and embarrassment. One particularly adamant response criticized managers who enact policies before all employees are informed. Confusion about how to approach policies and embarrassment in dealing with the public were mentioned as likely outcomes of limited information sharing. Further expanding on the idea that all staff need to be informed, one participant encouraged managers to be absolutely certain the information they share actually reaches all employees. As indicated in the survey results, for many individuals sharing information is a necessary, complex skill for fostering positive relationships between managers and staff.

Related, survey respondents made it clear that information needs to be made explicit by managers. "Don't assume employees can read your mind" was a common theme. Managers need to give clear and precise instructions if they expect their results to be met. If the manager is uncertain about how much information staff have about a topic or understand about a project, she should ask them whether they have what they need and whether instructions are clear.

Expecting a response to a question or issue is the top rule of another respondent. Managers should try to follow up on issues when they are posed by employees. Although this appears easy, it does require true management skills be performed effectively. An acceptable timeframe in which to respond must be established. To stay on top of response times, a manager can make entries into a time management tool, whether a datebook, calendar, or other electronic device, to be sure too much time does not elapse. If the individual with the question does follow up requesting a response, then a progress report is warranted. Follow-up requires analysis: does this lie within the manager's purview and, if not, are there other alternatives for the employee for resolution?

BE POSITIVE, RESPECTFUL, AND FAIR

"High performing companies have employees with very positive emotional states. . . . Managers in these organizations foster positive emotions in employees by paying attention to their needs and recognizing their unique contributions" (Quinn 2005, 80). Numerous Gallup polls have demonstrated that a positive work environment frees employees to focus on succeeding in their work (Corey, Keyes, and Haidt 2003).

Managers have the capacity to set a positive example for success by promoting a positive work environment. Survey respondents reminded managers of the importance of showing empathy by following the "Golden Rule." One simply stated, "Do unto others . . . [as you would have them do unto you]." Another both echoed and challenged this sentiment, stating, "Instead of treating others the way you would like to be treated, treat others the way *they* want to be treated." To do this, managers must know their staff, understand where they're coming from, and show staff they are cared about as individuals.

Another way to demonstrate caring is by building trust. Several librarians expressed the importance of openness and honesty from library leaders. One expressed it this way: "Let employees know your expectations and follow through when they aren't being met." Another respondent emphatically stated, "I would choose honesty as the [#1] rule that I wish supervisors would follow." According to Robert Fulmer, "Top management sets an important tone by encouraging openness and honest communication so that employees feel empowered to raise issues" (2004, 311).

This is not to say that ineffective leaders are dishonest—it just underscores the importance of being open and sharing information equally. One librarian declared, "I think the best thing a supervisor can do is to tell everyone the same thing. Keep it simple." Another encouraged equality in all interactions—"Treat everyone equally"—while also pointing out the importance of overall respect: "support and do not undermine staff" and "disagree in private."

A third encouraged leaders to "always seek the most respectful interpretation" when interacting with staff, and to "listen for what someone is trying to convey, avoiding defensiveness and giving the benefit of the doubt." Regarding interpersonal skills, one librarian believes library leaders need "empathy and understanding" and another encouraged leaders to "say thank you" and to "ask, 'What do you think?'"

Treating coworkers with equality and respect encourages a state of well-being, which leads to higher job satisfaction and, in turn, better job performance. This creates a positive, successful work environment—a win-win for all. One respondent suggests that managers "provide a 'safe' environment for people to say what they really mean, and what their concerns/likes/are, so they can be honest and open without fear of judgments or criticism. [It] takes a listener who doesn't need to always react to what they hear, and who can phrase reaction in a nonthreatening way."

According to Jennifer Rowley (1996), a major motivator for staff is knowing their contributions are appreciated through acknowledgment. Our survey results support this claim. "Listen and let employees know that you value their input. Thank and appreciate. Show value and that you care in a genuine fashion," one respondent stated. Two survey participants encouraged managers to "[give] positive reinforcement!" and "give performance feedback in a timely manner." Positive reinforcement and acknowledgment of efforts require little work on the part of the middle manager, but, as N. J. Campbell (2007) points out, something as simple as treating employees with respect can actually increase productivity and efficiency.

BE A ROLE MODEL AND
MODEL DESIRED BEHAVIORS

In addition to the themes already discussed, a large percentage of responses fell into a general category of desirable communication behaviors. Since behavior of management sets the tone for how workers communicate with each other and what behaviors are tolerated, these can be grouped as "model behaviors."

As one respondent put it, "Lead by example, be willing to do what you ask others to do." Another response suggested that the top rule should be that "the supervisor knows how to do what they are supervising. If they cannot work on the 'front line,' then how can they really know what needs to be done?" Brought back into relation with communication, one might say that good managers must be able to walk the walk, or at least competently talk the talk of all whom they supervise. It may not be realistic to expect a manager to understand the minutiae of MARC records. But in a situation where she may not be intimately familiar with the tasks being performed, the need for communication becomes even greater. Supervisors need to ask questions to understand the challenges of their subordinates, and to be careful not to make decisions without comprehending the full implications.

Of course, every supervisor makes mistakes. These are noted in another response, which suggested that the top rule for library leaders should be apologizing and saying "I'm sorry, I was wrong" when the manager makes a mistake. This acknowledges that making mistakes is part of the learning process, and that learning from mistakes is valued by management.

One response centered on emotional intelligence: "Find your and your team's personal styles of learning and craft the communication chains in your department accordingly." Ideally, assessment of staff learning and communication styles, and training in these areas, would be helpful to managers crafting messages suited to each learning style. Although in large libraries assessment obstacles may be daunting, it may work best in the instance of a single employee with whom the manager is experiencing difficulties. If the issue is one of learning style, assessment would give managers the information they need to adapt their message to reach specific individuals.

Other suggestions from respondents are that middle managers should articulate clear objectives and time lines for projects; state their communication preferences; avoid acronyms, jargon, and abstractions; communicate information in an organized manner; and provide clear agendas for meetings.

CONCLUSIONS

Managing people is not an easy task. Supervisors frequently must learn the craft on the job. Fortunately, many have significant work experience, so it is an achievable mandate. The best practices identified by our MPLA survey participants offer some excellent ideas and starting points for managers seeking to improve staff relations.

REFERENCES

Campbell, N. J. 2007. "R-e-s-p-e-c-t in the Workplace." *Employment Relations Today* 34:61–69.

Fulmer, Robert M. 2004. "The Challenge of Ethical Leadership." *Organizational Dynamic* 33 (3): 307–317.

Harter, James K., Frank L. Schmidt, and Corey L. M. Keyes. 2003. "Well-Being in the Workplace and Its Relationship to Business Outcomes: A Review of the Gallup Studies." In *Flourishing: Positive Psychology and the Life Well-Lived*, ed. Corey L. M. Keyes and Jonathan Haidt. Washington, DC: American Psychological Association, 2003.

Quinn, Brian. 2005. "Enhancing Academic Library Performance through Positive Psychology." *Journal of Library Administration* 42 (1): 79–101.

Rowley, Jennifer. 1996. "Motivation of Staff in Libraries." *Library Management* 17 (5): 31–35.

Stewart, Susan. 1991. "The Importance of Effective Communication to Library Leadership; Or, Communication, Communication, Communication." In *Library Communication: The Language of Leadership*, ed. Donald E. Riggs, 55–63. Chicago: American Library Association.

PART II

THE MIDDLE GROUND

13

FORMAL AND INFORMAL COMMUNICATION IN MEETINGS

ROBIN L. EWING

SUCCESSFUL MIDDLE MANAGERS HELP LIBRARIES ACHIEVE THEIR GOALS BY working through people, and that work most often takes place in meetings. During meetings, effective middle managers employ formal and informal communication techniques to work productively with their supervisors, peers, and employees. Formal communication in meetings centers on the concrete record of what's discussed and decided. Informal communications during meetings are those "accidental" or haphazard exchanges that draw on verbal and interpersonal skills rather than written communication. After a brief consideration of the importance of transparency in all forms of communication, I outline ways the middle manager can productively leverage the formal and informal aspects of communication during meetings.

TRANSPARENCY AND TRUST

As a middle manager, you are the conduit between leadership and frontline staff. Transparent communication is the sine qua non for effective formal and informal exchanges. First, by developing a reputation for transparent communication, middle managers are able to create high-trust relationships with their director, peers, and employees. Trust is important because it allows speakers to avoid miscommunicating with each other. As Stephen Covey and Rebecca Merrill note, "In a high-trust relationship, you can say the wrong thing, and people will still get your meaning. In a low-trust relationship, you can be very measured, even precise, and they'll still misinterpret you" (2008, 6).

Covey and Merrill (2008, 157) describe two traits possessed by leaders who communicate transparently:

- They "Talk Straight"—that is to say, they speak with integrity. When you speak with integrity, you speak honestly, but not hurtfully.

- They also actively "Create Transparency." They "tell the truth in a way people can verify. Get real and genuine. [Are] open and authentic. Err on the side of disclosure. Operate on the premise of 'What you see is what you get.' Don't have hidden agendas. Don't hide information."

The very nature of transparent communication means you communicate openly with everyone: your director, peers, and employees. For most of us, communicating transparently with our director is difficult but crucial. Perry Smith writes, "Without good feedback from many sources, a leader is partially blind and, over time, can become isolated from the real problems and the real issues" (2002, 94).

Finally, you must facilitate an environment of open communication for your employees, which will actively engage them in advancing the library's goals. Your default communication setting should be to share rather than hoard information. Naturally, you sometimes are privy to confidential information that cannot be shared, but in all other cases strive to share. In times of high stress in your library, you may need to repeat information several times using both formal and informal communication methods. Robert Sutton advises, "When people are freaked out, skilled bosses make their explanations as simple as possible and repeat them over and over—and do so through multiple communication channels. When fear is in the air, your mantra should be: Simple, Concrete, Credible, and Repetitive" (2010, 188).

FORMAL COMMUNICATION

Formal communication in the workplace centers on written reports and projects, or in the case of meetings a record of what was discussed and decided. Unsurprisingly, middle managers spend many hours in meetings with larger groups or in one-on-one meetings with employees. In addition to running meetings effectively, you must also participate proficiently in meetings that include your supervisors, peers, subordinates, or any combination of the three. Many librarians describe meetings as the bane of their existence and something to be avoided at all costs. Middle managers don't have that luxury. You have to recognize that meetings are an essential part of your work and not interruptions to your day. In fact, they function as critical communication channels for managers.

If you are new to conducting meetings, I suggest you consult resources on how to lead them effectively. Although it applies to a more corporate workplace than most libraries, *The Manager's Guide to Effective Meetings* (Streibel 2003) does include advice that resonates in all work environments. Each chapter is straightforward and

includes tips, key terms, cautionary notes, and a manager's checklist. In the chapter on preparing for meetings, Streibel recommends that you do the following before a meeting:

- Determine your purpose for meeting.

- Develop and distribute the agenda in advance.

- Set your goals for the meeting and communicate them in advance.

- Be specific in your agenda.

If you can't determine why you are meeting, don't schedule one. Once you conclude that a meeting is necessary, convey to participants its purpose and provide detailed agenda items. By including descriptive agenda items, you are better able to keep the meeting on track. Unambiguous agendas also allow participants to prepare for the meeting in advance. Streibel offers extensive advice on running a meeting:

- Start and end meetings on time.

- Take notes on decisions, action items, and key discussion points.

- Follow the agenda, but recognize that it is not set in stone.

- Summarize the main points, decisions, actions, and assignments.

- Decide if another meeting is necessary.

- Share the summary widely.

I cannot stress enough about agendas not being set in stone. Sometimes tangents are necessary, and as you become more skilled at facilitating they won't derail the meeting. In fact, your attempt to stop a tangent can be more of a distraction than the digression itself. Streibel states, "The facilitator should always keep in mind that *purposes* are more important than *minutes,* that it's more important for the group to be *effective* than *efficient*" (2003, 66). Finally, in the spirit of open communication, you should disseminate the minutes of the meeting to a wider audience than just meeting participants.

In *Good Boss, Bad Boss,* Sutton (2010) describes what not to do when conducting meetings. Bad meeting behaviors are really power displays that have no place in a library with a transparent communication culture. These behaviors include arriving late to most meetings and sometimes showing up very late, canceling a meeting after everyone has gathered, and keeping people past the scheduled ending time.

Throughout *Good Boss, Bad Boss,* Sutton portrays good bosses as leaders who do not waste the time of their employees or peers. When you meet with your employees, you should be respectful of their time, for it is as valuable as yours. Additionally, once the work of the meeting is completed, you should end it. You also should conclude a meeting early if it is unproductive: "Declaring defeat before the scheduled ending provides an escape from useless, boring or destructive meetings. Doing so is far better than prolonging the misery or allowing the damage to keep piling up" (Sutton 2010, 159).

INFORMAL COMMUNICATION

In contrast to formal communication, informal communication is haphazard, with a focus on verbal and interpersonal skills rather than written communication. Informal communication permeates all workplace interactions, especially meetings. Robert Moran offers tips on how to prepare and conduct meetings while acknowledging how interpersonal and informal communications affect meeting participants: "Meetings are not merely discussions of work-related issues. They are small-group interactions with all the dynamics of small groups" (2006, 135).

Moran further discusses what may happen to transparency in a meeting with participants at different hierarchical levels. The presence of senior leaders can inhibit a participant's desire to be straightforward or willingness to ask clarifying questions. A participant may attempt to impress the boss by forcefully arguing a point. These issues can quickly derail a meeting and prevent you from determining a course of action. For open communication to happen in a meeting, Moran advises that "all participants need to be seen as colleagues with hierarchical roles put aside temporarily" (2006, 137).

Meetings that include your director, which for the purposes of this chapter could mean supervisor or administrator, represent an opportunity to advocate your department's needs. Your primary role as a middle manager is to connect the people you work for with the people who work for you. In meetings, you have an obligation to speak for those not present. An in-person appeal may result in immediate action from your director. Stating the obvious, I recommend that you explain how the library's goals will be advanced when you argue for resources from your director.

Furthermore, meetings with your director offer a chance to inform her of any projects you have started. I have yet to meet a library director who likes surprises, good or bad. No director first wants to hear about a library problem or project from someone outside. One caveat about meetings that include your director is that you should not raise an issue concerning another department without first speaking with the manager of that area. Using face time with your director is not a good strategy to solve a problem with another area unless you have exhausted all other avenues. It is essential to maintain positive working relationships with other library department heads.

Meetings can serve as information-gathering hot spots. Chatting with peers before and after them strengthens lines of communication, which can lead "to more action, more experiments, more learning, and simultaneously to the ability to stay better in touch and on top of things" (Peters and Waterman 1982, 124). Management by walking around is another practice that encourages impromptu conversations with people in your library. Such regular communication helps you attain your goals and enables you to build up a well of credibility with peers. Use these lines of communication to be an advocate with your peers. Ackerman and Mackenzie (2006) describe this as nudging as opposed to bulldozing.

Strong relationships with colleagues help you navigate conflicts. Sometimes I find conversations hardest with peers in other departments when theoretically they should be the easiest. Joseph Grenny calls these "crucial conversations," noting that "our ability to handle controversial discussions determines how influential we are in our career and personal lives" (2003, 68–70).

These difficult conversations occur when another department is creating a problem for yours, as when reference librarians may be giving incorrect information about how interlibrary loan works. If you are the interlibrary loan manager, you need to give the correct information to the reference manager. To conduct this difficult conversation, Grenny recommends not assuming the worst of others and starting with facts, not feelings (2003, 69).

CONCLUSIONS

Middle management is not for the faint of heart or the tongue-tied. You will constantly be pulled between your competing responsibilities to your director and your staff. However, effective communication skills do position you to navigate those waters and contribute to your library's success. Your ability to negotiate for your unit and lead and participate in meetings depends on your commitment to transparent communication in all directions.

REFERENCES

Ackerman, Richard, and Sarah V. Mackenzie. 2006. "Uncovering Teacher Leadership." *Educational Leadership* 63 (8): 66–70.

Covey, Stephen M. R., and Rebecca R. Merrill. 2008. *The Speed of Trust: The One Thing That Changes Everything.* New York: Free Press.

Grenny, Joseph. 2003. "Crucial Conversations." *T+D* 57 (12): 68–70.

Moran, Robert F., Jr. 2006. "Meetings: The Bane of the Workplace: It Doesn't Have to Be So." *Library Administration and Management* 20:135–139.

Peters, Thomas J., and Robert H. Waterman Jr. 1982. *In Search of Excellence: Lessons from America's Best-Run Companies.* New York: Warner Books.

Smith, Perry M. 2002. *Rules and Tools for Leaders: A Down-to-Earth Guide to Effective Managing.* New York: Perigee.

Streibel, Barbara J. 2003. *The Manager's Guide to Effective Meetings.* New York: McGraw-Hill.

Sutton, Robert I. 2010. *Good Boss, Bad Boss: How to Be the Best—and Learn from the Worst.* New York: Business Plus.

14

THE POWER OF UN

MAUREEN DIANA SASSO

Meetings are indispensable when you don't want to do anything.

—John Kenneth Galbraith

MEETINGS ARE A UNIVERSAL PHENOMENON IN THE WORKPLACE AND IN ALL types of libraries. This chapter introduces library managers to the "unmeeting" as an alternative to conventional meetings. Conventional meetings, both face-to-face and virtual, take place synchronously with participants interacting with each other in real time. The unmeeting format complements rather than replaces conventional group meetings altogether. It allows for interaction but assumes that participants are in separate locations while actively engaged in a predetermined task, and that the manager is available to them during the designated unmeeting time.

The term *unmeeting* has been used at Duquesne University's Gumberg Library since as early as 2008 to describe a type of staff meeting in which participants don't meet face-to-face unless they need or choose to do so. The name is inspired by the memorable "uncola" soft drink advertising of the 1970s (Idsvoog 2007). The goal was to introduce a new meeting format to boost productivity and give staff a "refreshing" feeling of accomplishment. The term has also been used recently in the blogosphere to espouse the viewpoint that businesses should not hold meetings unless absolutely necessary (*Unhurd* 2011), and in association with the term *unconference* to describe a nontraditional approach to professional meetings (*Internet Time Wiki* 2009).

DOING HARD TIME: MEETING JAIL

The literature across many disciplines is replete with advice to managers on how to make meetings work better (Hudson 2009; Ressler and Thompson 2008; Shelton and Bauer 1994). Most library literature on effective meetings discusses professional meetings and conferences rather than staff meetings. Business literature, as might be expected, is rich in both articles and books, with many titles focused on overcoming the negative aspects of meetings. Advice ranges from commonsense tips such as setting agendas in advance and ending meetings on time to the more dramatic, such as Khawand's (2010) "Managers, don't lock your people up in meeting jail" and Lencioni's (2006) how to avoid "death by meeting."

Like our counterparts in business, library managers and staff may dread meetings even though they are necessary to our work. Janice Francisco captures this feeling well, noting that "everyone has been there—trapped in a useless, frustrating, unproductive meeting wondering what they are doing and why so many others have been invited to do it with them" (Francisco 2007, 54). Spending several hours a day in back-to-back meetings can indeed feel like meeting jail if managers don't take steps to ensure that meetings are productive.

Meetings can be problematic for many reasons, particularly since librarians lead such highly scheduled professional lives. Academic librarians work in a hybrid environment in which they perform as faculty, engaging in scholarship and service. They teach classes and hold office hours like other faculty members but are also accountable for librarianship—selecting, acquiring, and cataloging materials, taking shifts at the reference desk, and more.

Public librarians face similar challenges since service is the primary job of many. Depending on the size of the library and its staff, the professionals' schedules may have little overlap. Time off the desk must be spent on a variety of activities including programming, materials selection, cataloging, weeding, professional development, and administrative duties. Given the workload and differing shifts that must be covered daily, it is a challenge to find the time to meet. Therefore, it is essential to make certain there is return on the time invested.

Workplace meetings generally have one of two purposes: to provide information to participants, or to reach conclusions on agenda topics (Moran 2006). In their discussion of why meetings fail, Nelson and Economy (1995) stress that the power to call a meeting carries with it the responsibility to ensure that the meeting is worthwhile. They suggest that managers ask themselves whether there is another way of resolving the issue or communicating the information before scheduling a meeting. For example, informational meetings can often be replaced by e-mail and other forms of communication.

Managers hold decision-making meetings, such as departmental meetings, on a regular basis. Often, however, less time is needed for discussion and making of decisions than for doing the work necessary to implement them. As a result, time spent meeting can be perceived as impeding rather than facilitating work, particularly when deadlines loom.

As Moran (2006) states, the solution to the complaint that meetings waste time rests with the participants, primarily the person who calls the meeting. The savvy manager calls meetings only when needed, creates clear agendas, keeps meetings on track, and ensures follow-through on decisions. By adding a dose of creativity, managers may also boost productivity and provide staff with a break from routine.

THE UNMEETING: YOUR GET OUT OF JAIL FREE CARD

Conventional meetings are best suited for interpersonal interaction—group discussion and decision making. The unmeeting is an alternate meeting format that can be employed to facilitate group process and projects. Unmeetings differ from open-space meetings and unconferences, which assume that participants set and take responsibility for the agenda, often spontaneously, rather than agree to an agenda in advance (Lawson 2010).

Instead, the unmeeting assumes that group discussion has taken place previously and a course of action has been chosen. The manager sets the agenda with the agreement of the participants. Unmeeting participants are engaged, empowered, and expected to achieve results in the time allotted. No minutes are taken; rather, group progress on agreed-upon tasks documents the results of the meeting.

How It Works

The technique is simple: when a manager schedules an unmeeting, the participants are expected to be in designated locations (usually their offices) working on predetermined tasks. The manager sets the time and agenda in advance, explaining in writing what specific tasks the unmeeting time will be used for and articulating expected outcomes and deliverables. Participants are free to work without distraction while the manager answers individual participant's questions and provides feedback to those who need it. At the conclusion of the meeting, participants send their deliverables to the manager and receive feedback.

Examples of tasks appropriate for unmeeting agendas include these:

- Shared writing tasks with common deadlines, such as completing annual reports, self-appraisals, and performance evaluation documents

- Complex tasks that can be broken into segments, such as developing a customer service or collection development plan, proposal writing, and program planning

- Time-critical tasks that require group input, such as creating and reviewing instructional materials like course syllabi, assignments, user guides, and web pages

- Long-term tasks with individual responsibility, such as research and scholarship and preparation of promotion documents

Why It Works

Used in combination with regular face-to-face meetings, the unmeeting allows managers to bring focus to their priorities in a positive and collegial way. By providing a clear charge and the resource of time to those who need it, the unmeeting reinforces both the priority of the tasks assigned and the value of participants' time. A well-planned unmeeting can improve morale because participants experience a sense of shared purpose and of having accomplished their work instead of just talking about it.

Unmeetings promote productivity because they empower participants to set aside other competing priorities and take a break from the stress of managing multiple deadlines; provide participants quiet time and space to think and be attentive to the task at hand without interruption; guarantee participants that the manager is available to answer questions and give feedback immediately; and make participants accountable for attending to the manager's identified priorities and meeting agreed-upon deadlines.

Potential Pitfalls

Even though participants are likely to view unmeetings as opportunities for tangible accomplishment—and therefore welcome them—managers should prepare for the fact that unmeetings can go off course just as face-to-face meetings can. For participants, the distractions of solitary time are many. Chief among them is the temptation to complete other pressing work or answer e-mail. There is also the potential for participants to surf the Internet or simply procrastinate rather than attend to the unmeeting agenda. To avoid these pitfalls and build accountability in the unmeeting process, managers should set mutually agreed-upon deadlines for the tasks to be completed; have participants send progress reports or the completed tasks at the end of the designated unmeeting time; give prompt feedback and follow up with an expression of appreciation for the work the participants have completed; and follow up individually and reaffirm expectations if a participant does not show evidence of cooperation or does not complete an agreed-upon task.

Happily Unmeeting Ever After

Many library managers find themselves in a seemingly paradoxical situation. They are expected to work collegially and encourage participation in decision-making processes while ensuring that projects are completed on time. Both unmeetings and conventional meetings have advantages, and both should have a place in the manager's toolkit. Conventional meetings are the best choice when significant interpersonal interaction is needed. The unmeeting format works well when participants have a shared task and deadline.

The unmeeting allows managers to provide those they supervise with time to focus on tasks that are important to the department or institution that might otherwise be delayed due to competing priorities and deadlines. Managers can use unmeetings to ensure that priorities are addressed effectively and on time by providing guidance, clarifying expectations, and setting aside sufficient time for participants to accomplish their work. The unmeeting is empowering because it gives participants a sense of control over their assigned tasks, as well as productive because it gives managers a way to assure that sufficient time is devoted to shared priorities—thus avoiding a last-minute scramble to meet deadlines.

USE CONVENTIONAL MEETINGS FOR . . .

Exchanging ideas

Problem solving

Setting goals and priorities

Facilitating planning and decision making

USE UNMEETINGS FOR . . .

Follow-up tasks from conventional meetings

Time-critical tasks requiring input from each participant

Routine shared tasks with common deadlines

Long-term projects that can be done incrementally

MANAGER'S UNMEETING PREPARATION CHECKLIST

Are you ready to try an unmeeting?

- ○ Meet with the participants for discussion and decision making prior to calling an unmeeting.

- ○ Examine your priorities and upcoming deadlines to select a shared task that all participants must complete individually or contribute to.

    - ○ Make sure to choose a task that has been discussed previously and basically understood by the participants.

    - ○ Determine whether the task can be completed in one meeting; if necessary, break it into discrete segments to be completed over several meetings, and set the deadline(s) accordingly.

    - ○ Prepare the agenda.

    - ○ Set the date and time and expectations for the locations the participants will work from.

    - ○ Explain the expected outcomes/deliverables for the unmeeting.

    - ○ Explain how to communicate questions to you (in-person, e-mail, phone) during the unmeeting time.

    - ○ Explain how to provide deliverables to you (e-mailed files, printouts in your mailbox, etc.)

    - ○ Explain how and when you will provide feedback.

REFERENCES

Francisco, Janice M. 2007. "How to Create and Facilitate Meetings That Matter." *Information Management Journal* 41 (6): 54–58.

Hudson, Kathleen. 2009. "Maximize Meeting Success." *Nursing Management* 40 (10): 52–54.

Idsvoog, Karl. 2007. "Uncola: The Video History of a 7UP Breakthrough Ad: How Actor Geoffrey Holder Brought Down a Racial Barrier." *Advertising Age,* May 7, http://adage.com/article/news/uncola-video-history-a-7up-breakthrough-ad/116484/.

Internet Time Wiki. 2009. "Unmeetings." http://internettime.pbworks.com/w/page/20095958/unmeetings.

Khawand, Pierre. 2010. "Managers, Don't Lock Up Your People in the Meeting 'Jail'! 5 Ways to Help You Meet Less and Accomplish More." *Less-is-more* (blog), August 2, www.people-onthego.com/blog/bid/44351/Managers-don-t-lock-up-your-people-in-the-meeting-jail-5-ways-to-help-you-meet-less-and-accomplish-more#emart-form-anchor.

Lawson, Steve. 2010. *Library Camps and Unconferences.* London: Facet.

Lencioni, Patrick. 2006. *Death by Meeting: A Leadership Fable about Solving the Most Painful Problem in Business.* San Francisco: Jossey-Bass.

Moran, Robert F., Jr. 2006. "Meetings: The Bane of the Workplace. It Doesn't Have to Be So." *Library Administration and Management* 20 (3): 135–139.

Nelson, Robert B., and Peter Economy. *Better Business Meetings.* New York: Irwin, 1995.

Ressler, Cali, and Jody Thompson. 2008. *Why Work Sucks and How to Fix It.* New York: Penguin.

Shelton, Maria M., and Laurie K. Bauer. 1994. *Secrets of Highly Effective Meetings.* Thousand Oaks, CA: Corwin Press.

Unhurd. 2011. "The Unmeeting" (blog). April 14. http://unhurd.com/2011/04/14/the-unmeeting/#more-373.

15

CHECKLIST FOR PRODUCTIVITY

SAMANTHA SCHMEHL HINES

LIBRARY WORK, WE TELL OURSELVES, IS KNOWLEDGE WORK. EVERY DAY IS DIFferent. We always handle different items, changing questions, varied tasks. In this kind of malleable environment, some might say it doesn't make sense to use checklists to manage how we do what we do. Checklists help individuals work through rote tasks in which we forget things because our minds are focused on other less tedious things.

This is what I thought about checklists until I read Atul Gawande's bestseller, *The Checklist Manifesto: How to Get Things Right* (2009). The author sets forth the argument that checklists can be an excellent tool for assisting professionals in dealing with increasingly complex duties. As a doctor, Gawande begins by examining the medical profession, but he moves along to architecture, finance, and cooking. In examples from each, he demonstrates that workers today have to deal with an enormous amount of know-how in their fields—in some cases an overwhelming amount of knowledge. This causes us to slip up. We can forget the basics when we are conscious of everything else we might need to know in a situation. To overcome this and to manage what we need to get done, Gawande suggests checklists.

In the context of middle management, checklists make sense. Middle managers may be new to juggling lots of projects, new to sharing responsibility for a team's progress rather than their own progress, and new to supervisory tasks. Checklists can help new middle managers keep track of all the details which may escape them, things they know but sometimes forget in the bustle of everyday work. Keeping track of details allows them to apply that mental energy toward higher-level thinking.

The concept that seems to resonate with most people when thinking of checklists is of a pilot running through preflight paperwork. Pilots want to ensure that their planes are absolutely ready to fly, with no mechanical problems, supply issues, or other needs. Lives depend upon getting these things right. The checklists extend from preflight to cover most aspects of flying. They provide a framework for actions that provides safety, communication, and forward momentum. They keep minds free to focus on higher-level issues that may arise.

Checklists differ from to-do lists. To-do lists are continually generating lists of varying tasks with deadlines. Checklists are not meant to be algorithms or teaching tools. Rather, they are intended to manage simple steps involved with performing a single large task, like preparing an airplane for takeoff.

We library workers definitely have to deal with an overabundance of knowledge in how we can and should do our jobs. A simple checklist, for example, could help us remember to hit all points in a reference interview. For the most part, we internalize the elements of a typical reference interaction since we repeat it so often, but occasionally I remember only as a student walks away that I forgot to ask just the right probing question, or to assure him he can come back if he has any further need.

I am not sure I would recommend just yet that we have a checklist out at the reference desk to run through with every interaction (but would it hurt?). Instead, I'd like to examine the concept of checklists with regard to management, specifically with providing and supporting a productive work environment within the library. What factors would we need to check off to ensure that we are providing a productive atmosphere for our employees?

Gawande provides an online "Checklist for Checklists," which we can use as a template for creating such a checklist (Gawande 2010). The first factor is development of the checklist. The first item listed for development of a checklist is "Do you have clear, concise objectives for your checklist?" My particular objective, providing and supporting a productive work environment within the library, is fairly clear and concise. I likely want to define the beneficiaries of this environment. Whom do I manage? As a case study, let's consider an individual who manages students and staff at a reference desk.

Once we have clear and concise objectives, we need to develop items for the checklist, run through the rest of the steps for development, and then move on to drafting. The development section of the Checklist for Checklists has two items for consideration that are best to think about from the start. One is "Have you considered involving all members of the team in the checklist creation process?" This is obviously a great idea for building buy-in from your team and also helps guarantee that you are addressing issues of relevance. The second is "Have you considered adding items that will improve communication among team members?" This is also a great idea since a big part of a productive work environment is clear, consistent communication.

Directives for developing checklist items include that items be actionable and affected by the use of a checklist. Let's revisit our objective. Our reference desk manager wants to provide and support a productive work environment within the library. That's a good concept, but how can we make an actionable and practical checklist out of this? One way is to create a checklist for starting our manager's day. Every day when our manager arrives at work, she will have a brief checklist to run through that helps focus her efforts on fulfilling the objective.

With that in mind, I propose five items for our checklist:

A Checklist for Starting the Day

1. What are our manager's most important tasks to accomplish today? This should be limited to three objectives and written down.

2. What are the team's goals for today? Our manager needs to ask herself and write down: Will they be performing routine tasks? Is there an upcoming meeting for which I need to provide an agenda or other information? Are deadlines approaching? Do they need anything from me?

3. What emerging circumstances need to be dealt with immediately, delegated, or noted for later? Examples include people calling in sick and a class planning a last-minute tour. Our manager will review her notes and make any needed changes to her tasks or her team's goals.

4. What upcoming events need to be dealt with? How are we fitting in with the big picture? Our manager again will review her notes and make any needed changes to her tasks or her team's goals.

5. Based on our manager's notes for today, when will she check in with her team, and how? Some days a quick e-mail or stop by their workspace suffices. Other days she may need to set up a more formal meeting.

((()))

The development section of the Checklist for Checklists asks us to consider whether each item is a critical safety step in danger of being missed, and whether the steps are checked by other mechanisms. Though none of the above is life-threatening, these steps are essential in modeling and providing a productive work environment. Even though these steps may seem like a commonsense way to start your day, they are often lost in the shuffle of arriving at work and being bombarded with information from phone calls, e-mails, and in-person conversations so common for middle managers. Taking a few minutes to run mindfully through these steps starts the day off in a way that is far more conducive to productivity for ourselves, those we manage, and our workplace overall.

The next section in the Checklist for Checklists deals with the physical drafting of the checklist. There are several design concerns Gawande considers that I do not address here, focusing instead on points that deal with content. The first listed is whether the checklist utilizes natural "pause points" in a workflow. The moment I arrive at my desk is for me a natural break in my workflow. My journey to my desk is often interrupted by coworkers or direct reports giving me information. I usually check to see whether I have phone messages. Once I sit down at my desk, I take a big breath and think, "How do I start this day?" This checklist takes advantage of that moment for our reference desk manager.

Some of the items on the drafting section deal with length. One asks whether the checklist is short enough to fit on one page, and another asks if there are fewer than ten items per pause point. These are both the case for my simple checklist. This keeps the list simple and focused. With this in mind, one should also use simple sentence structure and basic language.

I have some concerns on this point. My list does contain items that are a bit longer than I would like. I address this concern more fully and test it in the final part of the Checklist for Checklists—"validation"—where we get ideas about how to assess the efficacy of our checklist and implement concepts for improvement. But first this checklist must be trialed with frontline users.

Given the design suggestions above, I cleaned up my checklist and came up with the version in figure 1. Then I solicited help from three colleagues to utilize the checklist in their daily planning. The feedback I received was enlightening. All three pointed out that a daily check-in with a work group might be seen as micromanaging. Two recommended that the revision step should come last. All three had not read Gawande's book but are now planning to. The Checklist for Checklists recommends modifying your checklist based on these trials, then trying it out further. Based on feedback from my short trial, I came up with several changes in the design, laid out in figure 2.

As I, and perhaps my colleagues, adopt the checklist, the Checklist for Checklists suggests that we make sure it fits the flow of work, catches errors when they can still be corrected, and does not take up too much time. These points make sense. What use would the list be if it were

---

Checklist for a productive start to the day
Draft; created March 2011

○ **Write down my 1–3 most important tasks to accomplish today, personally.**

    1.

    2.

    3.

○ **Write down my team's goal(s) for today.** Ask myself: Will they be performing routine tasks? Is there an upcoming meeting for which I need to provide an agenda or other information? Are deadlines approaching? Do they need anything from me?

    Team Goal: _____

○ **Revise the above in light of emerging circumstances needing to be dealt with immediately, delegating, or noted for later.** Examples include people calling in sick, a class planning a last minute tour or so on.

○ **Decide when I will check in with my team today, and how, and arrange it.** Some days a quick email or stop by their workspace will suffice. Other days I may need to set up a more formal meeting.

FIGURE 1

First Checklist

Checklist for a productive start to the day
Draft; created March 2011

○ **Write down my team's success metrics for today.** Ask myself: Will they be performing routine tasks? Is there an upcoming meeting for which I need to provide an agenda or other information? Are deadlines approaching? Do they need anything from me?

    Today is successful if the team: _____

○ **Write down my 1–3 most important tasks to accomplish today for my own work.**

    1.

    2.

    3.

○ **Decide if I need to check in with my team today to ensure success, and how, and arrange it.** Some days a quick e-mail or stop by their workplace will suffice. Other days I may need to set up a more formal meeting.

○ **Edit the above in light of emerging circumstances needing to be dealt with immediately, delegated, or noted for later.** Examples include people calling in sick, a class planning a last minute tour or so on.

FIGURE 2

Revised Checklist

not catching problems or fit poorly into the workday?

Last, it is important to plan to review and revise the list at some point in the future to make certain it is functioning well and still meets your needs. Therefore, it is helpful to include a "last revised" date. Depending on the actual function of the list, there may be a natural break in your year, month, semester, or other time period to review it. If your duties change, this provides a great opportunity to review any personal or group checklists like this one. If you do not directly supervise a team but rather manage projects, some parts of the checklist may be less valuable, yet it still has merit. With regard to teams, you may have projects to work on jointly even if you don't directly manage team members. It would be useful to check in with those teams as indicated by your tasks for the day, emerging circumstances, or upcoming events.

Checklists can seem like such a basic tool, but they do so much to help us manage our "headspace." After I sent the checklist to my colleagues for review, all three mentioned how useful adopting something similar to their own work could be in order to review priorities and keep them in mind throughout the day.

Checklists can also foster an environment of self-evaluation, which is a key principle of a productive workplace. If we can't evaluate our own efforts fairly and openly, it is unlikely we will accomplish much meaningful work. A carefully vetted and trialed checklist can help us remember key factors that may get lost in our workday, free up mental energy, and focus us on getting things done for ourselves, our work teams, and our libraries.

REFERENCES

Gawande, Atul. 2009. *The Checklist Manifesto: How to Get Things Right*. New York: Metropolitan Books.

———. 2010. "A Checklist for Checklists." Project Check. www.projectcheck.org/checklist-for-checklists.html.

16

PROCRASTINATION AND WILLPOWER

SAMANTHA SCHMEHL HINES

ONE OF THE PROBLEMS I HAVE WITH WRITING ABOUT PROCRASTINATION IS that the task is rife with irony. I sit down at the computer to begin and am seized with the compulsion to check my e-mail, my voicemail, my Twitter account, perhaps review my to-do list to make sure I am really working on my priority projects. Before I know it, I have wasted half an hour and have yet to write one word on the topic of procrastination. Then I feel miserable—like a fraud. I wonder what qualifies me to write on this subject when I clearly have no willpower to stop procrastinating myself.

New middle managers face similar issues with procrastination. We have multiple and quickly changing responsibilities: for projects, to our employees, and to our employers. Procrastination often comes with the territory and can make you feel like you're undeserving of your position.

Maybe we should stop beating ourselves up. A new school of thought proposes that procrastination is the result of impulsivity. In our fast-paced, gadget-obsessed, social networking society, we have so many demands on our attention that we have a hard time differentiating between what is important and what is immediate. In this situation, the immediate wins out and we end up checking e-mail forty times a day, accessing Facebook repeatedly, and chatting with coworkers rather than working on that report due at the end of the week. We ask ourselves why we have so little self-control, but perhaps the answer is not that we have too little but simply that we have too many distractions calling on our willpower. In this chapter I consider procrastination in relation to impulse control and in light of the demands placed upon our willpower in our technological age, and I offer practical suggestions for how we can build up self-control to get things done.

Piers Steel, a psychologist at the University of Calgary, is pioneering the study of impulsivity as it relates to procrastination. He jokes that his work on procrastination is really "me-search" as opposed to research and says this explains why it took him ten years to publish on the subject after his initial investigations.

Steel summarizes his theory in an equation:

$$\text{Utility} = E \times V/I \times D$$

Utility is how likely you are to procrastinate on a given task, E is the expectancy of success at the task, V is the value of the task, D is the sensitivity to delay, and I

is impulsiveness (Steel 2011). "Expressed in words," says Stephen Kotler in an article on the theory, "how likely one is to delay depends on one's confidence multiplied by the importance/fun of a given task, divided by how badly you need the reward [for finishing], multiplied by how easily distracted you are" (2009, 73). Steel maintains that the largest variable in the equation is impulsivity, and that impulsive people have the most trouble with procrastination.

Temptations of the modern age are a large part of why procrastination seems to be getting worse. "It's easier to procrastinate now than ever before. We have so many more temptations," Steel declares. "It's never been harder to be self-disciplined in all of history than it is now" (2011, 105). All of our technological gadgets and gizmos add up to yet another demand on our time and attention.

Yet impulsivity need not imply a character flaw. Since it is defined as how distractable you are, this quantity can obviously fluctuate within the individual and depending on circumstances. Like most people, I am far more distractable when I'm in a bustling environment with many activities going on. It would be difficult for me to write this chapter at an airport or shopping mall. My preferred writing environment is at home—with a cat or two and a cup of tea—where I happen to be working now.

Then again, this sort of environment is quite boring for me when I'm trying to conceive new library services or make connections with information. My best environment for brainstorming is while taking a vigorous walk around campus or driving by myself.

My worst environment for most work is, ironically, sitting in my office in the library. I feel surrounded by distractions: other projects, coworkers calling and stopping by, students poking their heads in with questions or just to say hi, cell phone ringing, e-mail dinging. It makes me feel valued, certainly, that so many people seek out my opinions and assistance, but getting anything done other than some light reading or web design can be challenging.

Further, my work computer setup is very modern, allowing me to multitask in all sorts of interesting ways that prevent me from getting much work done. My clunker iMac at home can barely run word processing, and my home Internet is slow in a way that's upsetting for downloading things from Netflix but perfect for working without distractions.

The previous two paragraphs may be giving you some ideas. First, distractions lead to procrastination, no matter how much willpower you have. Second, your work environment has a huge impact on how much you are distracted. The logical conclusion is to work where you feel least distracted. To do this, you have to be aware of what works best for your particular tasks and have the freedom to make some changes.

This first task is a bit easier than the second. One way to discover where and how you work best is to keep a time log. Keep track of your time as if you were a contractor who bills by the quarter hour. In addition to keeping track of what you're honestly working on, keep track of when and how you're distracted.

Another idea that helps with the time log is to set two to four important tasks each day to complete. This can give your time log some focus. You will know at the start of the day what you intend to accomplish, and now you can keep track of when and how you work on it, as well as when and how you get off track.

Once you have done this for a while, you may see some patterns. For example, you note that you are interrupted each day around 11:00 a.m. by a particular employee or student, or perhaps you notice an after-lunch lull. Start thinking about how you can adapt or adopt these patterns to work with your tasks. Could you create an "office hour" from 11:00 a.m. to noon when people can freely interrupt you in exchange for shutting the door the rest of the day? Could you hold off answering e-mail until the after-lunch lull and instead use your freshest early morning work hours to produce work requiring more intense concentration? If you have many projects requiring total concentration in a way you cannot get in your office or workspace, could you work from home or a café one day a week? One afternoon? One hour?

One complaint I often hear is that workplaces do not allow employees to work from home, work flexible hours, or even close their office doors. This is an unfortunate situation, and it suggests that employers care more about appearances than actually getting things done. Try discussing this situation with your supervisor or those you supervise. Sometimes a written contract that somehow quantifies your increased productivity and lessened procrastination helps. Sometimes these sorts of inflexible rules are a sign of deeper trouble within the workplace, an environment you may need to consider leaving.

Still, working from home or elsewhere off-site is a privilege that must be earned. If there is a way to earn it legitimately and then wow your supervisor or employees with how productive you have been, this is an excellent path to take, and it also provides benefits to others in your organization.

For those who do not have the option of changing work environments, there are still ways to deal with impulsivity and distractions. One way to minimize our natural tendency toward impulsivity is to visualize the future, to help make the not-so-immediate deadline more of a reality. Think about how accomplishing or not accomplishing your task will affect your concrete visualization of the future. Realize also that giving in to procrastination to satisfy immediate desires hurts in the long run.

If you find yourself procrastinating because it's just easier to check e-mail or indulge in any other more attractive and immediate task, take a moment to acknowledge that feeling of discomfort. Do not give in to the feeling, but allow yourself to feel it before moving on to the tips below.

The primary advice I give to those complaining about procrastination and distractions in the workplace is to shut off your Internet. Physically unplug your computer to get rid of those distractions at the source. Set a timer for a period of time, perhaps 25 minutes to start, and then once you have successfully worked without distractions for that time allow yourself to plug back in and check e-mail or other distractions for five minutes.

Once five minutes are up, unplug again and dive back into work. If your phone is the problem, take it off the hook or turn off the ringer. Nearly anyone calling can wait 25 minutes for a callback. If fellow workers are interfering, try to find a time when they are in meetings or not yet at work to do anything requiring concentration. For me, this is 8:30–10:00 a.m.

A variation is to schedule set times for activities and stick with them. If you simply must check your e-mail first thing every morning, limit the time you spend doing so to 30 minutes. Triage your e-mails by answering anything that can be answered in two minutes or less, filing away anything you need later and deleting anything you won't, then choose a time later in the day after your most important tasks are completed to finish up any remaining e-mails. Be generous with the delete key. Most of the time deleted e-mails that later become important can be retrieved or resent. Once you are done with your e-mail, shut down the program. Turn off any e-mail alert noises or popups you have on your computer or mobile device. According to Steel, just turning off e-mail alerts can save us a month's worth of time each year. Each time you are derailed by that e-mail alert, it takes up at least fifteen minutes to stop what you're doing, read the e-mail, think about what action to take, and follow up. That really adds up over the course of the day, the week, the month—and that is time you can use for getting important things done.

Make sure you build some downtime into your day. A problem many procrastinators have is getting to the point where they feel they really must devote an entire day to a project. At that point, they plunge completely in and do not emerge until they are done. This makes work seem like punishment. Every work project, no matter how tight the deadline, can survive your taking a 5-minute break to get up and stretch or a 15-minute snack. This provides an important release valve and can make work more pleasant. When your work is more agreeable, you may be more likely to start working before the crunch and therefore not stress as much.

As the old joke goes, the best cure for procrastination is to just do something. Once I finally sat down to draft this chapter, it took me one hour to write 1,600 words. Something that I put off for weeks was off to a roaring start by just sitting down and doing it. This is excellent advice, but the best treatment for procrastination is to be aware that it is not a personal failing but rather a situation that can be adjusted for a better outcome.

Accept the negative emotions that can arise when starting a new project, but then put them away and take action. Beware of falling into the "backward ploy" of feeling that you have to understand the relevant factors that contributed to your procrastination before you can do anything to change your life for the better. Accept the fact you are human and distractable in an increasingly distracting world, then work to reduce distractions to get the job done.

REFERENCES

Kotler, Stephen. 2009. "Escape Artists." *Psychology Today*, September/October, 73–79.

Steel, Piers. 2011. *The Procrastination Equation: How to Stop Putting Things Off and Start Getting Things Done.* New York: HarperCollins.

17

THE CRITICAL PATH FOR MIDDLE MANAGERS

A Project Management Technique for Librarians

DOROTHY A. MAYS

MIDDLE MANAGERS ARE OFTEN RESPONSIBLE FOR OVERSIGHT OF COMPLEX library projects. Perhaps you have been charged with design of a new web page, reorganization of a department, or implementation of a federated search database. Such projects involve numerous people, tasks, and careful orchestration of several outside variables. All it takes is for one deadline to slip and the whole project can be thrown off schedule. Meanwhile, the library director is breathing down your neck for an update on the timeline, but how can you provide an answer when you don't know how long an employee's sick leave will last? Or the vendor just failed to deliver its product for the third time? Or the hurricane looming off the coast is about to fling chaos onto the entire state for at least a week?

Sadly, these variables are no excuse. Your task as project manager is to define the scope of the project, coordinate personnel and supplies, set a timeline, and get the project across the finish line. One unfortunate quirk of contemporary librarianship is that librarians are frequently promoted into management positions because they are excellent librarians rather than because of their potential for leadership or project management. Thus, many librarians have no relevant training before they are charged with steering a large project through to completion. Work tends to proceed in a haphazard manner, timelines are not properly articulated, and confidence in the project suffers.

Two factors loom large in the success of managing a project: planning and communicating that plan. This chapter outlines a technique that requires middle managers to plan and communicate using project management techniques borrowed from the business world. It is surprising how many managers begin tackling a project based on a gut instinct for how to proceed rather than starting with a series of meetings involving the key people who will be executing the project, defining the parameters, and setting deadlines. Project management techniques and software can help define and communicate the plan.

Many techniques of project management grew out of the research and development world and, frankly, their cumbersome systems have rarely translated well into the culture of libraries. But one aspect of these planning systems is relatively easy to learn and implement. The Critical Path Method (CPM) is a project management technique that enables a middle manager to design a schedule, identify critical components, and assign proper relative importance to each activity. Rather than explore all the project tasks

CPM can help accomplish, this chapter reduces the CPM technique to a streamlined format that can be incorporated into libraries and adhered to by staff.

REASONS FOR PROJECT FAILURE

A lack of up-front planning is the likely culprit when large-scale projects devolve into chaos. A typical organization spends 5 percent of the total project effort on advance planning, whereas more successful organizations spend as much as 45 percent of their time developing careful plans before delving into the work (Wamsley 2009). Kappelman and colleagues' (2006) research into the failure of IT projects listed dozens of warning signs of project failure in order of importance. Fully eight of the top ten reasons projects are doomed to failure were directly related to poor planning or communication, including failure to research project requirements, lack of milestones and due dates, undefined project success criteria, and communication breakdown among stakeholders.

The good news is that all these problems can be substantially addressed by establishing a sound critical path at the outset of a project. Although construction of a critical path involves a lot of preliminary planning and communication, the time you invest in these early meetings pays huge dividends later.

PRINCIPLES OF THE CRITICAL PATH

All complex projects require multiple activities to be carried out in parallel, but this array of tasks can distract and overwhelm a manager. By using software to create a critical path, the manager is required to determine which of these tasks should take precedence, potential slips in the schedule, and how to allow for necessary adjustments.

By sliding less urgent tasks to the side, the manager is able to spot problems that threaten initiatives on the critical path and take corrective action more quickly. Thus, the manager can identify tasks that are less time sensitive, can be assigned more leeway (known as "float time") in the schedule, or can be delegated to junior members of the department. This leaves the manager free to concentrate on keeping tasks on the critical path on target. If a crisis occurs and an important piece of the puzzle is delayed, the manager can use the software to learn the implications immediately, implement workarounds, and mitigate delays in the schedule.

There are numerous free software programs available on the Internet, such as Viewpath (www.viewpath.com) and TaskJuggler (www.taskjuggler.org). These are stream-lined versions of full-blown project management software packages and may be adequate for library use. For purposes of this chapter, I used Microsoft Project 2010, but I am not here trying to train anyone to use CPM software; rather, I hope to enlighten managers about advantages of such scheduling systems. CPM requires a good deal of up-front work, but having a critical path greatly improves the likelihood of bringing a project to completion on time, on budget, and with greater communication among all parties.

HOW TO IMPLEMENT A CRITICAL PATH

The first activity essential to designing a critical path is to define all activities of a project and people involved in them. Most large projects have several activities that must occur simultaneously. I recommend arranging these activities into two or three logical groups.

For purposes of an example, consider the installation of moveable shelving into one section of a library. Let's assume that the area of the library where moveable shelves will be installed will reuse existing shelving but it will be mounted onto moveable tracks. This requires purchasing additional shelving, for shelving capacity is going to be doubled or tripled.

A moveable shelving project generally requires participation from all major departments in the library. Librarians need to evaluate collection size, make growth projections, and weed the existing collection. The technical services department alters data in the OPAC. A good deal of physical labor is required to unload books, dismantle shelves, and find storage space for these materials during the construction phase. Finally, outside contractors will do the actual installation of the moveable shelves. Here is a listing of the major steps necessary for this project:

Administrative and Preparation Tasks

- Hire a moveable shelving company
- Hire a carpet company
- Hire an electrician
- Lease book carts for duration of project
- Measure existing book collection
- Project future growth of collection
- Identify ranges of books to shift
- Update location codes in OPAC

Weeding

- Flag books to be weeded
- Pull weeded books
- Ship weeded books to final destination
- Remove weeded books from OPAC

Construction Aspects

- Clear space to store construction materials
- Receive book carts
- Receive new shelves and materials
- Load books to be moved onto carts
- Disassemble existing shelving system
- Remove carpeting
- Install new electrical wiring
- Obtain electrical inspections
- Install moveable shelving
- Install new carpet
- Replace books onto shelves
- Change physical signage

These tasks involve people from most departments in the library as well as outside vendors. Unless you have a memory like a computer chip, it is unlikely that you can think of all the people, tasks, and unforeseen variables that come into play during implementation of this project. Therefore, I suggest the following:

- Gather a team with representatives from each department.

- Using an oversize whiteboard, encourage brainstorming of all steps needed to complete each task.

- For each activity, note who should perform the task.

- Give a rough estimate of how many days it will take to accomplish each task.

- Note which tasks must be completed before another commences and which can be carried out simultaneously.

These initial planning meetings are designed not only to generate your action steps but to educate your staff about the complexity of the project ahead. Being part of the planning process is a classic technique to encourage team members to become invested in the mission.

The manager then streamlines these action plans into logical groups and in chronological order. Much of the work requires one task to be completed before another can begin. For example, you cannot remove books from the shelves until the rented book carts arrive. Nor can you disassemble existing shelving units until all books are removed. These tasks must be scheduled sequentially. On the other hand, some tasks have more flexibility and can take place concurrently. Changing the location code on thousands of books takes a great deal of time, but it can be done throughout the process without hindering the orderly progress of the other tasks.

Most CPM software allows you to enter your tasks into a Gantt chart, which is a bar chart designed to track the start and finish dates of a project. For tasks dependent on completion of another task, the software asks you to link those tasks. You can identify which tasks can start simultaneously, which must finish before another can begin, and which should reach completion at about the same time. Some tasks can be scheduled with more float time if they are not tied to a specific task. Creating this chart forces the project manager to sequence tasks properly, set deadlines, and assign appropriate personnel. Some of the more sophisticated software packages send alerts if the same person's name appears in too many tasks that converge around the same chronological spot on the calendar.

Figure 1 is a streamlined version of a Gantt chart generated in Microsoft Project, showing major activities involved in the moveable shelving project. Lines connecting the bars on the chart indicate which tasks must be completed before another commences. You can also see which tasks are unfolding concurrently.

A tremendous amount of work goes into creating the initial version of the Gantt chart, but this preplanning pays off as the project unfolds. Not only does it force the project manager to consider all the tasks, sequencing, and necessary personnel, the chart itself is a great communication tool. For those staff members who may not be familiar with Gantt charts, you can choose to print the chart in a calendar view.

Now let's introduce a little real-world chaos into the time line. Let's say an event beyond your control is about to destroy your carefully prepared schedule. A hurricane blows into town, and as a result all the electrical inspectors in the state have been pulled in for emergency duty. The county has informed you that there will be no electrical inspections for three weeks. There is simply nothing you could have done to foresee this, but the project cannot proceed without inspection of your newly installed electrical wiring, so you must revamp the schedule to take that three-week lull into account.

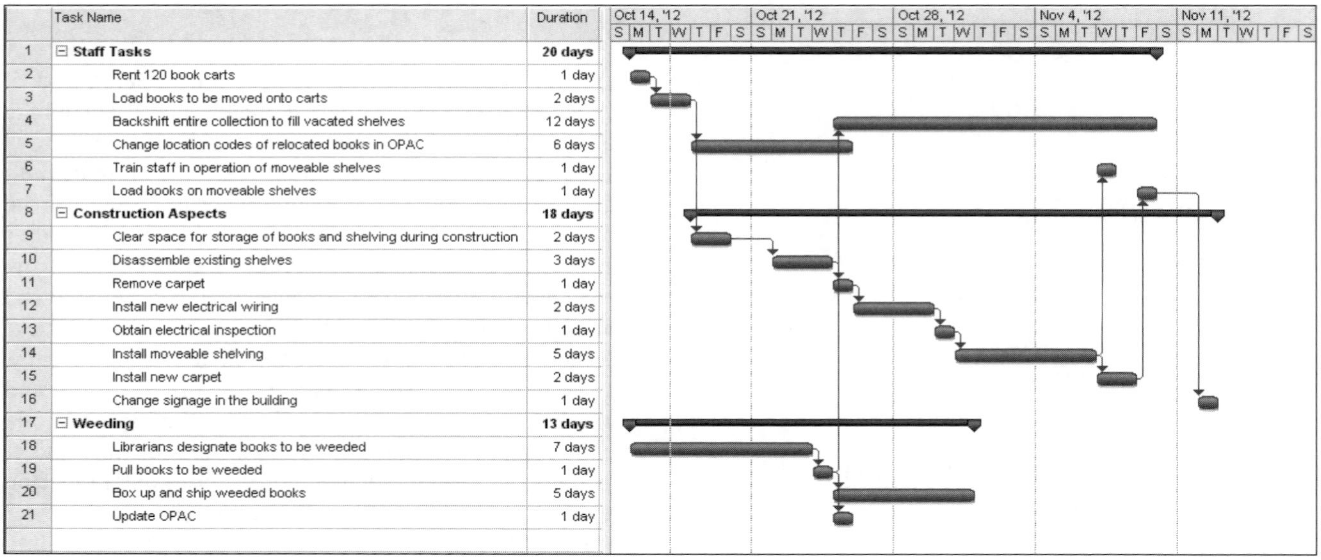

FIGURE 1

Gantt Chart

Using CPM software, you can create a new time line in less than a minute. When you move the date of the electrical inspection back three weeks, the software automatically recalculates the schedule. Because you have preloaded each task with its various dependencies, the software knows how to keep the delayed electrical inspection from affecting tasks not associated with the wiring and construction aspects. Only tasks that require the electricians are reshuffled; the majority of the weeding, record updating, and shifting of the collection can proceed without interruption.

On the upside, what happens if a task is completed well ahead of schedule? When you shorten the time line for that task, the software recalculates the schedule to let you see if it is possible for you to shorten the overall schedule.

One of the biggest complaints in organizations carrying out large projects is lack of communication (Cervone 2008). Middle managers are often responsible for shuttling information between frontline workers and upper-level management. Keeping the flow of information going can be a challenge, but putting the project online allows all stakeholders immediate access to the plan. A simple chart that can be rapidly updated and distributed to team members is perhaps the most efficient way to communicate the state of a project as it unfolds. Even if the project manager is out on sick leave, the critical path is easy enough for anyone on the team to interpret.

All libraries evolve, whether well planned or not. The use of sound project management techniques dramatically increases the likelihood of a middle manager being able to get projects across the finish line in a timely and successful manner.

REFERENCES

Cervone, H. Frank. 2008. "Good Project Managers Are 'Cluefull' Rather Than Clueless." *OCLC Systems and Services* 24:199–203.

Kappelman, Leon A., Robert McKeeman, and Lixuan Zhang. 2006. "Early Warning Signs of I.T. Project Failure: The Dominant Dozen." *Information Systems Management* 23 (4): 31–36.

Wamsley, Lori. 2009. "Controlling Project Chaos: Project Management for Library Staff." *PNLA Quarterly* 73: 5–6, 27.

18

SUPERVISION

DEBBIE SCHACHTER

BY THE TIME MANY LIBRARIANS BECOME MIDDLE MANAGERS, THEY LIKELY HAVE experience in both being supervised and supervising others. The quality of their supervision may vary, though, depending on innate skills and abilities (emotional intelligence being a significant factor) as well as personal experiences with their own supervisors. Organizational culture is crucial in setting type and quality of supervision undertaken in the library. To be most effective in all aspects of supervision, middle managers must be closely engaged with their staff.

In this chapter I cover a variety of general supervisory activities and skills of managers in libraries and other organizations, with an emphasis on the nature of supervision at the middle management level.

Overall, fundamental supervisory skills include the following:

- Communication skills
- Interpersonal skills (or emotional intelligence)
- Leadership skills
- Interest in staff development
- Fairness (praising and reprimanding)
- Modeling positive behaviors
- Technical skills

Supervision encompasses a wide array of activities, generally acknowledged to include these:

- Planning, organizing, and controlling work
- Motivating staff
- Communicating
- Performance management and development

- Coaching
- Managing conflict and discipline

PLANNING

Planning is an activity in which middle managers as well as supervisors are involved when developing strategic plans, annual operating plans, and standing plans such as policies, procedures, and budgets, among others. Within the supervisory context, strategic and tactical plans provide the multiyear overall vision and direction for the organization, with linkages to the departmental tactical or operations plans usually developed on an annual basis. The middle manager, as supervisor, must ensure that staff understand the overall organizational direction. At the same time, the manager or supervisor works with employees to develop their own specific goals for the year, which provide a context for their work within the overall plan. Depending on the organizational culture, staff or representatives from different levels of the institution may also be involved in development of the overall strategic plan.

Middle managers and other supervisors are essential in communicating the purpose of the strategic plan to employees. This also serves to empower staff with a greater understanding of their connections, inputs, and contributions to the overall organizational direction. The plan should answer the following questions (Robbins and DeCenzo 2010):

- Where are we now?
- Where do we want to be?
- How will we get there?
- How will we measure our progress?
- How will we know how successful we are?

The purpose of plans is also to develop goals. For the supervisor and middle manager, goal setting with employees is fundamental to good performance within a division.

ORGANIZING

If one is to supervise effectively, staff must be organized appropriately to fulfill their functions. This means developing teams or departments to meet particular work objectives. In addition, sufficient authority must be provided to employees to ensure that they are able to complete tasks for which they are responsible. Middle managers often err by one or the other of these two factors—responsibility or authority—rather than the two together. Other questions to consider:

- Are the right skill sets represented in the department or division?
- Should staff work in teams or individually?
- Are staff job descriptions current?
- Are reporting structures and responsibilities clear?

CONTROLLING

Once organization of the work is determined, how does the supervisor monitor the work or output of staff? This is accomplished by setting and communicating targets. Controls are then put in place to manage costs and ensure the appropriate quality and quantity of work.

In the library environment, cost management is essential, for there is rarely a revenue-generating side to balance increasing costs. Middle managers supervise work processes and manage costs, in a supervisory context, in the following ways:

- Improving methods
- Regulating workflow
- Minimizing waste
- Providing appropriate equipment
- Performing selective cost cutting

DECISION MAKING

How decisions are made within a department, or indeed an entire organization, is often based on the institutional culture and past practice. Decisions may be centralized or decentralized, individual or team-based. Most modern organizations recognize the benefit of tapping into staff expertise at all levels for ideal decision making. Supervisors provide opportunities for discussion and input from employees, including idea generation, to assist the development of high-quality decisions.

The organizational culture affects whether and how staff input is sought during decision making. It is, however, the middle manager's job to guarantee that decisions are shared with staff, regardless of whether senior management seeks input into decision making or not.

MOTIVATION

Although it is argued that supervisors and managers cannot actually create motivation, they can certainly create the environment or assign work based on employee skills and interests that does improve motivation. Research has shown that empowerment in the workplace and the interpersonal bonds of colleagues and supervisors provide more motivation than monetary rewards.

Conversely, by not empowering employees the organization is left in danger of failing to achieve its objectives or, worse, suffering an actual disaster. Employees who are not empowered may actually feel powerless. One of the ways managers create powerless staff is by limiting the flow of information to them. Empowerment, then, begins with sharing information and extends to granting staff control over, and responsibility for, solving problems and making decisions.

Different organizational cultures allow for different levels of empowerment. The middle manager is key in advocating and ensuring employee empowerment by sharing information, engaging staff in decision making, and encouraging them to be creative and innovative. Empowered employees help managers provide better service, avoid pitfalls, and make better decisions. Even in the most difficult circumstances, empowered employees are more resilient in the face of change.

Supervisors must delegate work and, to accomplish this, they should provide employees with the resources and authority to complete these tasks, including formal communication of the delegation, so other staff are aware; authority to access resources they require; and additional support that may be needed from supervisors. Most employees feel motivated by being given responsibility for work or projects.

PERFORMANCE MANAGEMENT

Good planning involves a process known as continuous performance management. An effective performance management system includes processes that engage supervisor and employee in annual goal planning, regular review and feedback, and a formal review at least once a year. Performance management is intended to help employees understand their roles in the organization and the purpose of their work. Annual goals link the employee's work with organizational planning, including the strategic plan. Regular review meetings allow for timely feedback and help employees achieve their goals. Further, regular meetings allow employee or supervisor to identify problems as they arise and provide a process for modifying goals or helping to address any performance issues.

Individual employee development objectives should be shaped on an annual basis, or they may arise during the course of the year as it becomes evident that an employee does not have all of the skill sets to achieve intended goals. Performance plans may simply be identification of training courses, or they may be explicit processes and procedures that address real performance problems.

It is essential to ensure that a functioning performance management system is working through the supervisory level. Assuring that supervisors themselves receive regular performance reviews helps model this practice, which feeds back into their reviews of their own line staff.

COACHING

Effective coaching helps employees learn and develop in their positions. Coaching is a day-to-day method that takes advantage of problems or situations that benefit the employee in a learning moment. Coaching should take place when the supervisor identifies a gap between the quality of service an employee should provide and his or her current performance. Coaching is intended to provide a learning context for employees, rather than a disciplinary action, when a work situation does not meet performance standards.

Thus, to be effective at coaching, the middle manager must actively participate in the work environment, whether by working side-by-side with supervisors and staff or by maintaining close contact with day-to-day work of the department. Sometimes employees recognize the need for assistance with a particular type of problem and come to their supervisor seeking coaching. But some won't always do this. A manager or supervisor cannot rely solely on staff identifying their own need for coaching.

Problems must be addressed at the point they occur and should be viewed as a teachable moment, intended to correct a lack of knowledge or misunderstanding of policy, practice, or procedures. Coaching helps the employee perceive the need for improvement and allows the manager and employee to develop a strategy to resolve the gap together. As always, any corrective or learning experience must be documented, then followed up to ascertain commitment by the employee to improve performance.

CONCLUSIONS

Personnel issues are often cited as a major reason for staff turnover and lack of productivity, so middle managers must be aware of these best practices in supervision and make certain they are being enforced. Even for those who have supervised for years, refreshing your knowledge of best practices will improve performance management activities, morale, and staff motivation.

REFERENCE

Robbins, Stephen P., and David A. DeCenzo. 2010. *Supervision Today!* 6th edition. Upper Saddle River, NJ: Prentice Hall.

19

FIRM BUT FAIR

Dealing with Problem Employees

CEES-JAN DE JONG

WHEN YOU MANAGE A STAFF, YOU ARE WORKING WITH SOME DEDICATED AND hardworking individuals. But there are always one or more employees who prove to be problematic in one way or another. As a result, you find yourself spending time monitoring behavior, determining ways to measure productivity, recording problems, communicating issues, and meeting to discuss the employee to a degree that may end up overwhelming you.

Of course, you have other responsibilities, and problem employees can really get in the way. Understandably, the impact of problem employees can be significant and can result in a dysfunctional workplace. For instance, a tardy employee may make other staff question why they show up on time; a disruptive employee can make other staff members feel uncomfortable or create divisiveness in the area.

Clearly, the middle manager cannot let staff discipline slide. To minimize the time drain, focus on spending some time organizing yourself to handle staff in a firm, but fair, manner.

GETTING ORGANIZED

You need to invest a fair amount of time getting organized when you accept a position with a staff reporting to you. There are likely collective bargaining agreements, forms, and processes you must familiarize yourself with when it comes to monitoring the success of your staff.

Collective Bargaining Agreements

If you are in a union environment, your staff is most likely governed by a collective bargaining agreement. Though they don't make for very exciting reading, you should acquaint yourself with the sections relevant to supervising staff (hours of work, illness, overtime, performance reviews, vacation, etc.). Whenever you plan to do something out of the ordinary such as move an employee to a different work location, it is advisable to consult with someone from library personnel or human resources and together identify applicable sections from the agreement. Take advantage of others' experience with the agreement. They may point out things you never thought of, such as rights of the employer, which may be important in the disciplinary process.

Performance Reviews

In most instances, your library has an annual performance review process that you need to utilize with your staff. Specific forms are generally required as part of this process, and they have probably been in place for some time. Become familiar with both forms and process. If you are not satisfied with this system, there may be opportunities for you to provide input. But since you need to devote a fair amount of time getting up to speed, choose your battles wisely.

The next step should be to review past performance reviews and job descriptions of your staff. This helps provide context for performance issues as well as expectations established for the upcoming performance review. In the long run, it is valuable to meet as soon as possible with each staff member to review the expectations determined in the previous performance review. You can then establish follow-up meetings as needed.

Remember that nothing should come as a surprise to an employee when it comes to the performance review. Any issues you identify should have been shared with the employee well in advance with guidance on rectifying them. Hence, meeting once a year to discuss performance issues is not enough. If you have a large staff, it is even more important to be aware of upcoming performance appraisals, giving yourself and employees enough time to review expectations and address any issues.

Disciplinary Processes

An employee may feel reprimanded if requested to come to your office to discuss a behavioral problem. Actual discipline, however, as understood in a collective agreement, is a highly formal process that often involves representation for both parties. You may discover that there is a predisciplinary process that must be followed before a disciplinary meeting can take place. Disciplinary meetings frequently are extremely uncomfortable for most parties, since all previous attempts to resolve the issue have been unsuccessful, or the issue is so severe that the supervisor cannot act without having a human resources representative present.

Before any disciplinary meeting, have thorough documentation to demonstrate that you have followed the predisciplinary steps. Such actions generally include discussing the issue with the employee, monitoring it over time, and providing formal feedback as well as training,

if necessary. It is essential that after every one-on-one meeting with a problem employee you put in writing the issues discussed and what was agreed to. It is possible that library personnel or your human resources department has a form for this purpose, but make certain you retain a copy of every document you provide the employee. Dealing with issues in a formal manner can often put your employee on the right track, and usually it is unlikely you will need to go as far as a disciplinary meeting. Nevertheless, be familiar with the process and documenting procedures, so you are always prepared.

Setting the Tone

Be firm but fair. I have found this approach effective in establishing the right tone for addressing problem employees. In a firm but fair work environment, staff expectations are clear, everyone is held to the same standard, and exceptions are rare. For example, the tardy employee may think it is all right to come in late regularly and work a little later at the end of the day. Before addressing the individual, all staff should be clear that everyone is expected to show up on time for work. Once this expectation has been clearly stated, if the problem remains then it is time to deal with this issue on an individual level. Again, the issue should come as no surprise to the employee. If there is more than one tardy employee, they should be addressed in the same way to avoid a situation in which someone feels singled out.

The final step must be to follow through on your decision to hold people accountable, in this case for showing up on time. When are exceptions appropriate? Naturally, you have to be flexible at times. After all, there should be a suitable level of trust between supervisor and employee. As long as you are aware of the "optics"—how things are perceived and interpreted—and you are not dealing with a "trendsetter"—someone who will lead others into unacceptable work practices—there can be some flexibility. Keep in mind that, whatever you do, it should not interfere with the tone you want to set for your department.

ADDRESSING THE PROBLEM EMPLOYEE

Once you have prepared yourself sufficiently, you will be in an excellent position to address issues surrounding the problem employee. If your boss has not pointed out specific staff who require some extra guidance, it is likely that through meetings circumstances will be made apparent that require you to pay close attention to the behavior of particular individuals. Your goal is to ensure a positive work environment where people feel fairly treated, so make sure expectations concerning problem behaviors are clearly stated.

Communicating expectations can occur at staff meetings, via e-mail addressed to all staff, written into performance appraisals, and during one-on-one meetings that could result in an addendum to the performance appraisal. For example, if you have a few staff members who are not taking responsibility for carrying out specific tasks and are being perceived as not pulling their weight, you declare the expectation that everyone is required to demonstrate initiative in taking responsibility for shared tasks. It is useful to articulate an expectation at a staff meeting where most members are present. Everyone recognizes that you are dealing with this issue, and you can avoid singling out any one person.

On the other hand, a one-on-one meeting may be necessary to address the specific problem. This meeting should focus on the situation, allow you to propose a solution or course of action together, obtain a verbal commitment from the employee to meet your expectations, and be documented with a follow-up in writing that summarizes major points and what was agreed to. Discussions often go off on different tangents, so make sure you are both clear on what the issue is, and bring the discussion back on topic if it strays too far off course. It is important to stay on topic.

During your discussion, allow the employee to come up with ideas on how to resolve the issue. If the employee has some ownership of the plan, he or she could be more strongly committed to making it work. Just make sure the ideas are realistic and in line with your staffing model and workflow. Once you have a plan, make sure the employee commits to it by giving specific targets or deadlines that can be evaluated. It is also helpful to set a follow-up meeting, which gives you the opportunity to either celebrate the improvements made by the employee or, if things did not go so well, undertake a fresh evaluation of what went wrong and decide on next steps.

Though you may have the best intentions when meeting, things can go poorly for a variety of reasons. Emotions on both sides must be held in check; prior assumptions can lead to misunderstandings; the employee may not take responsibility for the situation; new information revealed may change the entire context; or both parties may not reach agreement. When it becomes clear that the issue will not be resolved, end the meeting with a concrete plan to continue discussion at a later date. This may give you an opportunity to discuss the incident with your supervisor or human resources staff to determine a fresh strategy.

If you find it challenging to confront people on issues, consider participating in a program or consult books that focus on building this skill; Kerry Patterson and colleagues' *Crucial Conversations* (2011) and *Crucial Confrontations* (2004) are two books worth looking at. Building confidence to address issues and learning techniques to help conversations go smoothly facilitate maintaining a positive work environment.

One situation that really tests the middle manager's abilities is conflict between coworkers. In this instance, you must also deal with how the conflict is handled. If handled by all parties in a respectful manner, the manager may be able to resolve the conflict by simply providing clarity and direction. But when civility breaks down, things can degenerate quickly. You must immediately intervene, separate the employees, and allow them to calm down. Ultimately, you must bring the coworkers together again to acknowledge their inappropriate behavior, acknowledge more effective methods of addressing this situation, and then apologize to each other.

CONCLUSIONS

A dysfunctional work environment can take up more of your time than dealing with problem employees. Although you need to invest time getting organized, it is time well spent. You not only refine your skills in dealing with problem employees but keep performance appraisals on track and maintain clear expectations of your staff. When your staff believes everyone is treated fairly, morale improves and everyone benefits from this change.

REFERENCES

Patterson, Kerry, et al. 2004. *Crucial Confrontations*. New York: McGraw-Hill.
———. 2011. *Crucial Conversations: Tools for Talking When Stakes Are High*. 2nd. ed. New York: McGraw-Hill

20

PERFORMANCE MANAGEMENT

Making Difficult Conversations Easy and Managing Soft Skills

ROBERT BARR

WHAT KIND OF WORK DO YOU DO? THIS IS A COMMON QUESTION NEW acquaintances often ask each other. How you answer this question helps define your job. Do you respond with your title? Perhaps you say a brief phrase right from your official job description. A cataloger might describe creating a MARC record. Reference librarians might discuss answering patron questions and instruction or programming. Managers could cite some difficult patron interactions they have dealt with recently, their budgets, or their staff. We are naturally inclined to list the "hard" skills, the "what" of the job.

For many managers, particularly those recently promoted, engaging in conversations about an employee's performance and behavior, the "soft" skills of the jobs—"how" the job should be done—is one of the most challenging aspects of supervision. Managers who supervise the performance of others are more effective if they help their employees with the "how" as well as the "what." They help staff understand the kinds of behavior required for successfully completing their work.

I examine performance management by comparing and differentiating job performance and employee behavior. Practically, I look at three employee performance issues, their underlying behavioral causes, and a series of steps for engaging in productive manager-employee conversations.

OVERLOOKING OR ADDRESSING THE SOFT SKILLS

The phrases we use to describe jobs and those we find in job descriptions usually address goals and objectives we are easily able to describe. They tend to omit the soft skills of the job altogether. Consider the following phrases taken from recently posted job descriptions:

- Responsibilities include collection development and maintenance, young adult and adult programming, and promotion of library services to the community.

- Competent in written and oral communication skills including business writing, report writing, summarizing, editing, and presenting.
- Coordinate inputs from other selectors, front-line librarians, vendors, technical services, and web content.

These are hard skills describing what the prospective employee will accomplish, if successful. They don't inform applicants what kind of person they need in this job—they simply indicate what types of activities and responsibilities the position entails. Descriptions of desired behavior or necessary attitudes are often omitted. Behaviors and attitudes can be difficult to describe. Phrases like "contributes to a cooperative and welcoming work environment" and "cheerfully and empathetically serves internal and external customers" can mean vastly different things to different people.

Understandably, good behavior is an unstated expectation. Hard job skills and performance objectives are acquired through past education or experience. The mechanics of how to conduct a good reference interview were learned in library school. The ability to serve cheerfully and help facilitate a welcoming environment was taught . . . when, exactly? Whether or not you perform well can be attributed to your education, training, and experience. On the other hand, behavior is much more personal. It is a product of how you were raised, what experiences you've had, as well as your worldview and beliefs.

In many instances, "problem" employees encounter difficulties with the behavior (how) aspects of their jobs more than the performance (what) aspects. Conversations about behavior are something many supervisors dread. Discussing an employee's behavior can be much more difficult than having a conversation about his or her job performance. There are, however, a few steps one can take to make these conversations more palatable and productive.

STEP 1
COMMIT

The first step is to commit to having this conversation sooner rather than later. Although this might appear obvious, it is all too easy to ignore or avoid problems. Unfortunately, performance problems are rarely resolved without any corrective action. Managers who don't address problems end up undermining their own effec-

tiveness in the eyes of their subordinates. By permitting poor performance to continue, the middle manager unintentionally sends the message that this poor performance is in fact acceptable. Further, performance problems have a tendency to compound. Colleagues viewing poor performance as acceptable may model their own behavior accordingly.

STEP 2
UNDERSTAND THE PROBLEM: KNOWING WHEN BEHAVIOR IS THE ISSUE

The second step is to identify whether the *root* of the problem is related to performance or behavior. When attempting to distinguish between performance and behavior, it is often helpful to consider whether this problem can be resolved through training. Behavioral issues are much more complex than performance issues. An employee can be trained to perform in the following areas competently and efficiently: technical skills, knowledge of policy, organizational/hierarchal structure, shelving speed/accuracy, even professional ethics and customer service. Training in behavior—effective communication, personal accountability, having a customer-centered attitude, being a self-starter, and fostering a fun, collaborative work environment—must be paired with significant, managerial follow-through in order to be successful.

Behavioral training sessions are helpful in establishing an institutional culture. They send a clear message regarding the kinds of behavior senior management expects and supports. Rarely does an individual behavioral training session alone establish a new behavior, but with continuous feedback and reinforcement from middle managers problem behaviors can be changed.

Another way to distinguish performance issues from behavioral issues is to examine how much of the problem is within a staff member's control. We choose to act in certain ways—to empathize or not, to allow a heated discussion to annoy us, to shower before going to work. Though we would like to claim to have a similar level of control over our job performance, such skills do not come without significant education, training, or experience. Evaluate the following situations for how they pertain to an employee's behavior or performance:

Emily is frequently late for work. There is no pattern to her lateness. When asked about it, she blames either her alarm clock or traffic. Other staff have to cover her responsibilities for opening the library.

Norman is friendly and, for the most part, provides first-rate customer service. Some patrons refuse to be helped by any other staff member. Norman spends far too much time assisting these individuals, making other patrons wait. He also conducts personal discussions not related to the library.

Clifford appears depressed and struggles with customer service. Although he handles external customers acceptably, he talks negatively about them behind their backs. Further, he is rude and unresponsive to staff in other departments.

All these examples are rooted in behavioral problems—but all have performance aspects. Emily's lateness is primarily a behavioral problem. It could be easily confused with a performance issue. Although customers respond positively to Norman's friendliness, it results in customer service performance issues. Clifford's customer service behavior is inconsistent and not productive.

STEP 3
INTERACT

After determining whether the problem is rooted in performance or behavior, the third step is to plan for a meeting. It is critical to keep in mind the effect problem behavior has on performance. You might make a list detailing behavioral aspects of the problem and how they affect performance. Even when behavior is the root of the problem, it is beneficial to ease into conversations by beginning with observations about performance before addressing underlying behavior. Start with what's simple and address issues from a performance perspective. Think about the following:

Does the behavior affect more than one area of performance? Consider Norman: in most situations, particularly with one-time or infrequent patrons, his overt friendliness supports good customer service.

Is it unrealistic to deal with behavior in an employee-manager context? A mental health professional might be more appropriate for helping Clifford resolve his depression—though his supervisor must still address internal service issues.

Behavioral issues are frequently more demanding and time consuming than performance problems. Can you acceptably resolve an issue by focusing on performance?

It is important to begin the meeting with an empathetic attitude. Ask yourself how you would interpret what you are going to say and how you think your employee will interpret it. Every person is different, and responses to criticism vary wildly. With an employee sensitive to criticism, begin the conversation with specific statements about observed performance. Be critical of the performance—not the person. The best way to address the behavioral cause of an issue is first to identify the issue, then ask open-ended questions or make observations that allow the employee to bring up the cause and (one hopes) take responsibility for the problem.

Emily's tardiness is fairly straightforward. Getting to work on time should be under her control. Start by saying, "I notice you've been coming in late recently. Is there something going on?" How *not* to begin this conversation: "Emily, you've been coming in late recently. I'm sure you're aware how your tardiness is affecting your coworkers, who have to do your work for you. One of the values of our institution is respect, and by arriving late you're not respecting them." Although some of these points are most likely valid, this is not a good way to begin.

Norman's situation is a bit more complex. The majority of his behavior is valuable. The problem is not his behavior so much as the combination of his personality with those of a small portion of his patrons. A positive and empathetic way to broach this topic: "Norman, I've noticed that some of our more demanding patrons make it difficult for you to help others once you've filled their request," then illustrate this with an example. This is nonaccusatory. It doesn't put Norman on the defensive and is likely to provide a transition into brainstorming ways of ending patron interactions after their needs have been met.

For most managers, having difficult conversations about behavior in which they provide constructive feedback is not easy to master. But it is one of those skills every manager needs to acquire. Behavior is much more difficult to change than performance. Still, permitting and encouraging discussion on the *how* aspect of a job in addition to the *what*—in conjunction with being receptive and open to addressing issues as they arise—provide opportunities to increase morale and employee collaboration, fostering a positive workplace and, ultimately, patron satisfaction.

21

PERFORMANCE IMPROVEMENT

An Overview for Middle Managers

BARBARA PETERSOHN

MIDDLE MANAGERS FREQUENTLY HAVE RESPONSIBILITY FOR MANAGING EVERY-thing from major organizational policies to the finer details of front-end delivery of services and resources in libraries. They manage either the public's point of contact or the point of information for staff on technical issues. As the people likely to manage staff who interact with the public or carry out policy, middle managers struggle with the challenges of ongoing training and improvement of staff: how they perform their duties and responsibilities "on the line" or at the desk, and how they interact with customers.

Managers' ability to identify and correct performance problems is key to how well they do their job, how well their service points serve communities of users, and even how closely their institution or organization comes to meeting its strategic goals. Because middle managers help identify barriers to performance on both the individual and organizational levels, they benefit from understanding the concepts of performance improvement and how they can be applied in work environments, including libraries.

The practice of performance improvement, sometimes called *human performance technology*, is defined by the International Society of Performance Improvement as a "set of methods and procedures, and a strategy for solving problems, for realizing opportunities related to the performance of people. It can be applied to individuals, small groups, and large organizations. It is, in reality, a systematic combination of three fundamental processes: performance analysis, cause analysis, and intervention selection" (International Society for Performance Improvement 2011).

Performance improvement draws from disciplines including behavioral psychology, human resources management, and instructional design. Distilling the process into a simplified model is complicated by the many different models that exist, perhaps because of the wide range of backgrounds of those who write on the topic. Nevertheless, some elements are shared by performance improvement models (James A. Pershing 2006):

Gap analysis: the comparison of optimal performance (by an employee or organiza-tion) to actual performance. The difference between the two creates a gap that identifies a need to be addressed.

Performance analysis: formulating questions and collecting data based on the iden-tified performance gap, to get to the root cause of a performance problem.

Intervention selection: a change in the environment or behavior selected to address the problem and close the gap between existing and optimal performance. Usually more than one intervention is used to address a performance issue.

Implementation: application of a well-designed and developed plan for the interventions selected.

Evaluation: measuring the impact of a performance improvement intervention through feedback or data collection.

To make performance improvement meaningful to middle managers, in this chapter we first look at Gilbert's behavior engineering model, a widely used method for identifying individual performance problems, and then apply that model to a typical middle management situation. I also provide a brief overview of performance improvement tools, with another scenario and the tools and process used in that case.

THE BEHAVIOR ENGINEERING MODEL

Thomas Gilbert's behavior engineering model (BEM) is almost universally used in some form by performance improvement experts. Though revised by others over the years, Gilbert introduced the model in the late 1970s as a kind of checklist of both the individual's internal collection or repertory of behaviors—knowledge, skills, abilities, motivations—and the external, environmental, or workplace factors that either support or hinder performance. Distinguishing external from individual factors and identifying three categories of each, the BEM provides middle managers with a list of areas to explore when getting to the root of an individual's performance problem and suggests a systematic and process-oriented approach (Gilbert 1978).

Gilbert identifies three categories of environmental support in the workplace: data/information, resources, and incentives. These are collectively labeled "Workplace Environment" in table 1.

Data/information support in the workplace includes the communication that should go on between employer and employees and among employees. The information exchanged informs employees what is expected of them, how tasks should be performed, when, where, and why. Data/information also includes feedback to employees about whether they are meeting expectations, how their department and other departments are doing in meeting overall goals and objectives, whether there is a per-

formance deficit or failure, and examples of correct performance. As most middle managers have learned through experience, information or data flow in the workplace as described in the model is crucial. Lack of information sharing or communication, says Gilbert, is by far the single biggest cause of performance problems.

Resources are the tools and materials employees are given to do their jobs. Software, workflow, equipment, and arrangement of the workspace should be designed to match the needs of those who do the job.

Incentives are the monetary or nonmonetary rewards or compensation employees receive for their work. Nonmonetary rewards include employee recognition, performance incentives, advancement, career development, and leave time. Incentives also may include how difficult, punishing, easy, or rewarding it is to complete tasks on the job—the positive or negative consequences of doing a good job.

What the individual brings to the job, the "Worker's Behavior Repertory" in table 1, includes knowledge, capacity, and motives.

Knowledge describes the education or skills employees need to perform the tasks given successfully. Job responsibilities should be suitable to their individual knowledge, skills, and abilities.

Capacity is how well employees can learn or adapt to perform successfully. An employee may be a "good match" for a job based on his or her adaptability, temperament, or personality.

Motives include the individual's internal motivation to work and how compatible the individual and the organization are in terms of culture, ethics, and mores.

Table 1 is an adaptation of Gilbert's BEM divided by workplace/environment support and individual repertory for the general categories "Information," "Instrumentation," and "Motivation." This table gives some specific examples and descriptions for each category as they might be rewritten by a mid-level library manager.

In his discussion of the BEM, Chevalier (2003) focuses first on environmental factors affecting performance. Environmental factors are frequently the cause of a performance problem and present the greatest potential for improving performance. Because they frequently "pose the greatest barrier to exemplary performance," they are also easier to address or remediate than individual behavior. "When environmental supports are strong,"

TABLE 1

Gilbert's Behavior Engineering Model

	Information	**Instrumentation**	**Motivation**
Workplace Environment	DATA, INFORMATION • regular meetings with supervisor • clear guidelines on desk responsibilities, guides or job aids to help performance • performance expectations with timely feedback • updates on department productivity	RESOURCES, TOOLS • ergonomically appropriate workstations and work areas • intuitive equipment, hardware, and software that accommodate workflow • workflow processes that suit worker skills	INCENTIVES • incentive programs • career-development opportunities • appropriate leave programs • consequences to good (or bad) work performance • schedules (or leave time) to accommodate personal needs • employee recognition
Worker's Repertory of Behaviors	KNOWLEDGE • adequate training preparation for duties • timely training on desk procedures • ongoing training on new library software, services, or resources	CAPACITY • employees can learn what they need to know to do the job • employees can adapt to the job requirements/ environment	MOTIVES • why employee works/ wants this job • workplace culture, ethics, and motives aligned with those of the employee • employees hired based on how skills match job realities

says Chevalier, "individuals are better able to do what is expected of them" (2003, 9).

Changing environmental factors offers greater impact on performance improvement at less expense than changes at the individual level. If a performance problem points to individual factors (motives, capacity, readiness, knowledge, and skills), implementation of corrective actions has less immediate influence and the cost in generating the desired improvement is likely greater. Performance improvement experts note that training or training programs (i.e., improving the knowledge and skills to do the work) is usually the most expensive and least effective means of improving work performance (Rothwell 2005). Many recommend leveraging the BEM by first looking for performance issues caused by workplace or environmental factors, then moving on to the indi-

vidual's behaviors in the following order (from Chevalier 2003):

Environmental Factors	Individual Repertory
1. Information	1. Motives
2. Resources	2. Capacity
3. Incentives	3. Knowledge

Using the BEM as a structure to assess and remediate the environmental or workplace factors, and working through the model in the order suggested here, the middle manager can "walk" through each category, looking for elements to investigate. For example, starting in the "Data/Information" category, a manager might explore whether there is clear communication with the supervisor, regular meetings, feedback on performance, and clear guidelines on desk responsibilities.

Using the Behavior Engineering Model: The Disappearing Reference Stats

Rose, an information desk manager in a busy urban library, notices that her reference statistics show atypical declines for certain morning hours in the week for the previous few months. Statistics are reviewed regularly to help make staffing decisions. Though the overall daily counts are within range, a drop in counts might prompt the director, struggling with continued budget cuts, to reduce hours on those days.

Statistics are recorded using a web-based application on the reference desk PCs, which requires that staff select a check box for the type of transaction and then click a button to record the transaction. Based on previous schedules, Rose identifies three employees who would have been responsible for working the desk during the times in question. All are highly regarded librarians with several years' experience.

Using the BEM prescribes looking first at information, tools, and incentives for employees. To follow the process, Rose interviews each employee individually. She asks them to describe how they record statistics, if they have questions about the software that records statistics, and if record keeping interferes with other work. The first two employees describe how they record statistics as expected, but the last librarian interviewed, Marie, volunteers that she appreciates the importance of statistics and carefully keeps a paper record of reference transactions, which she adds into the system once she is off the desk.

"The web-based form is simple enough," Marie adds, "but I found that the desk is too busy for me to keep patrons waiting. So I started coming back and adding my counts in before the end of the day." Not knowing that the application adds a date and time stamp on each recorded transaction, and that administration looks at a graph of transactions based on hourly counts, Marie unwittingly has skewed statistical records by adding her counts after her desk hours.

Both a failure to communicate information about the statistics-keeping process (Data/Information) and the competing tasks to both serve the public and record statistics (Incentives) were BEM contributing factors here. The statistics application was a mystery to Marie, who did not understand how data were kept and then applied. And the process of recording statistics while on the desk created competing priorities, or made keeping statistics "punishing" for her.

Rose realizes from the interview that Marie needs more information about the software and how statistics are used by the administration to make budgetary and other decisions. Marie, trying to serve patrons first, needs some accommodation for recording her statistics accurately, so Rose investigates whether the web form can be altered to allow the user to adjust the date and time stamp.

THE PERFORMANCE IMPROVEMENT TOOLKIT

Performance improvement is grounded in the systematic collection of data, which can assess needs, analyze performance, analyze the workplace, suggest what is required to solve performance problems, and show progress (or lack of progress) in application of a performance solution. Here are some of the best known and most frequently used data collection tools in the performance improvement toolkit:

Observation: observing and documenting behaviors of workers as they perform work tasks. Quantitative and qualitative data can be derived from observation, which varies in the amount of overtness and degree of participation by the observer. Observation requires extensive planning and training but can identify subtleties like nonverbal behavior, gestures, and voice inflection, which are difficult to glean from other types of data (Marrelli 2005a).

Interviews: data collection based on a series of questions, which can be structured, semistructured, or unstructured, depending on the information needed and the range of limits to allowed responses, from fixed response to open-ended. Interviews often provide detailed information about problems on the job, potential causes or solutions, describe working relationships and common practices (Jana L. Pershing 2006).

Focus groups: small groups of participants assembled by a facilitator to discuss a series of questions. They can provide feedback based on perceptions and attitudes and groundwork for more focused questions for interviews, surveys, or other types of data collection (Marrelli 2008).

Work samples: data gathered from the products of work performed on the job. Unlike observations or performance tasks, they are not scheduled tasks but samples of work collected from the output over a period of time. They are particularly useful for determining the effectiveness of a performance improvement intervention (Marrelli 2005c).

Process mapping (also known as task analysis): analyses of inputs, action sequences, and outputs as part of work tasks, which can be diagrammed or graphed in a flowchart. Process mapping can identify errors, lack of work support, or redundancies along with communication problems in workflow (Marrelli 2005b).

Content analysis: investigation and analysis of the content of communications or textual documents in the workplace. Because written documentation and communications exist in most work environments, content analysis is considered one of the more frequently used data-gathering tools in the "toolbox" and may vary widely depending on the types of documentation available (Gilmore 2006).

This short list suggests the array of data collection and analysis that might accompany the performance improvement process, whether to assess a need or to identify a performance intervention. Some of them are used in the case study that follows.

Performance Improvement Tools in Context: The Elusive Library Schedule

At first, occasionally posting an inaccurate schedule at a campus branch library seemed to Jonathan, the branch manager, like an insignificant problem. But the schedule for the Highside Center's library was now being rewritten almost every other week during the semester. The need to make changes was constant and seemed out of control. Notices about updated hours were posted and reposted, sometimes with little or no advance warning to students or staff. For Jonathan and his staff, the organizational goal for their branch library begins with developing and posting an accurate, reliable schedule.

Jonathan noticed that for most semesters the schedule of operating hours for the library did not accurately target needs of the library's users: (1) there were several occasions over the year when the library was not open enough hours during exams; (2) there were several occasions when the library did not plan to accommodate classes on campus for atypical weekend hours; and (3) the library had failed on occasion to adapt operating hours for external or public groups using the facility.

To determine the cause of this performance gap, unstructured interviews of key personnel from the main library, branch library, and the Center's administrative staff were conducted with open-ended questions about

processes and tools. Work samples from the scheduling calendar and personnel records documenting schedule changes were collected for content analysis or document review. The data gathered were sifted and sorted in a search for similarities and patterns, then graphed.

The content analysis showed that (1) errors in the semester schedule related to exam scheduling were most frequently due to library staff not gathering information about exams offered in the building at the right time and failing to ask for this information from Center staff in a timely way; (2) errors in scheduling related to requests originating from the College of Business to add class meeting times were beyond library staff's control and would have to be addressed by other means; and (3) library staff did not have a prompt for gathering schedule information. Further, interviews of the Center's administrative staff indicated that use of the facility by outside groups occurred with little advance notice but contributed to a limited number of errors in the schedule.

All these issues affected scheduling, but the data graphed from the content analysis showed that issues 1 and 2 most frequently caused the errors. Based on his analysis of data, Jonathan presented three recommendations for change to library administration and Center staff: (1) establish a systematic process and "tickler" file for staff with calendared events for checking exam schedules and classes offered in the building to predict needed changes in library service hours during exams accurately; (2) since errors caused by class schedule changes from the College of Business could not be anticipated by the library, abandon the semester-based schedule in favor of a month-to-month schedule to minimize or eliminate those errors; and (3) not change the library's schedule to accommodate public or nonuniversity users or events. Jonathan also suggested reviews after six and twelve months to evaluate effectiveness of the interventions and adjust if necessary.

Basic steps of the performance improvement process, reviewed earlier, can be related to the Highside branch case:

A gap analysis compared actual level of performance to desired level, in alignment with the goals and objectives of the organization. The analysis compared actual to desired level and determined that the branch was not meeting its performance standard of few or no schedule changes as part of its goal for good customer service.

A performance analysis looked for performance problems in the organization, management, facilities, and technical, social, and individual arenas. Data were collected: instances of schedule changes, interviews with Center administration, branch and main library staff, and a document review. Some remedies like regulating School of Business class schedule changes were not within the control of the branch manager.

The branch manager selected interventions based on data, targeted to the problem and cost effective.

The branch manager selected solutions that were low cost and required limited retraining. Staff were not collecting the right information at the right time to make an accurate schedule. A tickler file will prompt staff to gather timely information for the schedule, a change in policy will target the schedule more to students, and the process was changed to develop the schedule in a monthly, not semester, time frame. Finally, the manager will be responsible for a follow-up review of the solution in six and twelve months and for gathering data to measure impact.

((()))

Gilbert states that the "ultimate cause" of any performance problem, whether immediately caused by the work environment or the individual or both, "will be found in a deficiency of the management system" (1978, 76). As part of the management team, mid-level managers have the best vantage point from top to bottom—from the overall objectives and perspectives of top-level management, to details of the work of organizational units, to routines of staff on the front lines. Middle managers have the best opportunities to identify and correct performance problems and to correct deficiencies in the management system. They are the best hope for performance improvement within the library organization.

REFERENCES

Chevalier, Roger. 2003. "Updating the Behavior Engineering Model." *Performance Improvement* 42 (5): 8–14.

Gilbert, Thomas F. 1978. *Human Competence: Engineering Worthy Performance*. New York: McGraw-Hill.

Gilmore, Erika R. 2006. "Using Content Analysis in Human Performance Technology." In *Handbook of Human Performance Technology*, ed. James A. Pershing, 819–836. San Francisco: Pfeiffer.

International Society for Performance Improvement. 2011. "What is HPT?" www.ispi.org/content.aspx?id=54&terms=what+is+hpt.

Marrelli, Anne F. 2005a. "Observations." *Performance Improvement* 44 (2): 39–43.

———. 2005b. "Process Mapping." *Performance Improvement* 44 (5): 40–44.

———. 2005c. "Work Samples." *Performance Improvement* 44 (4): 43–46.

———. 2008. "Collecting Data through Focus Groups." *Performance Improvement* 47 (4): 39–45.

Pershing, James A. 2006. "Human Performance Technology Fundamentals." In *Handbook of Human Performance Technology*, ed. James A. Pershing, 5–34. San Francisco: Pfeiffer.

Pershing, Jana L. 2006. "Interviewing to Analyze and Evaluate Human Performance Technology." In *Handbook of Human Performance Technology*, ed. James A. Pershing, 780–793. San Francisco: Pfeiffer.

Rothwell, William J. 2005. Selecting Human Performance Enhancement (HPE) Strategies." In *Beyond Training and Development*, 175–193. New York: American Management Association International.

22

CONSULT ME FIRST

Building Consultative Relationships between Top-Level and Mid-Level Library Managers

JEFFREY A. FRANKS

LIBRARY DEPARTMENT OR BRANCH HEADS, IN BOTH ACADEMIC AND PUBLIC libraries, are true textbook examples of mid-level management. They serve as a conduit for the movement of information from top-level management downward and from library patrons and subordinates upward. As communicators, interpreters, and facilitators of the organization's mission and strategic plan, they receive and process information from both directions in order to facilitate actions required to carry out plans and achieve mission goals.

Department head knowledge is broad ranging. By virtue of their supervisory responsibilities and day-to-day interactions with staff and patrons of all types, they acquire a great deal of knowledge about how services and processes are functioning. From their interactions with fellow department heads, they gain insight into the intricacies and subtleties of daily interdepartmental interactions. In many respects, department heads are in a far better position to know how things work than those above them.

Top-level administrators who aspire to be truly effective can benefit from facilitating the flow of information up and down the channels of communication with department heads. To maximize their value to administrators, department heads should be prepared to offer insights whenever an opportunity arises. As a result, administrators working together at many levels make better informed and more effective decisions.

Mid-level managers are usually the first level of management to witness results of upper-level management decisions. When these decisions affect library operations, services, or morale negatively, middle managers experience the fallout firsthand, for better or worse. Although these instances can be challenging, they provide opportunities for middle managers to both acquire additional leadership skills and demonstrate leadership to the organization. As an example of leadership in the organization, middle managers are in the position to cultivate leadership skills in others. Be acutely aware that your leadership behavior is on display and that this behavior has a direct effect on the job performance and leadership behaviors of subordinates. You can inspire superior performance and serve as a role model toward developing leaders in the organization.

UNDERSTANDING UPPER MANAGEMENT'S RELUCTANCE TO CONSULT

Decision making is one of the most important activities of management at all levels. In his *Overview of Decision-Making*, E. Frank Harrison (1982) states that competence in this activity differentiates the manager from the non-manager and the good manager from the mediocre manager. It would be difficult to find many managers who don't consider themselves good decision makers. Any suggestion that a given manager might improve her decision-making techniques would almost surely elicit a highly defensive reaction.

Understanding this reluctance to examine one's ability as a decision maker may provide insight into why some managers fail to consult adequately prior to making important decisions. Some administrators maintain the erroneous notion that the need to consult is evidence of a lack of ability, or that through consultation one becomes vulnerable. Neither is true. If administrators are willing to consult others openly, including their department heads, they might find that, rather than seeming weak or ill prepared, they actually appear confident and capable.

Administrators may also be disinclined to seek out assistance when making decisions because they have had experiences in which they felt like the emperor in "The Emperor's New Clothes." We know this story. Those upon whom the emperor relies for truth continue to supply bad information. Such experiences may be especially prevalent where there is an intermediary administrative layer between the top-level and department heads. Careerism can lead individuals to subordinate their ethics to the desire for recognition, power, status, and control. To avoid the possibility of conflict, top-level administrators should not refrain from consultation but should provide a check in the system. Occasional direct one-on-one communication between top-level administrators and department heads provides an opportunity to bridge potential communication and values gaps while increasing mutual understanding.

Mid-level managers may, however, be reluctant to offer their expertise if in the past they have been kept at arm's length and only minimally consulted, or if they have experienced the same careerism in those around them and have observed the pervasiveness of false information spread for personal gain. Middle managers must be willing to speak truth to power even when it is uncomfortable to do so. If they want to be consulted, they must be open, honest, and fair. If there have been instances

of miscommunication, department heads should seek an avenue of direct input.

WHEN IS CONSULTATION A GOOD IDEA?

Successfully orchestrating the many facets of collaborative consultation requires a bit of thought on the part of senior management about two of its major components: When is consultation necessary, and when is it not? How much consultation is required?

Just as there is much to be gained by consulting, there is much to be lost in failing to do so. The more significant the decision, the more important it is to consult. Top-level administrators should ask, What's at stake? Is there potential for large-scale negative outcomes or consequences that will affect large numbers of individuals? Or is the decision in question one which, even if misguided, can easily be reversed? Consultation should be standard practice when decisions and actions meet any of these conditions:

- Directly affecting the workplace environment, workspace, or office space

- Directly affecting employee safety and well-being

- Directly affecting workflow and work processes or the availability of necessary tools and resources

- Shifting job responsibilities from one individual to another or from one department to another

- Affecting workload or an employee's ability to perform work responsibilities

- Affecting a unit's budget or personnel allocations

- Affecting an individual's career potential

Failure to consult before acting in the above situations may lead to lasting negative outcomes in productivity and employee morale. Top-level managers can avoid negative outcomes by being sensitive to individuals who may be affected. Department heads can provide that insight if they are prepared to offer their expertise, and if they remain approachable. They can prepare themselves by listening closely to their subordinates and envisioning potential outcomes; they can make themselves approachable by maintaining an open, sincere, and constructive demeanor with superiors and subordinates through all types of experiences, good and bad.

HOW MUCH TO COMMUNICATE?

Having come to the conclusion that consultation would be a good idea and having met with positive reactions from mid-level managers, top-level managers then must decide how much communication is necessary. Consultation is not meant to be an obstruction to progress; rather, it should be a facilitator. The goal of consultation should be to gain as much knowledge and gather as many perspectives as needed to make an informed decision. When consulting, it is important that administrators avoid giving the impression that they are taking a vote or asking others to make decisions for them.

Prolonged consultation that prevents leaders from taking action in a timely manner can have a destructive effect on the administrative process, as well as on the productivity and morale of subordinates. It may also lead to an aversion to further consultation. The act of consulting also should not be mistaken for or used as consensus building. Although some consensus may be gained through consultation, consensus building and similar empowerment and teamwork exercises are different processes with different objectives, meanings, and outcomes. It becomes the administrator's responsibility, then, to listen without making promises that a department head's ideas will necessarily be implemented.

Mid-level managers must keep in mind that ultimately the decisions they have been asked to collaborate on will be made by upper administration. It is important that they appreciate being approached and heard and not feel slighted if all their ideas are not used. If subordinates' perceptions of these decisions are poor or negative, the department head, as part of the management team, is expected to interpret and support the choices of top-level management even when they are not what the department head expected them to be. These are the cases in which the department head perhaps has the best opportunity to model leadership within the organization.

Although there is little that managers at different levels can do to prevent bad communication in others, there is much they can do to prevent it in themselves. Mid-level managers who are good communicators increase the likelihood that upper-level administrators will provide opportunities for them to express their opinions and contribute more directly to the achievement of missions and goals. Top-level administrators who are good communicators gain the trust of their subordinates and are, therefore, better able to make sound decisions for the institution.

MAXIMIZING THE VALUE OF CONSULTATIVE MEETINGS

Having developed effective communication skills, both top-level and mid-level managers then can make use of those skills in consultative meetings by tending the lines of communication with classified staff and other employees. Of all the employees in the organization, those on the front lines who are not in management positions may be at the highest risk of feeling marginalized, alienated, or even completely irrelevant to the processes that drive the organization. Department heads can encourage upper management to utilize these individuals and, as a result, reap the benefits of uplifted morale and increased productivity.

Although group meetings—those forums in which upper- and mid-level administrators meet with groups of classified staff or other employees—can be an effective way to provide announcements and updates, managers at all levels should also realize the tremendous potential of these meetings as an opportunity to mine the collective knowledge and institutional wisdom of each individual. To do so, there must be an exchange of ideas at these meetings. "Ideally, meetings allow both for information to be presented and ideas and issues to be discussed." In all meetings, "it is important that the forum be appropriate for the issue, that the message be clear and direct, that there be some opportunity for questions and discussion, and that all affected and interested staff members be involved" (Stevens 1983, 107, 110). Department heads can demonstrate leadership by initiating discussion and inviting others' participation. Upper-level administrators can openly solicit contributions to discussions from all stakeholders.

CONCLUSIONS

Department heads, if they are willing and active participants in the consultative process, can be valuable sources of useful information. They serve as institutional repositories of wisdom and experience and provide access to the collective knowledge and ability of each successive subordinate layer. Effective upper-level administrators not only seek but also cultivate relationships and avenues of communication, both formal and informal, that maximize the value of department heads to the organization. Department heads should also develop these relationships. In doing so, these groups of leaders, in collaboration, increase the prevalence of success at many operational levels and facilitate achievement of library missions and goals in general.

REFERENCES

Harrison, E. Frank. 1982. "An Overview of Decision Making." In *Strategies for Library Administration: Concepts and Approaches*, ed. Charles R. McClure and Alan R. Samuels. Littleton, CO: Libraries Unlimited.

Stevens, Norman D. 1983. *Communication throughout Libraries*. Metuchen, NJ: Scarecrow Press.

23

MANAGING PERCEPTIONS

LIZA WEISBROD

SOME HAVE COMPARED WORKING IN MIDDLE MANAGEMENT TO WALKING A tightrope. I prefer to think of it as an exercise in managing perceptions. Influencing how other people in an organization think, feel, and act is an essential managerial pursuit, especially for middle managers. Balancing the perceptions of your staff should be a regular part of your job, but perhaps middle managers' most crucial relationship is with their bosses. Knowing what your supervisor expects from you and how to communicate effectively can make a big difference in your success as a manager.

What does a boss expect from a middle manager? Recognizing what makes your boss happy isn't rocket science—a lot of it is common sense. But keeping in mind the following general principles, along with presenting your work in the best way, can make your job easier and you a more successful manager.

TAKE RESPONSIBILITY

Take responsibility for your work, unit, and employees. You want your boss to perceive you as a go-to employee—someone who can get the job done. Give your boss enough information to make sure she knows you're on top of your job. The perception of you as a competent manager will put your supervisor's mind at ease and prevent her potential micromanaging instinct from kicking in.

When you are given an assignment, complete it, or you had better have a good explanation of why you cannot. Don't let things drift. When your boss comes to you with a project, listen and evaluate it carefully. No boss wants to hear "That's not my job" or "I'm too busy," even if it *isn't* your job and you *are* too busy. If your boss has asked you to do something, it is probably not optional.

What if you really don't have time for another project? Don't say, "Sure, no problem" to something you cannot reasonably complete. You will end up looking unreliable when you don't finish it. Being perceived as undependable is not the way to get ahead. Ask your boss about her priorities and structure your discussion around them. Explain why this project cannot be done right away (you are in the middle of a project with a deadline; two of your staff are out for an extended period of time), then present a workable time line to get started and complete the assignment. If the project falls outside the scope of your position as you understand it, have a discussion with your boss about why she is asking you to do it. Be up front about your concerns but open to work that needs to be done. Again, you want to be seen as someone who can accomplish things.

Take responsibility for your staff. You want to be perceived as a good manager and your department as a reliable, contributing unit to the library. Personnel issues can be challenging, but addressing staff concerns and keeping everyone on the right track are essential parts of a middle manager's job. Although you should keep your supervisor apprised of what's going on, don't ask her to solve problems you can solve yourself. As John Gabarro and John Kotter state in their landmark article "Managing Your Boss," "Your boss is probably as limited in his or her store of time, energy, and influence as you are. Every request you make of your boss uses up some of these resources, so it's wise to draw on these resources selectively. This may sound obvious, but many managers use up their boss's time (and some of their own credibility) over relatively trivial issues" (1980, 100).

Of course, there are times when you need to bring in your supervisor. If you can't resolve a problem, talk to your manager. Don't just hand off the problem, though— propose possible ways this problem could be resolved. As Janis Johnston writes, "When you report on a problem you should also present some solutions. This tells the boss that you see the problem as a shared concern, not just something you are dumping in his lap" (1997, 28).

Finally, take responsibility for your own actions. Although owning up to blunders may be the last thing you want to do, if you make a mistake or do something with unwelcome consequences for your supervisor or the organization, admit it. Your boss is going to hear about it from somebody, and it is better to hear details from you— sooner rather than later. This speaks to issues of trust and dependability. Your boss needs to know she can depend on you to give her important information, good or bad. As Johnston says, "Don't hesitate to tell your boss bad news. Sometimes we can delay a bit to find a better time to break the news, but your boss needs to know that she can rely on you to provide the information she needs, even when it's not good news. Don't hide your mistakes. Let your boss know that you are willing to take responsibility for both your achievements and your failures" (1997, 28).

BE CREATIVE

Libraries change constantly, and if you are the one with the new ideas you are in a better position to shape policies and procedures. Being perceived as someone who can solve problems and bring new ideas to the table is a great

position to be in. As Rosabeth Kanter writes, "Because middle managers have their fingers on the pulse of operations, they can also conceive, suggest, and set in motion new ideas that top managers may not have thought of" (1982, 96). Letting your boss know about possible ways to streamline procedures, enhance services, or even *save the library money* is one of the most important services a middle manager can provide. You benefit when your boss sees you as someone who finds opportunities to improve the library.

Creativity requires hard work, a clear and open mind, and a good dose of bravery. Not every creative idea is a good one, but your creativity has a better chance of being appreciated if you temper it with some practicality. A new approach needs a good reason to recommend it; nobody wants change just for the sake of change. That said, there are almost always things that can be done in a better way: users' needs change; library resources go out of fashion or become obsolete; a new, important service becomes available.

Let your boss know how your idea could be implemented and what the benefits would be. If your boss looks good, you look good, too. Give him reasons to support your proposal and present them in the way he prefers to receive information. It is important to learn the best way to communicate with your boss. As Johnston writes, "Do not just pass along information; consider *when* and *how* to present it" (1997, 28). Does your boss like facts and figures? Does he like to brainstorm? Does he like to know just the results rather than all the details? Tailor your presentation to the style your boss responds to best. Give him the information he needs to support your ideas, in the format with which he is most comfortable. Framing your idea in the right way increases the chance your boss will love your plan.

KNOW YOUR BOSS'S GOALS AND PRIORITIES

It is crucial you understand what is important to your boss. Don't assume you know what your boss's priorities are. Your perception of what the library needs and where it is going may not be the same as your administrator's. As Gabarro and Kotter write, "The subordinate who passively assumes that he or she knows what the boss expects is in for trouble" (1980, 99). No matter how exceptional your work is, if it is not what your boss wants it won't make your boss think of you as a valuable employee. If you focus on creating collection guides for your area, but your boss wants you to weed your collection to make more floor space, no matter how great your guides are you are still not helping your boss achieve her goals.

As a manager, you have to make sure your staff have a clear idea of what your unit should be trying to accomplish. Although you may understand your boss's priorities, your staff may have very different perceptions of where the library is headed. Their job responsibilities and places in the library may not facilitate seeing the "big picture." Rumors always circulate in a workplace, but try to make sure your staff have an accurate idea of what's important to your administration. Take time to make certain your staff's perceptions align with what is *really* going on.

DEMONSTRATE A POSITIVE ATTITUDE

David Antonioni writes that "people follow positive leaders because they have a compelling vision for the common good of the group" (2000, 29). Your attitude, enthusiasm, and energy filter through your department and set the tone for your unit. You are the link between your administration and your staff. Creating a positive atmosphere in your unit can make a big difference in how your staff views its work and environment.

John Baldoni writes in *Lead Your Boss* that managers should cultivate "leadership presence," which comes from a combination of passion and enthusiasm. He defines leadership presence as "earned authority" and the "tangible essence of power that flows from an individual's ability to do a job." Part of leadership presence is generating enthusiasm in your staff. You should be committed to communicating your passion for your work and "a passion for the people who do the work" (2010, 197–198).

As a manager, you have an opportunity to shape how your staff perceive the library and their work. In business literature, the term *sensegiving* is defined as the "process one uses to influence how others construct meaning" (Smith, Plowman, and Duchon 2010, 221), that is, shaping how others "make sense" of their world. Middle managers have an especially important role as sensegivers. The best units in any organization are those that get different personality types to work together and focus on common goals. Sensegiving is the daily, ongoing effort to shape how employees view and understand their workplace and get everyone to work toward the same end.

You lead by example. A confident, positive attitude makes a big difference in how your unit handles unpopular tasks. An effective middle manager is part cheerleader and part therapist. When faced with difficult changes or circumstances, take time to work with your staff and explain the situation in a way that is meaningful to them. Though you may not make everyone happy, your concern and attention will go a long way toward making changes more palatable. You need everyone on board to do their best job.

BE LOYAL

Make sure your boss views you and your department as his allies. Give him respect and let others know you respect him. You both are on the same side. To the best of your ability, support your boss's plans, but don't let him appear uninformed. Give him as much information as possible about how a decision will affect the department and the library. As a middle manager, you have a lot of insight to share. You owe it to your boss to inform him if you detect a fatal flaw in his plan or can foresee an unanticipated consequence.

A middle manager needs to be a "positive critic." As Quy Nguyen Huy writes in "In Praise of Middle Managers," a positive critic is someone who is "constructively critical" (2001, 75). Don't just give your boss reasons why a proposal won't work. Suggest a counterproposal and back it up with evidence. Look for alternative means to achieve your boss's objectives.

As mentioned, bosses don't like surprises. As Johnston writes, "If there is something significant going on in your library or department that others know about, be sure that your boss knows about it, too. . . . A surprised boss is likely to feel that he looks incompetent to others because he doesn't appear to know what is going on within his own organization" (1997, 27). Be your boss's eyes and ears and let him feel confident you will keep him informed.

Never undermine your boss. Although this may seem obvious, negative statements have a way of getting back to those about whom they are said. There are very few secrets in the workplace. If you have problems with your boss, discuss your concerns with him privately. Being perceived as disloyal does not help anyone's career.

BE AN ASSET

Be seen as an asset to your boss and the library. When your boss thinks about her responsibilities at work, you want her to smile when she thinks about you and your unit. Help her create a positive perception of the library. Usually your supervisor reports to someone, possibly a library director, library board, or maybe a university provost. She needs your help to "sell" the library. Let her know about your unit's achievements. Clearly written reports, talking points, and memos give her information she can use. They also serve as a way to inform her about what you and your unit are doing, creating the perception of your department as productive and essential.

Bosses love numbers. Statistics—even very basic ones—are a good way to illustrate your value to the library and its goals. Choose the right way to present your information to create the best impression of your department. Stating that your unit cataloged five thousand microfiche may not have the same impact as saying that you provided access to a set of five thousand historical manuscripts. Keep your audience in mind when you compile reports.

CONCLUSIONS

Knowing what your boss expects from you and framing your work in the best way can make a big difference in what you accomplish. The perceptions of both your boss and your staff influence how successful you are as a middle manager. Creating a good perception of your work and your department makes your job easier and you a more successful manager.

REFERENCES

Antonioni, David. 2000. "Leading, Managing, and Coaching." *Industrial Management* 42 (5): 27–33.

Baldoni, John. 2010. *Lead Your Boss: The Subtle Art of Managing Up.* New York: AMACON.

Gabarro, John J., and John P. Kotter. 1980. "Managing Your Boss." *Harvard Business Review* 58 (1): 92–100.

Huy, Quy Nguyen. 2001. "In Praise of Middle Managers." *Harvard Business Review* 79 (8): 72–79.

Johnston, Janis L. 1997. "Managing the Boss." *Law Library Journal* 89 (Winter): 21–29.

Kanter, Rosabeth Moss. 1982. "The Middle Manager as Innovator." *Harvard Business Review* 60 (4): 95–105.

Smith, Anne D., Donde Asmos Plowman, and Dennis Duchon. 2010. "Everyday Sensegiving: A Closer Look at Successful Plant Managers." *Journal of Applied Behavioral Science* 46 (2): 220–244.

24

SURVIVING LAYOFFS

CURT FRIEHS

I T IS IMPERATIVE THAT A LIBRARIAN AND MIDDLE-LEVEL MANAGER UNDERSTAND the effects a layoff can have on library staff, middle management, and even senior management. Downsizing done right—"rightsizing"—though painful, can leave a library in a better position to fulfill its mission. Done wrong, downsizing can demoralize layoff survivors and lead to a downward spiral of discontent.

In this chapter I consider the library middle manager's position in the layoff process from two perspectives. First I consider how the mid-level manager can work with senior management to mitigate the negative consequences of necessary downsizing. Then I present a fictionalized case study of a layoff gone wrong and provide suggestions on what to do when senior management have serious lapses in judgment.

Layoffs that are handled well—those that bring about necessary cost savings without undermining survivors' morale—share several characteristics (Brockner 1992; Mishra, Spreitzer, and Mishra 1998):

- They occur after all other cost-saving possibilities have been collectively considered and attempted.

- They are developed transparently in consultation with a broad cross-functional team capable of representing and addressing the needs of all interested parties.

- They are announced clearly, directly, and truthfully to everyone in the same way with plenty of advance notice.

- They include support plans for laid-off workers—job placement or job retraining services—as well as support plans for middle managers, who are typically the bearers of bad news and most likely to suffer employee backlash and "terminator" or "survivor's guilt."

Middle managers should have primary responsibilities in both the development and implementation phases by working with senior management as messengers and consultants. In the 2009 follow-up to their seminal 1998 article "Preserving Employee Morale during Downsizing," Mishra, Mishra, and Spreitzer emphasize that "frontline" mid-level managers "are the links between the downsizing strategy" and senior managers "who execute it" (2009, 43).

At all times—not just in a bad economy—it is important that senior management keep line workers informed of organizational finances. Middle managers should be conduits of financial information between senior management and frontline workers. Regular transmission of financial information can foreshadow any difficult transitions an organization may need and thereby "minimize the surprise element that characterizes most downsizing announcements" (Mishra, Mishra, and Spreitzer 2009, 43).

As Mishra, Spreitzer, and Mishra note, "Employees who have full knowledge" of an organization's finances "feel personally in control amid uncertainty." "Downsizing" then "becomes less a crisis and more an expected path." They aver that financial transparency has the additional benefit of increasing employees' willingness "to trust management to be open and honest" (Mishra, Spreitzer, and Mishra 1998, 88).

Even before developing a downsizing plan, senior management must remember that middle managers know the on-the-ground situation of their departments. Middle managers should first be consulted about possible restructuring or cost savings that might be found in their units, generating savings that could avert the need for layoffs—or at least more layoffs than necessary.

When layoffs become unavoidable, it is even more critical that middle managers be consulted. They know better than anyone the strengths and talents of their frontline staff. Lack of proper consulting with mid-level managers can lead to "the loss of key talent," thereby "minimizing . . . expected gains from downsizing." "Crucial skills [can] disappear, and organizational memory . . . [can be] disrupted or completely lost." Management can undermine productivity by "losing the very employees most able to revitalize . . . [an organization's] competitive advantage" (Mishra, Spreitzer, Mishra 1998, 94).

In the implementation phase, middle managers should again be utilized as messengers and consultants. "Frontline managers are . . . crucial in conveying the compassion that top management should be articulating" and should be "trained in the art of two-way communication" as well as "prepared . . . to help reduce uncertainty and anxiety among their employees" (Mishra, Mishra, and Spreitzer 2009, 43). To accomplish this, middle managers must be fully informed about details of the downsizing as well as empowered to share these details with staff. Part of this compassion includes "provid[ing] tangible caretaking services to help soften the blow for those laid off" (Brockner 1992, 13).

Middle managers can inform senior management about the needs of those at risk of losing their jobs and can help facilitate plans for severance pay, outplacement counseling, and other forms of help employees may need (Brockner 1992, 13). By expressing compassion through middle managers, senior managers can ensure the goodwill of those who remain while also easing the difficult transition of those departing.

But these are ideal practices. What does a middle manager do in the face of a botched layoff?

CASE STUDY

It's an early summer morning at a medium-sized public library. You check your inbox and find that a senior library manager has sent out an e-mail about a layoff that will result in a 20 percent reduction of staff. To make matters worse, the specifics surrounding the layoff are made public and appear in a local online newspaper before employees are informed directly by management. This news comes after library staff recently took pay cuts, which they believed would help avoid the first layoffs in the library's history. To top it all off, the manager facilitating the layoff recently received a substantial salary increase and purchased a new home and automobile.

As library staff suffer and face prospective lost income, morale hits an absolute nadir. The community expresses outrage at library board meetings, but that's only the start. Although one-fifth of the staff are facing a layoff, they soon learn that the budget shortfall is only 8 percent, making the scale of the layoff appear unjustified.

The Comments section of the online article becomes a forum where management and staff air their grievances in the public sphere. In a misguided attempt to assuage staff concerns, the library director sends another e-mail, which explains that senior management have been busy working on the impending budget crunch for nearly a year. This was news to most staff.

The middle manager who finds herself in the midst of a botched layoff is clearly in a trying situation. In this case, employees know there will be layoffs but don't yet know the effects. In essence, the middle manager is faced with angry and often confused people on their way out of the organization. Then there are "survivors." These are the employees uncertain about their future as well as those made newly aware of the dysfunctional nature of their workplace. On the one hand, it is still the middle manager's job to justify these unorthodox decisions made by a senior manager. On the other, the manager has to preserve the morale and trust of those who are going to stay while showing compassion to those about to lose their jobs. Here are some recommendations about how to achieve this precarious balance.

Library staff will inevitably approach middle management with complaints, some legitimate. Although one may be tempted to confirm their allegations, it is best not to abet them. Try the following commonsense responses:

> *I don't agree with every decision that gets made here, especially when I'm not consulted in advance. If you were in my position, what would you do—and how would that make this situation better?*

> *I understand what you must be feeling. This is a rough time for everyone. How can we work together to address this problem? What can we do to improve things here, given our positions in the organization?*

Such statements can redirect staff from complaining about the problem and encourage them instead to seek collaborative solutions. Though venting may be necessary in this initial phase of shock, try to focus attention on improving the current status. Don't worry about implying that it is someone else's decision and you had little or no input. Being kept out of the loop can have its advantages: you won't become the focus of employee anger and frustration.

CASE ANALYSIS

Joel Brockner (1992) at Columbia's Business School raises some pertinent questions related to addressing layoffs, which assist us in identifying realistic solutions to layoff problems.

Is the layoff congruent with the organizational culture?

When layoffs occur more frequently within an organization or an industry where the practice is more widespread, they come as less of a surprise. On the other hand, if library staff expect job security, then layoffs are more likely to undermine trust and morale.

A middle manager can do several things to reestablish trust among library staff. Immediately call a meeting to discuss the offending e-mail announcing projected job eliminations. First, explain that you currently don't have complete information but will share it as soon as you learn more.

Explain that you know that everyone brings special talents and abilities to the workplace. Ask your employees to e-mail a list of a few of their important job duties and activities that have made a big difference at the library. Before final decisions are made by senior management,

help staff improve their skills, so they can be seen as productive in any circumstances. Perhaps you can offer cross-training or new opportunities to stretch their professional knowledge. In this way, you transform yourself into their advocate—not adversary.

Is the layoff justified?

In our case study, staff soon realized that the layoffs were not proportional to the budgetary shortfall. The recent senior management salary raise only intensified the library's fiscal problems. To most library staff, the layoffs seem unjustified.

Even in an atmosphere of ostensible self-interest at the top, one of the most effective things a middle manager can do is to approach senior management with cost-saving alternatives to layoffs. If faced with an involuntary pay cut, there is a good possibility the library is coping with severe fiscal issues. Focus on solutions by asking yourself and coworkers if there are other ways to save money.

Faced with a similar situation in my own practice, I turned to staff to get feedback on possible areas for cost savings. In our case, employee suggestions such as cancelling out-of-town newspapers and other publications we had never seen patrons read saved the library tens of thousands of dollars in our department. This approach also helped build a level of trust in my leadership within our department, a key morale-building component during periods of crisis and change. Ideally, senior management in our case should have sought cost-saving alternatives from all departments before turning to layoffs. In other situations where that isn't the case, the middle manager needs to take initiative.

In implementing the layoff, how well did the organization attend to the details? Did management provide a clear and adequate explanation of the reasons for the layoffs?

The perception of "procedural fairness" is important. As Brockner notes, numerous studies demonstrate "that survivors react more favorably to the extent that they believe that the layoff is fair" (1992, 10). Mishra, Mishra, and Spreitzer assert that cost savings alone are not an adequate measure of downsizing success. Rather, major rationales for layoffs should be positioning the organization for future growth and innovation. They remark, "Innovations require trust and empowerment—the very qualities that often suffer during corporate downsizings" when details are mismanaged and rationales not clearly presented (2009, 42).

Communication channels used to announce staff reductions are crucial. If senior management is not communicating effectively, it is in your best interest to assemble related facts and transmit them to staff as transparently as possible. Talk to people face-to-face about the important issues at hand. Also, when possible, physically hand the employee something in writing outlining the specifics in order to prevent confusion.

Did the organization provide tangible caretaking services to help soften the blow for those laid off?

If management will not or cannot help former employees find new work, you can take the initiative by offering resume workshops, recommending appropriate books, or forwarding professional job postings. In a similar situation, when faced with employees confronting layoffs, I offered job-hunting workshops and résumé-writing help for patrons and encouraged staff to attend as well.

Further, continue to treat staff members with dignity and respect by acknowledging their work and special contributions. Remaining current in staff's personal issues or interests can also help build alliances and a positive atmosphere.

Last—but certainly not least—simply listen, intently and compassionately. As Mishra, Mishra, and Spreitzer recommend, "Employees and other stakeholders want to hear transparent and consistent information from their managers, but they also want an opportunity to ask questions, share feedback, clarify the situation and prepare for the future" (2009, 43).

CONCLUSIONS

Senior management missteps and errors in judgment pose serious challenges for managers caught in the middle during downsizings. Insensitive, self-serving managers neglect or simply overlook the basic needs and issues of their staff. Nevertheless, it is advantageous to remain neutral and professional and avoid conflicts between senior management and library staff. Rather than dwelling on problems, you have a responsibility to try proactively to seek solutions. Ultimately, you grow professionally by loyally supporting your staff through these trying times.

REFERENCES

Brockner, Joel. 1992. "Managing the Effects of Layoffs on Survivors." *California Management Review* 34 (2): 9–28.

Mishra, Aneil K., Gretchen M. Spreitzer, and Karen E. Mishra. 1998. "Preserving Employee Morale during Downsizing." *MIT Sloan Management Review* 39 (2): 83–95.

Mishra, Aneil K., Karen E. Mishra, and Gretchen M. Spreitzer. 2009. "Downsizing the Company without Downsizing Morale." *MIT Sloan Management Review* 50 (3): 39–44.

25

THE POOR ADMINISTRATOR AND YOU

Survival Tips for the Mid-Level Manager

JEFFREY A. FRANKS

MOST TOP-LEVEL ACADEMIC LIBRARY ADMINISTRATORS ATTAIN THEIR LEADER-ship roles through a record of consistent successes, but others arrive with records of minimal achievement and a less than adequate skill set. Some possess innate ability, others do not; the capacity for leadership varies greatly from one individual to another. Exceptional leaders usually produce empowered, productive mid-level managers and efficiently run organizations. On the other hand, poor leaders often produce a legacy of negative outcomes for the entire organization. Disparity in management ability is due at least partially to inconsistent preparation, both during the formal education process and along the career path. In his study of LIS program management courses, Budd (2003, 162) discovered that, although there is some agreement as to course content, including planning, fiscal management, personnel management, leadership, and evaluation. Other topics such as organizational culture, the political context of libraries, authority and responsibility, and ethics are far less frequently included.

Though the ability and judgment of mid-level managers is certainly an important factor for organizational success, those qualities in top-level administrators are absolutely critical to the healthy functioning of every library. That said, even the best prepared and most able administrators sometimes exhibit poor judgment. Most mid-level managers, new and seasoned, have, either directly or indirectly, experienced troubling or poor top-level administrative actions, comments, or decisions. How mid-level managers respond to these situations is largely dependent upon their own level of management preparation and experience. Attempting to cope with mistakes from above can be bewildering, confusing, and challenging, yet mid-level managers must respond to these instances with poise and balance, maintaining their own good judgment and displaying competent leadership qualities while navigating through the results. Having a predetermined survival strategy in place can lessen the difficulty and prevent cascading negative fallout.

Regarding mid-level managers, Yang and colleagues explain:

> They should be aware that their leadership behaviours have a direct effect on front-line employees' job performance and on the leadership behaviours of their immediate subordinates. Middle managers must be keenly aware of their profound influence on those in the lower level of the organization. They can inspire superior performance among the rank and file and can serve as role models towards developing leaders in the organization. (Yang, Zhang, and Tsui 2010, 674)

Understandably, there are times when such responsibility can seem overwhelming. During these times or when mid-level managers find themselves feeling isolated, the act of consulting with fellow department heads can lessen that sense of isolation. Further, one's peers may be able to provide constructive and objective input based upon their own similar experiences.

The brief case studies presented below are based upon actual events I've heard about over the years. They are intended as thought-provoking situations that can lead mid-level managers to insights of their own.

CASE
BETRAYAL OF TRUST

In response to a variety of factors, including the need for greater space for collections and personnel, the director of a large academic library, in consultation with a library management team consisting of several middle managers, resolved that the collections, services, and departments within the main library of the large parent university should be rearranged. The director proceeded by forming four ad hoc working groups, which he charged with recommending a new physical arrangement, to maximize positive outcomes for both library users and library services.

Though the groups were given a deadline, library administration announced a detailed account of its own plan for a new physical arrangement, arrived at without expected consultation with the team, in the campus newspaper approximately one week prior to that deadline. Given the amount of time and effort members of the working groups had put into developing a plan they thought would be beneficial, they were understandably shocked, angry, and disillusioned.

Analysis and Survival Tips

When trust has been broken, it is in the best interest of the institution as a whole for mid-level managers to step in and mend fences with an effort to understand the decision-making process that occurred. In matters as important as this one, top-level administrators ultimately exercise executive authority whether or not they consider or follow the recommendations of committees and other bodies. In this case, however, that authority could have been expressed in a more tactful manner. For example, the director might have convened the working groups to hear their ideas, however incomplete, and inform them that he would, for whatever reason, not wait for their final recommendations before deciding upon a plan.

It is not surprising that working group members and a great many others felt angry and betrayed by the director's seemingly unappreciative actions. It is important to remember, however, that in the end the administrative team would have likely tweaked recommendations to their liking. Further, it is also likely that some of the group ideas were leaked and in fact incorporated into the new design anyway.

A middle manager actively trying to quell the hurt feelings of other staff might point to the positive aspects of the plan rather than to the negative way it was carried out. Although this was not the optimal way to conduct a planning exercise, it was important for middle management to rally the disgruntled troops to regroup behind the new plan and move forward. Once the immediate grumbling subsided, the best reaction in fact was what occurred: mid-level managers prepared their units and collections for relocation, and the project was completed on time without incident. In the fall, library patrons returned to a more efficient library.

CASE
POOR LEADERSHIP

In a medium-sized academic library, the traditional functions of reference librarians were to provide the bulk of reference service and basic undergraduate library instruction. Subject bibliographers, members of a separate collection management department, provided less reference service but were responsible for all collection management and subject liaison duties as well as advanced subject-related instruction. After a period of rapid attrition through retirement of several subject bibliographers during a hiring freeze, reference librarians, who had long desired subject liaison and collection management responsibilities, willingly absorbed these duties.

Within a short period, librarians of both units were performing the same duties while reporting to two different department heads, or middle managers. The dean, desiring to eliminate the redundancy of the two units and remedy what some perceived to be unequal distribution of duties, charged members of both departments with recommending a new way to organize. Other than being told not to discuss their deliberations with either department head, the dean provided no specific instructions.

Most members of the group assumed, however, as did the two department heads, that some combination of the two departments was the intended outcome. Such a merger would require that one of the two existing department heads lead the new unit, while the other's fate would be uncertain. Since both department heads had been successful at their respective posts, this task would not be easy. Lacking a neutral facilitator, the group discussed the issue for nearly three months without reaching consensus. Personal feelings, loyalties, and fears permeated these deliberations, the results of which were injured feelings and damaged relationships. In response, the dean dropped the issue, leaving it unresolved. Although the two department heads continued to work together in a congenial manner, the overlap and uneven distribution of duties remained an issue for years following.

Analysis and Survival Tips

In response to poor leadership, it is important for middle management to model and foster a sense of unity rather than competitiveness and strife during a time of uncertainty. Without clear instructions, a mandate, or neutral facilitator, the group that had been asked to make recommendations was unable to discuss the issue constructively. Lacking an answer from the group, the dean might have exercised her executive authority by implementing her own plan, but she chose not to.

The two department heads were left to manage the negative fallout. To do so effectively, it was essential for both to behave professionally. Fortunately, their behavior during deliberations was exemplary. Throughout the process, they frequently took breaks or had lunch together. This activity projected a sense of neutrality and mutual support that later facilitated the mending process. Although the larger issue remained unresolved, members of both units eventually regained a sense of normalcy.

Although it is true that these two professionals, by their calm reactions to the situation, were able to mitigate the negative fallout, it is possible that they missed an opportunity. Sometimes bad senior management decisions, or a lack of any decision at all, can lead to opportunities for positive change facilitated by mid-level managers. If members of these two departments were unable to come to consensus on the issue, perhaps the department heads could have stepped in to make their own recommendations to the dean, and the overall issue might have been more productively resolved.

CASE
LACK OF SUPPORT AND POOR COMMUNICATION

The upper-level administration of a large public library became concerned about a disparity in the ratings of staff members by their respective department heads during performance evaluations. Specifically, some department heads regularly awarded a large quantity of top ratings, whereas others awarded a large number of low ratings.

TIPS FOR MANAGING BAD BOSSES

If the popularity of the 2011 film *Horrible Bosses* is any indication, working for a bad boss is one of the most common experiences of modern working life. One of the best books on the subject is *Working for You Isn't Working for Me: The Ultimate Guide to Managing Your Boss*, by Katherine Crowley and Kathi Elster (Portfolio, 2009). The book offers a four-step process for coping with and rising above twenty categories of bad boss behavior described.

Does your boss play head games by changing the rules on you or undermining your authority? Is he a "big shot" who always has to be right or in control? Does she cross boundaries by playing the confidant only to blab about your thoughts or feelings to others? Crowley and Elster provide tools for identifying which type of difficult boss you are working for, then discuss how to detect what stage your relationship with the boss is in, depersonalize the dynamic, detach from their behavior, and deal with the situation in a productive and positive way.

Crowley and Elster provide employees with a Myers-Briggs—type rubric to assess their own emotional tendencies in the workplace. If your general tendency is to nurture, harmonize, shine, and challenge people, or to stay under the radar at work (they describe many more than these), they recommend that you take responsibility for these attitudes and recognize the expectations, needs, and fears you bring to your relationship with your boss. They then tailor their advice for depersonalizing and dealing with the variety of difficult bosses to the general workplace tendencies of employees.

The benefits of this book are twofold for middle managers. While providing productive strategies for dealing with difficult senior managers, it also paints portraits of bosses the middle manager should do everything in her power to avoid becoming.

This disparity was perceived by the administration to be the result of differences in managerial perceptions of staff performance rather than actual staff performance. At the request of upper-level administration and with the goal of attaining a more standardized method of rating staff, department heads agreed upon and drafted several sets of staff performance expectations. It was understood that the application of new performance measures could result in some staff receiving lower than usual ratings and some receiving higher than usual ratings.

Despite the fact that this was explained to staff upon distribution of the new expectations and well in advance of the next performance evaluations, one staff member who had usually received all "excellent" ratings reacted negatively and disrespectfully toward her department head after receiving a mix of "excellent" and "very good" ratings. Following the performance review, the staff member met with the library director. A few days later, the staff member was transferred to another department with the explanation that it was the first step in a reorganization process. At no point prior to the transfer did the library director consult or brief the department head about the transfer.

Analysis and Survival Tips

Even when department heads cannot prevent difficult situations, they can look for opportunities for making the most of the change. The director's transfer of the staff member without affording the department head the courtesy of consultation compounded an already negative experience and sent a message to all department heads that support might not be forthcoming as they applied new performance measures.

Deleting a position from the middle manager's department added a burden to all other staff to absorb the extra duties. Perhaps most disconcerting, the department itself was left wondering if the director's motives for the transfer had been based on biased information. This action severely damaged the department head's trust in top-level management, yet there was no recourse other than to accept the situation and move on. Reaching out to other department heads facilitated the process.

Rather than lashing out at each other, the two affected department heads consulted with each other and their staffs about ways to cope with this challenging situation. Through this conversation, specific ideas for addressing workload were implemented and staff were encouraged by their department heads' understanding of their needs. When another staff member retired, the department head turned this setback into an opportunity by reassigning duties and hiring a new individual who brought a positive element to the interpersonal dynamics of the department. Without the department head's patience and ability to communicate, this positive change may not have followed from the previous negative decision on the part of the director.

CASE
MICROMANAGEMENT

As the unit most directly engaged in the provision of services necessary for student academic success, the reference department of this medium-sized academic library was charged by the dean with conceptualizing services for an already sanctioned learning commons. Led by their department head, the group began with an extensive literature search, followed with weekly meetings to discuss and conceive the array of services they would recommend.

Unfortunately, the department head's immediate supervisor took a personal interest in this project and began to scrutinize the group's work closely, imposing both his preferences and will upon their deliberations. Despite the department head's communication that the group preferred to function autonomously, this upper-level administrator continued to exhibit specific micromanagement behaviors, including giving explicit instruction to the department head each step of the way, interfering with workflow, blocking inquiry, assigning specific aspects of the project to individuals based upon his personal biases, creating meeting agendas, and editing the group's final report.

Analysis and Survival Tips

Although some top-level guidance is necessary, most department heads, by virtue of their having attained a level of managerial expertise, possess the knowledge and ability to complete most charges with minimal supervision. Regrettably, department heads must often learn to work under close scrutiny with poise and a positive attitude. Mid-level managers thrive in an environment of empowerment, trust, and support; micromanagement represents opposite qualities.

Upper-level administrators who regularly micromanage or interfere with the work of mid-level managers do not truly delegate responsibility to them. Nor do they empower them with the authority to exercise their skills and ability in the areas of problem solving, directing, decision making, and leading. Micromanagers subject their subordinates to undue scrutiny, overseeing them too closely and spending an excessive amount of time supervising projects and telling people exactly what to do and how to do it (White 2010, 72).

In this case, the department head was not permitted to lead, nor was he free to apply his knowledge, ability, or creativity to the project. The micromanagement behavior and usurpation of authority had a deleterious effect upon the morale of the entire reference department, such that further involvement in the project was undertaken reluctantly. But realizing that the department would ultimately be directly involved in the provision of services at the forthcoming learning commons, the department head continued to cultivate an interest in and enthusiasm for the project.

Fortuitously, the entire reference department was, in the end, given the opportunity to contribute to a larger, campus-wide planning process that began not long after. Numerous elements of their original vision were included in the learning commons service model. During the lag time between finalization of the planning process and construction and implementation of the learning commons, the department head began to integrate elements of that vision into the new reference service model.

CONCLUSIONS

The fallout from poor or troubling top-level administrative actions, comments, and decisions can impact library employees, services, and processes for months or even years. By remaining calm and maintaining a professional demeanor, department heads can be instrumental in lessening the negative effects of such experiences. Though navigating these situations can be challenging, mid-level managers have a responsibility to provide effective and positive leadership to those on the front lines, even under the most difficult circumstances.

REFERENCES

Budd, John M. 2003. "Management Education for Library and Information Science." In *Advances in Library Administration and Organization*, Vol. 20, ed. Edward D. Garten and Delmus E. Williams. Oxford: Elsevier Science.

White, Richard D., Jr. 2010. "The Micromanagement Disease: Symptoms, Diagnosis, and Cure." *Public Personnel Management* 39:71–76.

Yang, Jixia, Zhi-Xue Zhang, and Anne S. Tsui. 2010. "Middle Manager Leadership and Frontline Employee Performance: Bypass, Cascading, and Moderating Effects." *Journal of Management Studies* 47 (4): 654–678.

26

COPING WITH REORGANIZATION

An Interview with Sally Decker Smith

SALLY DECKER SMITH SPENT HER ENTIRE THIRTY-YEAR CAREER IN PUBLIC libraries, more than half in middle management positions. She is currently enjoying a second career as a public library consultant in the area of staff development. We sat down with Sally to discuss her experience handling a challenging reorganization process while serving as head of public services, the role of mentorship during such processes, and the rewards of a middle management career.

Tell us a little about your background.

I'm an accidental librarian. I was a teacher before starting my family, and my original plan was to go back to teaching once my younger daughter started school. I started working in a library instead and began my career in circ. I really liked what I saw—the library culture and atmosphere—and I was blessed with excellent mentors. When I asked them, "Do you think I can do this?" they said, "Sure, you can do this!" So I went to library school part-time. I got my MLS and never looked back. That was in 1987. I ended up working for the same system my entire career until I retired in 2010.

You worked your way up and retired as a middle manager?

Yes. From reference librarian to head of adult services to head of public services, which oversaw youth services. I also oversaw programming and interlibrary loan, among other functions.

The reason I retired as a middle manager is that, from the day I considered becoming a librarian, I never wanted to be a library director. The middle was where I wanted to be because it's where I thought I could be most effective. In my view, it's where the rubber hits the road. I wanted to make sure I still got to work at the reference desk because I loved it, but also to be responsible for helping others be good at the reference desk—be good for the patron, be good for themselves.

What were some of your challenges as a middle manager?

About four years before I retired, it was decided that it was time for a new strategic plan. We identified new priorities. But where it got difficult, in my opinion, was when the director at the time announced that we'd failed at the previous strategic plan. Right there I was tense because I don't think you can fail at a strategic plan. I think you hit some of your targets and you don't hit some of your targets, but you can't call that failure.

But she said we failed because we hadn't aligned our resources with priorities. So to meet the goals of the new plan, she tried something totally different. For example, since the community had indicated they wanted more programming, management then pulled a whole bunch of people from departments all over the building and put them in charge of programming.

The new strategic plan became the driver for some "out of the box" thinking, a real game of musical chairs. No one wants anyone to lose a job in a reorganization, but when people are reassigned to new jobs without being consulted not all of them are going to be happy, or consoled by being told by administration, "Well, at least you have a job."

A major challenge with the middle manager position is being a buffer between the director and staff. I had to be enthusiastic—"We're going to make this work, it's going to be great!"—when I was not entirely convinced this was the best idea. Management meetings did give me the space to express my concerns, but when I talked with staff I couldn't say what I really felt because I had to back the administration. I think this is a recurring theme in middle management, no matter what you're dealing with.

So what happened to your staff around the library?

Every time a new group was formed to focus on one of the strategic goals, public services seemed to get the short end of the stick. And when I brought it up, I was told, "Of course, we're going to have a reference desk with a staff." And I said, "But you're taking all of my bodies."

The reference librarians went to programming or purchasing, so where we had eight reference librarians including part-time people we suddenly only had three. At the end of the reorganization, I ended up with three former circulation clerks who had been happy, long-term employees in those positions, who were now reference assistants and expected to staff the reference desk, interact with patrons, and provide information. These were people who were not happy about this.

The thinking was that people didn't really ask reference questions, and you didn't need to have a reference librarian at the desk. You could just have assistants, and they could show patrons how to use the catalog and where the bathroom is, and on the off-chance a reference question came in a librarian could be called. It was an interesting experiment.

How did people who had been reference librarians take this as they ended up in other locations?

It was awkward because I had hired just about all of these people over ten or eleven years. And I'd looked for reference librarians who liked doing a bunch of stuff, people who were not narrowly focused—big picture people who were happy doing selection, computer training programs, staffing a reference desk, all the pieces of that. And then all of a sudden these multifaceted people were put into one job.

There was one poor woman who was a great reference librarian, but whose real strength was readers' advisory. They put her in charge of the collection development team, and all she did all day long was sit in front of a computer and read book reviews and order books. And she cried! If you're going to do this, then you're hiring a different kind a person. Many people were unhappy in their new positions.

How did you deal with this?

I had to do some career counseling and some serious cheerleading. And a number of people did leave the job they were put into. I helped them, because if you don't want to be in the position you're in then you shouldn't be there.

We were left fairly short-staffed in public services. All these newbies who were declared reference assistants found themselves working vastly more nights and weekends than they'd ever experienced before. When it was a reference department, we had a rotating schedule to distribute evening/weekend work. Suddenly, with a much smaller staff and with reference librarians given more responsibilities, people were working three weekends out of four and up to three evenings a week.

I had to counsel one of the new selectors, a children's librarian who was assigned to the selection team. One of the beautiful things about the selection positions after the reorganization was that they were allowed to set their own schedules and could work from 8:00 a.m. to 3:00 p.m. And so we had all these people who were working more nights than they'd ever expected in their lives, and she didn't realize people didn't take it well when she'd go around at 3:00 and say good-bye to everyone.

That librarian was a gifted storyteller. Taking her away from children's services was a real loss. She'd told stories to my own kids when they were growing up, and I knew how good she was. Then all of a sudden, she was one of these people who had a completely different set of responsibilities.

It seems like this was all brought about by a good impulse, to try to rethink the strategic plan of the organization. Did the administration consult with middle management to think out the consequences when developing the strategic plan?

There were meetings about things like that, and I participated fully. In theory, the management team was in charge of transitioning to the new plan. The reality was that a small subset of the management team had a vision of how it was going to work. And though we could voice our concerns in meetings, they were pretty much brushed aside. It was one of those cases where minds were made up and didn't want to be confused by the facts.

The goals that emerged were not bad goals. But they should have listened to the management team. We met together every week for a year and most of the people on that team had at least ten years' experience in their positions. Most of admin was new to the library, new to the profession, or new to the neighborhood.

Unfortunately, all of the management team didn't know their employees as well as they thought. When assignments were made, people were told, "You're going to be great at this." Those were the first people who came to me crying. But some of us did know the strengths of the people in our departments. In many cases, we had hired them or at least worked with them for many years.

How can middle managers make senior management aware of the individuality of employees?

I think it's difficult. And the larger the organization, the more difficult it is. The head of the children's department

knew what a good storyteller the woman I mentioned earlier was. Similarly, I knew what a good readers' advisory person the reference librarian was. The woman who left public services because of her schedule and children was a genius at children's collection development, and her new job focused on that, which was great for her.

Managers are responsible for knowing the strengths of their team. Communicating that knowledge to administration about individuals is not easy to do. It may get lost in the day-to-day work. This is why it's important for the administration to trust middle managers to know their people.

My monthly report, which was nominally a monthly report to the board, was actually my report to the director. The board didn't affect my life, but the director did. I made it a point to mention any significant achievement of anyone on my staff and mentioned them by name, especially if I got a written compliment from a patron. I'd copy that into the report, so the director could see that people were getting complimented for reference work. I tried to make sure individuals got recognition for the great work they were doing. I tried to communicate my understanding of the strengths of people that way to the director. But if you're a director and you're managing a staff of over one hundred, that's different from when you're a department head and managing a staff of twenty-five.

I think when they decided to reorganize the entire building the better approach would have been to let people apply for the jobs they wanted. It would have given people some sense of control over their lives and taken into account their preferences. It was suggested at the time, but admin said we needed to get this in place immediately, and there wasn't enough time to go through an application process.

It sounds like you have to be able to discover where peoples' natural strengths are, and how that maps back to the organizational goals, and make them feel good about that.

Yes. Not everyone is good at the same thing, and that's actually a gift to the organization. There's a quote I come back to repeatedly: "All of us are smarter than any of us." When there are problems to be worked through or things to figure out, get as many people as possible involved. The more brains you've got working on something, the better solutions you're going to find for whatever you're trying to do.

PART III
EMPOWERMENT

27

THE SELF-DETERMINED MIDDLE MANAGER

KRISTINE CONDIC

MIDDLE MANAGERS ARE CRITICAL TO A LIBRARY'S SUCCESS. THEY ARE PIVOTAL in opening lines of communication between the library supervisor and department employees. Effective middle managers communicate respectfully, listen actively, and engage in positive dialogue with all library staff.

You may believe that these characteristics describe you perfectly, but does your staff think the same thing? How are you perceived by library staff? One way to find out is to ask library personnel what they think of you. However, for a variety of reasons, you may not get a honest response. Another way to discover more about yourself is to examine the Leadership Grid developed by Blake and Mouton (Blake and McCanse 1991). The Leadership Grid is a model that helps middle managers understand their strengths and weaknesses and gives them a perspective on how they are likely to be perceived by others.

Using leadership models helps you find out more about yourself. This is essential since one of the keys to middle management effectiveness is self-awareness. You may learn that you perceive yourself one way but others perceive you in other ways. By learning more about management styles, you can find out more about your own style and adjust your actions and behavior to better reflect the style you desire.

MANAGER OR LEADER?

Just because you are a manager does not mean that you are also a leader—there is a vast difference between the two. A manager is a coordinator who makes certain things get done by accomplishing tasks such as developing a reference schedule, planning for implementation of a discovery tool, or coordinating a weeding project. A leader, by contrast, provides direction for reaching goals, inspiration toward a new vision, and guidance in achieving those goals. A leader sets the tone of the department, and that tone—also known as organizational culture—can range anywhere from helpful and courteous to innovative and daring to passive and complacent.

No matter whether you are a leader or a manager, you can decide how successful you want to be in that role. Self-awareness of your own management style and self-determination in being a better manager can guide you to successful middle management.

WHAT KIND OF MIDDLE MANAGER ARE YOU? THE LEADERSHIP GRID

Although your personality often unconsciously determines the type of manager you are likely to become, you can become more aware of your personality and decide what type of manager you ultimately want to be. Even within middle management, you can define your own style, which may be completely different from your supervisor's. To be effective, scrutinize yourself and select a style that highlights your strengths and diminishes your weaknesses. The key to becoming a better manager is to find out more about yourself. The more you know about yourself, the more you can become the type of manager you want to be.

The Leadership Grid fosters self-awareness and self-determination by describing leadership styles in terms of two factors: concern for production and concern for people. *Concern for production* means focusing on producing results, getting tasks done, crossing things off lists, or doing whatever the organization identifies as good production. Within the library world, this could translate into increasing the number of people helped at a reference desk or checking out more laptops. *Concern for people* means focusing on library personnel, including their personal satisfaction and motivation.

The Leadership Grid is illustrated in figure 1. The x axis records concern for production, the y axis concern for people. Values on each variable go from 1 (low) to high (9). Each pair of values on the grid represents a different leadership style. Let's examine five styles by describing the underlying theme, characteristics, and a sample scenario associated with each.

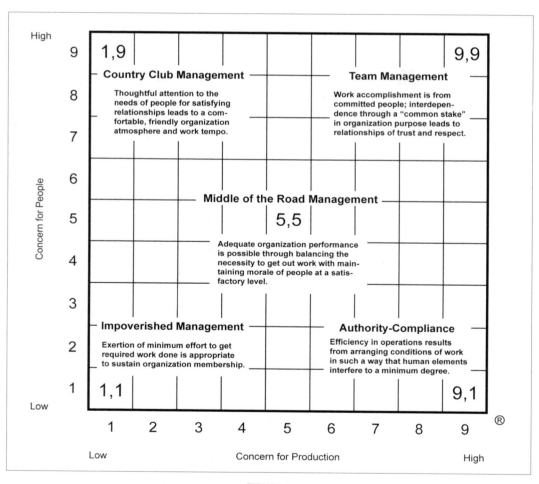

FIGURE 1

Leadership Grid

Impoverished Management (1,1)

Underlying theme: Little concern for production; little concern for people

Characteristics: This middle manager, the manager of a library reference department, avoids people as well as responsibility and remains uninvolved. An impoverished manager stays away from the decision-making process and does not engage in meaningful conversations with either the library director or other employees. This person's goal is to do the minimal amount of work but accomplish just enough to stay off everyone's radar. In all likelihood, this (1,1) manager is a constant clock-watcher, filling in time. Let's be honest. We know these people. They would rather be anywhere else than sitting behind a desk.

Scenario: The library director asks for annual goals and objectives from each library department, including the reference department. Our (1,1) reference department manager avoids seeking input from the reference staff and, therefore, submits objectives very similar to the previous year's. The library director does not call the middle manager to task for not submitting objectives, but at the same time the objectives are not a true reflection of the potential for the department in the coming year. The result is an unhealthy work environment that does little to promote growth within the department. Activities for the coming year are the same as in the previous year, and everyone, librarians as well as library users, suffers from this lack of growth.

Country Club Management (1,9)

Underlying theme: Little concern for production; high concern for people

Characteristics: "Don't worry, be happy." This manager wants to be friends with everyone, and since this is the primary goal it is unlikely that the managed department will be innovative and productive. The atmosphere is open and invites participation, but there is an overwhelming desire to reduce negativity and conflict so that contentious issues are avoided. To remain on a buddy-buddy basis with everyone, our (1,9) middle manager compliments employees incessantly, which is viewed by many as insincere.

Scenario: There are often negative consequences to such a country club approach, especially when difficulties arise. For example, let's say that in an economic downturn a library director requests that each department manager develop a plan reflecting a 10 percent cut from the department's budget. Our country club middle manager is unable to be the bearer of bad news and therefore refuses to discuss budget issues with department employees. As a consequence, the (1,9) middle manager does not have a plan ready for the library director, thus giving the appearance of a department that is ill prepared and uncooperative, and one that is at the mercy of arbitrary decisions from above.

Authority–Compliance (9,1)

Underlying theme: High concern for production; little concern for people

Characteristics: "Nice guys finish last." This middle manager is in control and, in no uncertain terms, tells employees what needs to be done. People are cogs; therefore, they need to be directed to perform tasks correctly. In fact, the (9,1) manager views most employees as obstacles who get in the way. Once all tasks are complete, this manager feels successful, which makes a good impression on the library director, even though loyalty and goodwill are lacking among the troops.

Scenario: Authority-compliant managers can point to the long list of items they have accomplished, but their productivity comes at a price. Let's say that bound serial volumes need to be rearranged to make room for current issues. The (9,1) authority-compliant middle manager develops a personnel schedule for the move but fails to double-check with employees beforehand. As a result, employees are scheduled to move volumes when many have previous commitments: one has a dental appointment, another has a committee meeting, a third planned to take the day off. To rectify this situation, employees have to swap among themselves to cover all the scheduled times, each cursing the manager for the inconvenience and lack of consideration. The task gets done, but library staff are dissatisfied.

Middle of the Road Management (5,5)

Underlying theme: Moderate concern for production; moderate concern for people

Characteristics: Middle-of-the-road means exactly that: compromise and concession. New, innovative ideas are not introduced because the middle manager does not want to encourage dissent. Extremes and conflict are unnecessary, uncomfortable, and need to be avoided. The middle manager is satisfied to maintain the status quo—maybe improving things just a little bit to show progress. Our (5,5) middle manager tends to bend whichever way the prevailing winds of the group are headed. New services are hindered since harmony is more important than improvement.

Scenario: Middle-of-the-road managers may have the self-perception that they are efficient (high on production) and friendly (high with people skills), but they compromise to attain goals and do not live up to their potential. For example, the library director wants to see the reference department implement a chat service, but reference personnel are not eager to launch this new service. Our (5,5) middle manager doesn't want to confront reference librarians since conflict will ensue. Instead, the middle manager stalls, avoids the issue, and tries to delay implementation. Once these tactics no longer work, the manager first is likely to touch base with the library director, then with reference employees, and then back to the director in an attempt to find a middle ground. The result in most cases is a service that is ill planned, has little support, and produces dissatisfaction all around.

Team Management (9,9)

Underlying theme: High concern for production; high concern for people

Characteristics: The (9,9) middle manager projects teamwork throughout by constantly interweaving production and people. Employees are eager to assist this middle manager since they have previously agreed to common goals and assisted in developing them. Employees are inspired to succeed, and mutual respect exists between all parties involved. Given this positive environment, disagreement and conflict are not avoided but addressed within a respectful atmosphere.

Teamwork, open communication, and delegation are hallmarks of this style.

Scenario: The team management approach relies on open lines of communication and respect. It is not enough to ask colleagues their opinions if it is viewed as lip service; the middle manager must truly appreciate dialogue and discussion. This type of management style can be time consuming, but it also can be immensely rewarding for the middle manager and library employees. Let's say the library director is urging the circulation department manager to consider offering 24/7 library service. The (9,9) circulation manager asks others within the department their thoughts on 24/7, and employees are eager to provide suggestions. Advantages and disadvantages of offering 24/7 service are openly discussed, and everyone participates in the decision-making process as a group. The organizational culture is one of cooperation, encouragement, and eagerness to try a new service.

USING THE LEADERSHIP GRID WISELY

Use the grid as a mechanism for understanding your own strengths and weaknesses and how they are perceived by others. The grid may also help you identify characteristics and behaviors you wish to attain as you strive to become a better middle manager. As a guide, it can help middle managers and library employees understand what behavior is appropriate and how to work best within that framework.

You might think that a (9,9) middle manager with high concern for people and high concern for production would be the best type of manager for almost any situation. In fact, this actually depends on the library's specific circumstances. For example, a building emergency may require the skills of a (9,1) manager (high concern for production, low concern for people) just to make it past the emergency. The death of a library staff member may necessitate the skills of a (1,9) manager (little concern for production, high concern for people).

What combination of concern for people and concern for production is right for you? As you learn more about the Leadership Grid, you may identify with some, but not all, facets of one leadership style. Are a few of these missing facets ones you would like to add to your own leadership repertoire? Once you are aware of the possibilities, you can mold your behavior to match the type of leader you want to be. Self-awareness is a powerful tool.

Think of these five management descriptions as guidelines to be used with flexibility, not viewed as black-and-white decrees. No one walks around saying, "I'm a (9,1) and I want to be a (9,9), but I'm not a good delegator, so I'll never become a (9,9)." Use these examples as guidelines, so you can identify your own leadership style and improve it.

REFERENCE

Blake, Robert R., and Anne Adams McCanse. 1991. *Leadership Dilemmas—Grid Solutions.* The Blake/Mouton Grid Management and Organization Development Series. Houston: Gulf Publishing.

28

DEVELOPING LEADERS

DEBBIE SCHACHTER

L EADERSHIP IS NO LONGER THE PROVINCE OF A LIBRARY'S SENIOR MANAGERS OR executives. Best-run organizations today recognize that leadership, in its many manifestations, should be diffused throughout the organization. This means there is a great need to be able to identify internal leaders and develop leadership skills more formally through mentoring and training programs. In this chapter I address leadership responsibilities in the middle manager position of libraries as well as the skill sets and styles of good leaders.

Leadership differs from management in several ways. Leaders provide the vision and mission the organization needs to move forward. Leaders may exist at many levels, but they are not necessarily managers. Managers are responsible for ensuring that staff have the resources and ability to undertake the work required, based on the over-arching vision and mission of the organization. As succinctly defined by Michael Useem in *Leading Up*, "The distinction [between manager and leader] is between *running* the office and adding *value* to it, between *discharging* our responsibilities and *exceeding* them" (2001, 2).

Today managers as well as supervisors are expected to take on more leadership responsibility than in the past, for a variety of reasons, including the need for succession planning and to develop the leaders of tomorrow. Middle managers need to build relationships and develop their leadership up, down, and laterally within an organizational hierarchy. This is one of the position's particular challenges.

In most organizations today, leadership is understood to be valuable throughout the organization. Middle managers can be assessed on the development of their staff, including development of leadership skills among supervisory and line staff. They also have the ability to exhibit leadership among their colleagues and to use positive leadership traits when leading upward in the organization.

Middle managers are also critical in ensuring that the organizational vision and broad goals are translated into day-to-day meaning for staff. This is one aspect of their leadership. They must also convey information and feedback from their staff to executives and senior managers, demonstrating leadership by helping staff contribute to the organization's direction.

CHANGING EXPECTATIONS OF LEADERSHIP

Leadership is defined in many ways. Traits have often been ascribed to good leaders (usually by analyzing the "in the field" work of good leaders). Leadership involves

- Assisting others in achieving a common goal

- Providing a vision for a common direction and inspiring followers to achieve common goals

- Having or developing the social skills and ability to inspire or influence others to follow a particular direction to achieve those goals

Leadership also requires many of the skills characteristic of good supervision: communication, employee development, team building, and implementing effective decision-making processes.

It was once believed that leaders are born, that leaders possess certain natural, personal traits. But evidence suggests that anyone can become a leader by focusing on the needs of followers. By developing attuned emotional intelligence (skills such as self-awareness, self-regulation, self-motivation, social awareness, and social competence), any middle manager may develop strong leadership skills.

LEADERSHIP DEVELOPMENT AT ALL LEVELS

Knowledge-based organizations are increasingly recognizing how employees at all levels contribute to organizational leadership. Middle managers are frequently pivotal, since they are the direct link in the chain from frontline staff to senior management or executives. Middle managers lead in several ways:

- Representing the leadership of the board, executive, or senior management to line staff

- Being leaders-in-waiting for senior management positions

- Developing leadership roles of supervisors with their staff

FOLLOWERSHIP

You can't do it alone. To be an effective leader, you must have staff willing to follow your direction. This leads back to essential skills in communication and the ability to define the vision and direction for staff. Emotional intelligence assists in developing followership. If you aren't a charismatic leader—and few truly are—work on your empathy and ability to understand the motivations and concerns of employees.

The editors of *The Art of Followership: How Great Followers Create Great Leaders and Organizations* (Jossey-Bass, 2008) define followership as a "moral practice," involving among other things "questioning leadership, and keeping leaders on purpose by sharing their ignorance with them." In fact, followership is an active role requiring many of the same skill sets as leadership. Followers and leaders are locked in a relationship that creates and sustains either effective or ineffective leadership.

Most employees want to contribute and feel part of the organization's success. As a leader, you create followership by being seen as someone whom people want to follow. Creating empowered, engaged employees helps engender effective followers. Followers don't merely follow the direction of their supervisors and managers, they help create better results through active involvement in problem solving, goal setting, and goal achievement.

A leader creates followership by providing employees with opportunities to receive information about the vision and direction of the institution and real means to contribute to it. True followership is thoughtful and constructive rather than a blind following of orders. If you find that you don't have followers, you must examine your own skills and abilities, then determine what you need to work on as a leader to inspire others to follow your direction.

Leaders foster followership in many ways, including these:

- Being direct about vision and goals

- Ensuring follow-through on actions

- Showing confidence

- Giving credit where credit is due

- Being honest when the leadership makes a mistake and offering corrections

- Demonstrating effective followership to senior managers and modeling this behavior for staff

Leadership cannot be achieved without trust. Trust must be developed with staff through clear, honest communication and transparent actions. These encompass being fair, open in your communication and intentions, showing consistency, fulfilling promises, and being honest about what you can and cannot communicate to staff.

EMPOWERMENT AND DECISION MAKING

Middle managers evince leadership within the organization by empowering their staff. Empowerment improves employee engagement and motivation. Empowerment demonstrates effective leadership when implemented by

- Involving staff in goal development for the department or division

- Involving staff in decision-making processes, whenever possible

- Identifying training needs and facilitating training for staff, including leadership development

- Providing resources staff needs to achieve goals

COMMUNICATION

One of the most important aspects of sharing vision is the ability to communicate effectively. Effective leaders are usually good communicators. They follow practices for good communication by

- Understanding the audience for the particular communication

- Communicating what employees need to know

- Communicating frequently, in many different ways

- Ensuring two-way communication, not just addressing staff

- Affording staff the opportunity to provide input and ask questions for effective two-way communication

- Communicating how employees' activities and input connect with the overarching vision for the organization

Understanding your personal communication style is important as you develop your own leadership. Written communication such as through intranet, e-mail, or memos is important, but personal communication is the most effective in demonstrating and developing leadership among staff. Particularly when the information a manager must convey is negative or involves a significant change, the most effective communication is in person. Middle managers may not always have complete information or answers, but their willingness to share information and staff input to the ultimate decision makers in the library helps staff see their middle manager's leadership.

PERSONAL LEADERSHIP SKILLS

Effective leaders generally exhibit a range of skills, which can be innate or developed through practice and study. Three key skills are important for leadership:

Persuasion—the ability to convince others your ideas have merit and should be initiated

Influence—the ability to exert power over others in a subtle fashion

Rapport—the art of creating a positive environment in which others wish to cooperate, something strongly connected to interpersonal skills

Again, most leaders hone their skills through hard work, courses, and studying employees and situations. Leadership ability is linked to motivation—the power an individual has to satisfy a need. Leaders act to provide satisfaction or are a means of satisfaction to others. You can establish the work environment to make this possible by understanding the needs of others and then applying persuasion and influence to show others how they will benefit.

TYPES OF LEADERSHIP

There are many types of leaders, but three commonly identified in the literature are *visionary*, *charismatic*, and *transformational* leaders. These three types have emerged as central to leadership success, whether that means leading change, leading innovation, or simply improving business results.

Visionary leadership arises when a leader has a clear vision she is able to articulate and share with others. This vision is inspirational yet also clearly achievable, and one that inspires employees to work to achieve that vision.

Charismatic leadership is possibly the best-known leadership style because of the many prominent and inspiring charismatic leaders in history and popular culture. Charismatic leaders have strong people skills. They motivate employees through identified character traits, including the ability to articulate and express drive toward an idealized goal, assertiveness and self-confidence, unconventionality, and ability to be seen as an agent of change.

Transformational leadership has significant literature devoted to it. Transformational leaders guide organizations through change while sharing a vision that inspires followership, motivation, and work satisfaction. Transformational leaders inspire employees to think beyond their own self-interest, leading to improved satisfaction: "The first characteristic of transformational leaders is their ability to elevate the interests of their employees, generate awareness and acceptance of the group mission, and look beyond their own self-interest to the greater good of the larger group" (Paarlberg and Lavigna 2010, 711).

LEADERSHIP STYLES

Leadership styles vary widely based on organization, industry, and culture. The style may depend on the nature of the work to be undertaken, and different situations call for different styles of leadership. Style refers to the strategies a middle manager uses to activate, direct, stimulate, and otherwise motivate employees. Some of the most common styles are autocratic, democratic, free-rein, and situational leadership.

Autocratic or directive: These types of leaders make all the decisions in an organization. This is most effective in a crisis or unfavorable circumstances. There is little expectation of relationship building or leadership development among staff.

Democratic or consultative: Leaders discuss the situation with the people they supervise before making a decision. This fosters strong teamwork and involvement and is often called *consensus management*.

Free-rein or participative: The leader acts as the information center and exerts minimum control. Employees are encouraged to find solutions and make decisions. There is the risk, however, of losing control of the operation. The employees involved need a high degree of responsibility.

Situational: The leader uses a particular style to meet the needs of a unique set of circumstances. It may involve using any of the other leadership styles and would likely need to change over time, as the work situation changes, to be effective.

Different situations call for different types of leaders. In emergencies, for example, an autocratic leader may be more effective and able to react to immediate needs than a democratic leader. The concept of situational leadership is that you, as a leader, should be able to utilize a specific leadership style based on the needs of the moment. It is helpful to understand what those leadership styles are, as well as what your innate leadership style is, in order to become a more effective leader. Certainly the expectation of your leadership role may be different for your superiors than for your subordinates. Understanding and drawing upon these styles and types make you a more effective middle manager leader.

LEADERSHIP SELF-DEVELOPMENT

Consistent personal development is helpful even when a manager has little experience or few of the personality traits ordinarily identified with strong leadership. With experience and focused attention on developing skills and self-confidence, any middle manager can become a strong leader. One of the most important aspects of developing leadership skills is an honest and thorough understanding of your own personal skills, strengths, and weaknesses. This may be accomplished through a variety of means:

- Taking self-tests that measure personality traits, communication skills, or leadership abilities

- Asking trusted colleagues and current or former supervisors for specific feedback on your leadership skills or areas for development

- Seeking a formal performance review specifically to request feedback on leadership abilities and potential

- Identifying a mentor or potential leadership role model

- Taking courses and reading literature on leadership

- Seeking opportunities as a leader within the organization, such as for specialized projects, whether in your department or not

As with any review, leadership critiques may prove a personal challenge. Discovering that aspects of your personality may need development can seem hurtful. It is therefore important to focus on the purpose of the development, if you truly want to become a better leader. There is something to learn from all experiences, whether positive or negative, something true in all aspects of personal development.

PRACTICE

As with any skill development, the most important aspect of focusing on middle manager leadership is practicing those skills. Conscious application of leadership skills, particularly when dealing with crises or change management, is an effective way to identify the positive or negative effects of this skills development.

Leadership development often needs to be self-directed, but there are other opportunities:

- Look for organizations that offer mentorship or training programs that concentrate specifically on developing the library leader.

- Volunteer with associations, particularly in board or executive positions that allow you to develop leadership skills in a formal and supportive environment.

- Seek out leadership training from professional associations with an interest in attracting and sustaining talented new leaders.

Nowadays middle managers are expected to be active leaders in libraries and other types of organizations. For some, leadership is a natural skill. For most, leadership is a skill and set of practices that can be developed through experience and dedicated self-development. Understanding the principles of good leadership and clear self-knowledge are the keys to effective leadership development.

REFERENCES

Paarlberg, Laurie E., and Bob Lavigna. 2010. "Transformational Leadership and Public Service Motivation: Driving Individual and Organizational Performance." *Public Administration Review* 70 (5): 710–718.

Useem, Michael. 2001. *Leading Up: How to Lead Your Boss So You Both Win.* New York: Crown Business.

29

BEING AN ENTREPRENEURIAL LEADER

JENNIFER ROWLEY

LEADERSHIP AND ENTREPRENEURSHIP ARE OFTEN DISCUSSED AS IF THEY WERE separate roles requiring different traits and behaviors. This may be partly because entrepreneurship has traditionally been associated with starting up new (small, commercial) organizations that may have small staffs, whereas leadership, concerned with influencing others, is typically associated with senior staff in larger, more established organizations, including those in both the public and private sectors.

There is an increasing level of interest in the public sector in general, and in libraries in particular, related to leadership, as well as entrepreneurship, innovation, and creativity—and the contribution they can make to success and survival. Although there is sometimes an implicit assumption that leadership is the sole concern of senior managers, there is increasing acknowledgment that the leadership journey starts with the first supervisory responsibility and continues through the layers of middle management.

Middle managers are typically sandwiched in the middle between those seen as responsible for setting the strategy and agenda for library services and "frontline" professionals and assistants. They can sometimes feel constrained by the expectations of senior managers and overburdened by the melee of day-to-day activities in maintaining good service delivery.

Yet middle managers are important in ensuring the success of their organization. In leadership literature, the value of a network of leaders within an organization, each leading in his or her own sphere of activity, is suggested with the concept of dispersed leadership. In entrepreneurship literature, there is increasing recognition of the importance of professionals and middle managers in "intrapreneurship" within their organizations. Finally, in the innovation literature, there is widespread recognition of the value of innovative teams and of innovative leaders in developing such teams—at all levels of the organization. As we see in this chapter, in changing and challenging times middle managers simultaneously need to be managers, leaders, innovators, and entrepreneurs. In other words, they need to exercise control and organize (management), influence and motivate people (leadership), and work with others to generate and implement innovations (entrepreneurship).

This chapter begins with consideration of the nature and importance of innovation and entrepreneurship in libraries, then considers the nature of leadership and the specific role of leaders in creating innovative and entrepreneurial libraries in challenging and changing times. The ideas presented challenge all librarians, but especially those in middle management and supervisory roles, to think critically and creatively about how they can act innovatively and entrepreneurially—for their own careers and for the survival and reenergizing of their library services and communities.

THE IMPERATIVE FOR INNOVATION AND ENTREPRENEURSHIP IN LIBRARIES

The information industry, including libraries, publishers, and technology providers, has already witnessed many changes resulting from the digitization of information resources and the way these resources are created, shared, distributed, used, and exploited. This means that all organizations in this sector, particularly those in the public sector such as libraries, need to embrace innovation, creativity, and entrepreneurial spirit and action to continue to make a valuable contribution to their communities.

The imperative for innovation has recently been strengthened even further with widespread public sector funding cuts. Library managers need to innovate in demanding periods of reduced funding and staffing. Middle managers, in particular, are responsible for sustaining efficient and effective service delivery under tighter resource constraints. As a consequence, they need to propose and advocate new ways of doing things and also engage busy and sometimes unmotivated and reluctant staff. In other words, middle managers need to act entrepreneurially, manage innovatively, and think creatively:

Act entrepreneurially. Entrepreneurs seek out opportunities, gather resources to make things happen, and put these new ideas into practice. They have a vision and passion for seeking opportunities for improvement or doing things differently. They enlist the support and help of others and are determined, resilient, and dedicated to making things happen. Most important, they seek and find ways to benefit from change or disruption. In fact, they see the dynamic, changing marketplace as an opportunity, not a threat.

Manage innovatively. Entrepreneurial actions typically generate innovation, and these innovations need to be managed. Innovation cannot be left to chance—it can consume considerable resources. Success or failure with innovation can have significant consequences for organizations. Successful innovation leads to enhanced quality of services as well as community enthusiasm and advocacy of library services. On the other hand, absence of innovation in a dynamic environment is a recipe for being regarded as increasingly irrelevant by users and community policymakers alike. Some organizations are better at innovation than others. They offer an innovative culture, which cultivates and nurtures innovators and innovations. Managers are central in promoting such a culture. Also, specific innovation projects need to be managed and coordinated through their various stages in order to lead to successful implementation.

Think creatively. Creativity, or the process of generating and developing ideas, underpins innovation and entrepreneurship. According to J. Bessant and J. Tidd, "Creativity is the making and communicating of meaningful new connections to help us think of many possibilities, to help us think and experience in varied ways and using different points of view; to help us think of new and unusual possibilities and to guide us in generating and selecting alternatives" (2007, 40). Managers need to develop their own capacity to think "outside the box" and cultivate and encourage similar abilities in others.

Middle managers in libraries have a significant responsibility to develop and support their teams to act entrepreneurially and think creatively. They need to assume a role in managing innovatively. It is important to remember that innovation and entrepreneurship in larger public sector organizations (sometimes called "intrapreneurship") are never easy.

Indeed, Pinchot's Ten Commandments for intrapreneurs assume that organizations are resistant to change (Pinchot 1985). They suggest that in many organizations an intrapreneur who wants to do things differently, or make things happen, is treated with suspicion:

The Intrapreneur's Ten Commandments

1. Come to work each day willing to be fired.

2. Circumvent any orders aimed at stopping your dream.

3. Do any job needed to make your project work, regardless of your job description.

4. Find people to help you.

5. Follow your intuition about the people you choose and work only with the best.

6. Work underground as long as you can—publicity triggers the corporate immune system.

7. Never bet on a race unless you are running it.

8. Remember that it is easier to ask for forgiveness than for permission.

9. Be true to your goals and realistic about the way you achieve them.

10. Keep your sponsors informed.

Intrapreneurs challenge the status quo and pose a threat to people who like things as they are. Pinchot implies that the route to success involves having a vision, believing in that vision and yourself, seeking out support of like-minded people, and taking control of making your vision a reality.

Acting like a maverick is particularly challenging for middle managers, who are accountable to both their staff and senior management. They have to develop a battery of strategies and tactics to create space and permission for them and their team to innovate and be creative. This might involve volunteering for working groups and special projects; networking both inside and outside the library; setting and committing to an appropriate agenda for ongoing staff development and training; or maximizing the level of autonomy for all group members, so less time is spent on controlling and reporting and more on thinking, reflecting, and communicating. It is likely to involve hard work, commitment, and clear agendas and targets so that managers and their teams can think carefully about how they spend their time and know when they have achieved a worthwhile outcome.

In addition, there is widespread recognition that innovation and entrepreneurship can be particularly challenging in some public sector organizations. Many are large and highly bureaucratized. Innovation can affect operating procedures, the institution's power structure and dynamics, and job descriptions and career prospects (Borins 2002). All this suggests the importance of good leadership to successful entrepreneurship.

LEADERSHIP FOR ENTREPRENEURSHIP AND INNOVATION

A study in which respondents were asked to identify the top three catalysts of innovation in their organizations provides a strong endorsement of the importance of management and leadership in promoting and encouraging innovation (Patterson and Kerrin 2009): almost half the respondents identified managers' support for and openness to innovation as critical; four out of ten referred to the role of leaders in modeling behaviors that encourage innovation; and almost a third underscored the importance of setting up the right team of people.

Leadership's pivotal role is emphasized by many commentators on creativity and innovation in the library and information field (Akeroyd 2000; Walton 2008). G. Paul (2000) asserts that a library manager who fosters creativity needs to be candid, highly communicative, and open to participation by others in decision-making processes. An ability and willingness to cooperate extensively on an equal basis with other staff is also

important. Therefore, managers must lead by example, demonstrating initiative and creativity in themselves. Consequently, to be a leader is to be an entrepreneur. Leaders are influencers—they influence others toward achievement of goals. They are externally focused, have vision, are strategists and catalysts. They look to the future, seeking out opportunities and turning them into innovations.

LEADERSHIP STYLES AND TASKS IN INNOVATION

Leaders have two principal and related roles in innovation (Advanced Institute of Management Research 2005): as motivators, inspiring people to transcend the ordinary; and as architects, designing an organizational environment that enables employees to be innovative.

Advanced Institute of Management Research distinguishes between leaders who primarily motivate through transformational actions (motivators) and those who have a more transactional approach, which focuses on the coordination of organizational tasks (architects). Table 1 shows the behavioral focus of these two different types of leadership and their associated competencies in four key areas of leadership. Most managers exhibit a preference toward either transactional or transformational leadership. The most successful entrepreneurial leaders achieve a balance between these two styles, so they both inspire people and create an organizational environment that promotes innovation.

A major skill required by leaders is the ability to adapt their approach to context. The most appropriate leadership is contingent on context. This is particularly true for innovation leadership. Different scales and types of innovation demand different levels of emphasis on tasks and people as well as varied approaches to establishing direction and strategy and managing their implementation. C. E. Shalley and L. L Gilson (2004) explain that leaders who promote creativity have specific areas of focus:

Developing a supportive work context. This takes into account how leaders interact with employees and how coworkers, team members, and even those outside of work interact with employees. This depends on whether sufficient resources are available, how employees expect to be evaluated and rewarded, and whether the culture is perceived to be fair. Such job-level factors should be prioritized because they have the most immediate and critical effect on an employee's experience and, therefore, creativity.

TABLE 1

Comparing Transactional and Transformational Leadership

	Transactional focus (Architects)	**Transformational focus (Motivators)**
Developing the vision: the strategy domain	Analyzing Learning and researching Entrepreneurial and commercial thinking	Creating and innovating Formulating strategies and concepts Adapting and responding to change
Sharing the goals: the communication domain	Presenting and communicating information Writing and reporting	Relating and networking Persuading and influencing
Gaining support: the people domain	Working with people Adhering to principles and values	Leading and supervising
Delivering success: the operational domain	Planning and organizing Delivering results Coping with pressure and setbacks	Deciding and initiating action

SOURCE: Advanced Institute of Management Research (2005)

Communicating that creativity is valued. Leaders should communicate clearly that creativity is welcomed. This may be achieved through setting goals and requirements. A clear message about the value of creativity is transmitted when leaders are creative themselves and encourage others who are creative to act as role models and mentor others. Rewards are an important indicator of desired behaviors.

Designing the team and social context for creativity. Leaders should ensure that individuals come into contact with people who offer a diverse range of skills and interests. They need to encourage interaction across functional areas, among team members, and with those outside the team. Moreover, leaders need to monitor and develop team cultures that value and support creativity.

Developing an individual's creativity. Leaders need to seek out and appoint creative individuals, placing them in contexts where their creativity is an asset and not a hindrance and offering them training in problem solving and other skills that support creativity.

GROWING ENTREPRENEURIAL LEADERS: DISPERSED LEADERSHIP

Information professionals who are not managers may be leaders. They may contribute to developing others or to building strong networks and relationships. The notion that leadership can be carried out at all levels of an organization and is not the exclusive domain of managers and senior staff is termed *dispersed leadership.* Middle managers can develop their teams by allowing and encouraging others to lead. In the context of innovation, several different leadership roles can be adopted by team members:

Technical champion or inventor: Has the critical technical knowledge to understand a problem, propose a solution, and solve developmental problems associated with bringing the innovation to fruition. This role requires inspiration, motivation, and commitment.

Project leader: Has overall responsibility for making the innovation happen.

Business innovator: Focuses on the market or user perspective and ensures fit between the innovation and market opportunity as both evolve during the development process.

Technological gatekeeper: Collects information from various sources (often informal) and passes it to key individuals; facilitates communication within a team and between the team and other stakeholders or groups. This role is significant in distributed or virtual teams.

CONCLUSIONS

Entrepreneurship, innovation, creativity, and leadership are different facets of understanding and embracing an uncertain future. Leaders exhibit entrepreneurial behavior and creativity themselves by serving as role models while creating organizational environments in which others are welcomed and expected to innovate. Middle managers who promote and embrace innovation are developing major facets of their leadership competencies and making important progress on their leadership journeys. They are preparing themselves to be the senior managers and leaders of the future.

REFERENCES

Advanced Institute of Management Research. 2005. *Leadership for Innovation*. London: AIMR.

Akeroyd, J. 2000. "The Management of Change in Electronic Libraries." 66th IFLA Council and General Conference, August 13–18.

Bessant, J., and J. Tidd. 2007. *Innovation and Entrepreneurship*. Chichester, UK: Wiley.

Borins, S. 2002. "Leadership and Innovation in the Public Sector." *Leadership and Organization Development Journal* 23 (8): 467–476.

Patterson, F., and M. Kerrin. 2009. *Innovation for the Recovery: Enhancing Innovative Working Practices*. London: Chartered Management Institute.

Paul, G. 2000. "Mobilising the Potential for Initiative and Innovation by Means of Socially Competent Management." *Library Management* 21 (2): 81–85.

Pinchot, G., III. 1985. *Intrapreneuring: Why You Don't Have to Leave the Corporation to Become an Entrepreneur*. New York: Harper and Row.

Shalley, C. E., and L. L. Gilson. 2004. "What Leaders Need to Know: A Review of Social and Contextual Factors That Can Foster or Hinder Creativity." *Leadership Quarterly* 15 (1): 33–53.

Walton, G. 2008. "Theory, Research and Practice in Library Management 4: Creativity." *Library Management* 29 (1/2): 125–131.

30

MANAGING CHANGE

A Reading Guide for Today's Middle Manager

KEITH PHELAN GORMAN AND JOE M. WILLIAMS

BUFFETED BY THE IMPACT OF DOWNSIZING, SHIFTS IN INFORMATION TECHNOL-ogies, global competition, and a historic recession, organizations are altering how they manage their planning and operations. These shifts in business management affect how organizations define mission, implement new initiatives, direct projects, evaluate programs, and repurpose staff. In many instances, traditional hierarchical models are giving way to more flexible, team-oriented approaches. In the case of middle managers, researchers and business consultants are discovering that many core managerial responsibilities have been pushed down to middle managers (Osterman 2008, 71). Middle managers are now being asked to act as general managers, work across departments, and make key decisions.

During this transformative era for libraries, it increasingly falls to middle managers to implement new initiatives, track and assess rapid shifts in user expectations and technology, promote staff development, and ensure clear communication across units (Lubans 2005; Young, Heron, and Powell 2004). In such fluid and demanding environments, a commitment to lifelong learning enables middle managers to develop and maintain effective managerial skills and strategies. The busy middle manager faces a significant challenge in staying current with the latest management tools and theory as well as managing change.

This annotated bibliography on managing change is intended to give busy managers an introduction to the latest research and trends. Unlike management webinars and workshops that provide practical advice, this literature review provides the reader with a broader perspective on management methods.

The bibliography is organized into sections that address effective leadership, library workforce, organizational culture, service models, strategic planning, scenario planning, and assessment. It is intended to offer middle managers the resources to devise a flexible and effective response to organizational change.

EFFECTIVE LEADERSHIP

The phrase *effective leadership* refers generically to the appropriate and consistent application of various leadership techniques or skills. Some elements often associated with effective leadership include articulating a vision, communicating effectively, decision making, selecting and rewarding employees, developing a leadership style, and utilizing strategic planning. Here are three useful resources for the middle manager:

Drucker, Peter F. *The Effective Executive.* New York: Harper and Row, 1965.

Though published in 1965, this book remains one of the definitive studies on the elements of effective leadership. Drucker opens and closes with the assertion that managers and other leaders are paid to be effective and his belief that effectiveness is not an innate gift but something that can be learned. The book is a collection of Drucker's practical and philosophical insights, observations, and real-world examples. The chapters on time management, self-assessment, prioritization, and decision making, in particular, offer managers practical tools for improving their efficacy.

Harvard Business Review Press. *HBR's 10 Must Reads on Leadership.* Boston: Harvard Business Review Press, 2011.

This book provides a compilation of articles that focuses on the ideas of leadership and identifying or developing leadership qualities. Taken as a whole, this collection provides the middle manager with a deeper understanding of what contemporary thinkers believe it means to lead. These ten articles, taken from the pages of the *Harvard Business Review* since 1990, address transformational leadership styles and assessment of one's personal leadership strengths and weaknesses and offer several definitions or visions of effective leadership. The importance of introspection and self-knowledge in leadership is a shared theme across most of these writings.

Stuart, Robert D., and Maureen Sullivan. *Developing Library Leaders: A How-to-Do-It Manual for Coaching, Team Building, and Mentoring Library Staff.* New York: Neal-Schuman, 2010.

This book provides managers with tangible, effective leadership principles and practices within the specific context of libraries and information services organizations. The authors take a hands-on approach to the topic by providing readers with self-assessment tools and exercises and offering techniques the manager can employ to engage staff and manage projects and performance.

LIBRARY WORKFORCE

With budget cuts, an ongoing technological revolution in communication systems, and the looming retirement of the baby boomer generation of librarians, libraries are being forced to reconsider how their functions are being accomplished (Mullins, Allen, and Hufford 2007). Middle managers are evaluating staffing levels, specific job tasks, and professional development needs. To meet emerging trends and needs, libraries are seeking to retrain existing staff, establish "blended" positions, and hiring professionals who do not hold an MLS degree. These three works shed light on library workforce concerns:

Goetsch, Lori A. "Reinventing Our Work: New and Emerging Roles for Academic Librarians." *Journal of Library Administration* 48, no. 2 (2008): 157–172.

By reviewing job announcements over the past fifteen years, Goetsch considers ways libraries are crafting new roles and responsibilities for librarians by reinventing more traditional positions and determining new skill sets. Middle managers will find her discussion of how workforce changes affect staff morale, service, and performance instructive. Goetsch argues that the success of realigning staff responsibilities rests with clear communication, resources for cross-training, and incentives for seeking professional development opportunities.

Marshall, Joanne G., Paul Solomon, and Susan Rathburn-Grubb, eds. "Workforce Issues in Library and Information Science." *Library Trends* 58, no. 2 (Fall 2009).

This special edition of *Library Trends* brings together a collection of research articles that provide a "life course" perspective on the education, recruitment, and retention of library professionals. Of special interest to middle managers is Gail Munde's study of age diversity in the workplace and intergenerational conflict. Resolution of workplace conflict, Munde contends, comes in the form of auditing workforce composition, determining generational career needs and characteristics, reviewing possible salary compression, and evaluating professional development needs.

Stanley, Mary J. *Managing Library Employees: A How-to-Do-It Manual.* New York: Neal-Schuman, 2008.

Stanley offers a well-organized manual for middle managers involved in hiring, training, evaluation, and mentoring of library professionals. Her chapters on training, retention, professional development, program evaluation, and performance appraisal best address the human resource challenges of managing an intergenerational workforce.

ORGANIZATIONAL CULTURE

An organization's culture is shaped by a set of values, norms, expectations, and practices. In trying to meet the needs of next-generation users, many libraries are concluding that they have to implement organizational changes and instill a new set of institutional values. They believe this shift in organizational culture will foster innovation, a responsive service culture, and encouragement of new library skills. Business consultants and scholars point to the need for effective communication among staff, middle managers, and library leaders to shape an organizational culture that supports continuous innovation (Schlosser 2011). These three selected works offer insights into how to facilitate institutional change successfully:

Harvard Business Review Press. *Harvard Business Review on Leading through Change.* Boston: Harvard Business School Publishing, 2006.

This selection of *Harvard Business Review* articles addresses the difficulty of successfully implementing organizational change. For the middle manager, authors Paul Strebel and Ram Charan offer ways to overcome employee resistance and organizational inflexibility by recognizing an employee's "personal compact" with the organization, ensuring that organizational values are aligned with operations, establishing open dialogue in all the organization's social operating mechanisms, and building a communication approach that values feedback and follow-through.

Maloney, Krisellen, Kristin Antelman, Kenning Arlitsch, and John Butler. "Future Leaders' Views on Organizational Culture." *College and Research Libraries* 71, no. 4 (2010): 322–347.

By surveying future library leaders, this study offers the middle manager a glimpse into peer preferences and perceptions regarding organizational change. The authors argue that organizations need to support more risk taking, become more externally focused, and embrace "disruptive change" to adapt to changes in information technology, research, and learning.

McDonald, Ronald H., and Chuck Thomas. "Disconnects between Library Culture and Millennial Generation Values." *EDUCAUSE Quarterly* 29, no. 4 (2006): 4–6.

The authors argue that libraries are not meeting the needs and values of the millennial generation. They call for a cultural shift that will create a "next generation landscape" that addresses current shortcomings of technology, policy, and unexploited opportunities.

SERVICE MODELS

With dramatic changes in information technology, learning, and user expectations, libraries are reconsidering their mission and core functions. In response to this realignment of mission, libraries are altering how they structure and deploy reference services, access tools, research and instruction services, as well as how they promote scholarly communication. The following publications provide middle managers with valuable insights into implementing new service models:

Bracke, Marianne Stowell, Michael Brewer, Robyn Huff-Eibl, Daniel R. Lee, Robert Mitchell, and Michael Ray. "Finding Information in a New Landscape: Developing New Service and Staffing Models for Mediated Information Services." *College and Research Libraries* 68, no. 3 (2007): 248–267.

With the reality of shrinking library budgets and changes in user behavior, the University of Arizona championed the idea of establishing a new service and staffing model to meet these challenges. For the middle manager, this study outlines a system of support that can be used to implement organizational change. This operational problem-solving tool consists of a leadership system, team system, planning system, process improvement system, and performance management system.

Johnson, Brenda L., and Ruth Lilly Dean. "Transforming Roles for Academic Librarians: Leading and Participating in New Partnerships." *Research Library Issues: A Bimonthly Report from ARL, CNI, and SPARC*, October 2010, 7–15.

Johnson and Dean argue that academic libraries are becoming "pull organizations" that conglomerate researchers, information, and ideas to generate scholarly communication and potential collaborative projects. For middle managers reconsidering the scope of their library services, the authors describe successful library and faculty partnerships at Indiana University and the University of Michigan that facilitate curriculum development, information literacy, digital projects, and new approaches to teaching.

Walter, Scott. "'Distinctive Signifiers of Excellence': Library Services and the Future of the Academic Library." *College and Research Libraries* 72, no. 1 (2011): 6–8.

Walter poses the provocative question of how libraries will continue to distinguish themselves from each other once access to content is no longer as competitive. He argues that distinctive services will be just as important in shaping a library's mission as resource sharing. Referencing the New Services Model at the University of Illinois at Urbana-Champaign, he notes that service will become a "signifier of excellence" and that the research library will distinguish itself by the quality and scope of its service programs.

STRATEGIC PLANNING

Strategic planning is an essential tool in any library's efforts to set goals, establish performance benchmarks, and determine allocation of staff and resources. This planning tool is part of a broader process that involves examining external markets and trends, evaluating internal strengths and weaknesses, and recognizing opportunities. The goal of this process is to generate or focus an organization's mission and vision, improve outcomes, or identify new directions for the organization. In conducting an environmental scan, many libraries employ a SWOT (strengths, weaknesses, opportunities, threats) analysis of both internal operations and external factors. The following are bibliographic resources to help with strategic planning:

Matthews, Joseph R. *Strategic Planning and Management for Library Managers.* Westport, CT: Libraries Unlimited, 2005.

This book provides an introduction to the strategic planning process, practices, and issues within the library and information services environment. The author outlines ten approaches to formulating strategy: conceptual, formal, analytical, visionary, mental, emergent, negotiated, collective, reactive, and transformative. He also discusses three different types of strategies that libraries can consider: "operational excellence" strategies that focus on providing efficient, often streamlined tasks and services; "customer intimacy" strategies that target particular segments of a customer base and can include personalized services or recommendations; and "innovative services" strategies that incorporate entrepreneurial moves or technological advances and applications through creative approaches. The importance of ongoing assessment and evaluation in the strategic planning process is underscored in this work. Matthews also points the reader to several online examples of library strategic plans.

Mintzberg, Henry. "The Fall and Rise of Strategic Planning." *Harvard Business Review*, January-February 1994, 107–114.

A widely read article from a management expert, this work addresses the place of strategic planning within the larger context of strategic thinking. Mintzberg believes the task of "planning" should not be separated from actual "doing." Instead, he argues that managers are vital in the strategic thinking process because they are deeply involved in the specific issues at hand. Managers can share their practical experiences and insights with planners, who can then help them creatively synthesize those lessons ultimately to shape an organization's vision and direction. Formalizing strategic planning, the author suggests, removes the necessary creativity and adaptability from the process.

Nelson, Sandra. *Strategic Planning for Results.* Chicago: American Library Association, 2008.

Nelson offers a detailed and methodical guide through a five-step strategic planning process: (1) identifying service priorities and assessing community needs; (2) defining organizational values; (3) writing goals and objectives; (4) communicating the plan; and (5) implementing the plan. Though geared specifically for public libraries, this guide is also applicable to a broad range of information services organizations.

SCENARIO PLANNING

Scenario planning is a mental exercise middle managers can employ to help them think strategically and plan for uncertainty. Through the scenario planning process, the manager develops multiple future scenarios based on current or perceived trends, determines the organization's response to each scenario, and then evaluates those responses. The goal is to help organizations prepare for an uncertain future, often by exposing opportunities or organizational weaknesses.

Association of College and Research Libraries. *Futures Thinking for Academic Librarians: Higher Education in 2025*, prepared by David J. Staley and Kara J. Malefant. Washington, DC: Association of College and Research Libraries, 2010.

This up-to-date example of academic library scenario planning briefly describes twenty-six scenarios for information organizations. For example, how would one's organization respond if thrust into a future where open access and open peer review are the norm, which speeds discoveries and creates a much more community-based dialogue among practitioners and researchers around new research? Scenarios were shaped in part through a survey of ACRL members. Activities are provided to help libraries engage in scenario planning and strategic thinking.

Association of College and Research Libraries. *The ARL 2030 Scenarios: A User's Guide for Research Libraries.* Washington, DC: Association of College and Research Libraries, 2010.

This publication provides four in-depth scenarios for academic library scenario planning. It also includes plans and steps libraries can adopt to conduct their own scenario planning as well as several helpful readings.

Ralston, Bill, and Ian Wilson. *The Scenario-Planning Handbook: A Practitioner's Guide to Developing and Using Scenarios to Direct Strategy in Today's Uncertain Times.* Mason, OH: Thomson South-Western, 2006.

This highly detailed guide to the scenario-planning process takes the reader from the process of forming the scenario-building team to generating and selecting appropriate scenarios, then moving from scenario analysis to the decision-making phase.

ASSESSMENT

Libraries are increasingly being challenged by administrators, accrediting organizations, and taxpayers to show greater accountability, transparency, and evidence of their value—a situation described as a "perfect storm" within the assessment community (Dole, Hurych, and Liebst 2005; Lewis 2010). This demand for assessment directly affects middle managers since they are responsible for the service and output of a department and are involved in staff reviews, program evaluation, and measurement outcomes. While continuing to track acquisitions and use, librarians now are turning to assessment tools, which measure the quality and effectiveness of services, library technology, and programs. The following publications serve as a valuable resource for middle managers:

Brown, Jeanne. "Informal Assessment for Library Middle Managers." *Library Leadership and Management* 24, no. 1 (2010): 18–22.

Brown offers a practical guide for managers who feel overwhelmed by all the existing assessment programs available. She argues that middle managers should employ an informal and continuous assessment approach, which does not require extensive preparation and resources and provides more timely information and more effective supervision. Brown outlines an evidence-based management model that generates patron or staff feedback. It is based on the simple practice of the middle manager "asking" staff and patron, "listening" to their feedback, "watching" operations and programs, and "acting" on the feedback.

Heath, Fred. "Library Assessment: The Way We Have Grown." *Library Quarterly* 81, no. 1 (2011): 7–25.

Heath gives an engaging historical overview of library assessment that pays particular attention to the past two decades and the role played by the Association of Research Libraries. An assessment scholar, Heath tracks the evolution and broadening of library quantitative analysis that has ushered in TQM, LibQUAL, and StatsQual.

Horowitz, Lisa. "Assessing Library Services: A Practical Guide for the Nonexpert." *Library Leadership and Management* 23, no. 4 (2009): 193–203.

Horowitz provides readers with a roadmap of the basic tenets of good assessment: (1) devise a set of performance standards based on the values of the library; (2) determine questions to be answered; (3) make sure to use the most appropriate data-gathering tool; (4) define plans for data use; (5) triangulate the data; (6) endeavor to maintain statistical validity; and (7) pretest data collection instruments. In addition, she offers practical steps to plan an assessment program by focusing on actions and implementing it by making it manageable. The article has a detailed bibliography and appendix that lists ALA standards and performance guidelines as well as other standards, guidelines, and metrics.

Matthews, Joseph R. "Assessing Organizational Effectiveness: The Role of Performance Measures." *Library Quarterly* 81, no. 1 (2011): 83–110.

This article and bibliography provide middle managers with a handy primer to understand performance measures such as dashboards, process improvement initiatives, and integrated management frameworks like the balanced scorecard. A balanced scorecard is a tool in which mission and strategic planning can be assessed via an array of performance measures. It is also a system that encourages feedback from all levels of the organization. Matthews states that the real value of performance measures is when they are tied to the organization's vision, goals, and objectives. He identifies good performance measures as those that are balanced and include both financial and nonfinancial measures, aligned to the organization's strategies, flexible and changeable as needed, timely and accurate, simple to understand, and focused on improvement.

REFERENCES

Dole, Wanda V., Jitka M. Hurych, and Anne Liebst. 2005. "Assessment: A Core Competency for Library Leaders." *Library Administration and Management* 19 (3): 125–132.

Lewis, Janice Steed. 2010. "The Academic Library in Institutional Assessment." *Library Leadership and Management* 24 (2): 65.

Lubans, John, Jr. 2005. "I Am the Very Model of a Modern Middle Manager." *Library Administration and Management* 19 (3): 140–142.

Mullins, James L., Frank R. Allen, and Jon R. Hufford. 2007. "Ten Top Assumptions for the Future of Academic Libraries and Librarians: A Report from the ACRL Research Committee." *College and Research Libraries News* 68 (4): 240–246.

Osterman, Paul. 2008. *The Truth about Middle Managers: Who They Are, How They Work, Why They Matter.* Boston: Harvard Business Press.

Schlosser, Melanie. 2011. "OSUL2013: Fostering Organizational Change through a Grassroots Planning Process." *College and Research Libraries* 72 (2): 152–165.

Young, Arthur, Peter Heron, and Ronald Powell. 2004. "What Will Gen Next Need to Lead?" *American Libraries* 35 (5): 32–35.

31

THE NEED FOR MIDDLE MANAGERS

Turning Today's New Librarians into Tomorrow's Leaders

BERNADINE GOLDMAN

THIS CHAPTER PROVIDES GUIDANCE ON HOW TO MAKE MIDDLE MANAGEMENT positions relevant and enriching. Developing the next generation of library leaders is a critical function the middle manager can assume, both in the interest of succession planning in a particular library and for the advancement of the profession as a whole. A focus on coaching and mentoring new librarians guarantees that the library will have viable candidates for management positions that may open up. Opportunities to perform rewarding work help retain librarians, and they are then prepared when the chance to advance arrives. Demonstrated upward mobility raises morale and aids staff development at all levels.

Here we consider how to give new librarians stepping stones to management positions by

- Changing the library organizational structure to give new librarians supervisory responsibilities

- Holding middle managers accountable for development of new librarians

- Intensively coaching new librarians to master the basics of their jobs while taking the initiative on assignments that lead to growth

- Connecting them to each other, the library management team, and the profession as a whole

- Deliberately preparing them for the next management level

- Giving them responsibility for their own professional development and that of others

JOBS FOR NEW LIBRARIANS

My workplace is a small- to medium-sized public library with one branch. Until a few years ago, our management team consisted of five senior librarians plus our director. There were no intermediate positions between the paraprofessional ranks and the senior librarians. We had, and still have, several degreed librarians working in paraprofessional positions. But unless they had supervisory and budgetary experience from another library, there was no way for our staff to move up.

This created problems with staff morale, retention, and recruitment. Because we are located in an isolated area of New Mexico, our retention problems were not as severe as they might be were we a big city library with many other options nearby. But our recruitment problems were more severe as we continued to see promising external candidates from out of state come for interviews and decide they really didn't want to live here. For the continued vitality of our library, we wanted to be able to address this lack of upward mobility for our staff and grow our own leaders.

CHANGING THE ORGANIZATIONAL STRUCTURE

The chance came with the beginning of a wave of retirements. Suddenly the logjam began to move and our library proved nimble enough to respond quickly. We laid the foundation by restructuring our organization to enable us to hire new librarians into professional positions.

Restructuring. We included more layers of management (counterintuitive in today's flat management environment, but helpful). This provided more opportunities for staff to work their way up. For most people, it had been too much of a leap to move from a paraprofessional to senior librarian position. Though many were high performers in their paraprofessional roles, their focus was naturally narrow and they did not normally enjoy the possibilities of gaining experience that would qualify them for management positions. We therefore created four supervising librarian positions, one for each library public service area: circulation, reference, youth services, and the branch library. Though we still preferred experience when recruiting supervising librarians, we could at last hire qualified and promising first-time, frontline supervisors into professional positions.

At the same time, we created an assistant library director position (my job) to be responsible for public services overall, to whom these new librarians would report. This new reporting structure also gave us a chance to integrate our public services and thus greatly benefit our patrons.

Staff development. We made staff development, including leadership training and succession planning, a focus of the assistant library director's job, making a true orga-

nizational commitment to staff that, if they would get the education and experience required, we would work to prepare them for advancement opportunities.

In the past few years, we hired four librarians, two of them internal candidates and two external. This alone has raised morale in the library, since staff now see that they have a chance to move up. This also encourages retention of this new talent as they acknowledge future possibilities.

HELPING NEW LIBRARIANS GAIN LEADERSHIP: MIDDLE MANAGERS AS FACILITATORS

Hiring is just the first step. The second, equally important step involves coaching, mentoring, and promoting librarians' professional development. If you find yourself as a middle manager in charge of supervising new librarians and you can see their potential to lead the library into the future, here are some tips to follow in preparing them for this future:

Coach librarians to perform their current tasks well. The demonstrated ability to excel at their current level speaks volumes when they apply for a promotion.

Hold operations meetings with each of them on a regular basis, once weekly to start. These meetings greatly improve communication between management levels, so it feels natural. No formal agenda is needed and both parties can contribute items for discussion. Sometimes you just need to touch base and check that all is going well; other times, these meetings can serve as problem-solving sessions or course corrections.

Be available for on-the-spot guidance as much as possible. Have an open door and demonstrate that you are always glad to see those you supervise. This should be easy since it is one of the pleasures of middle management to help people on their way up.

Be alert to patterns of problem areas for each librarian. As you become familiar with their strengths and weaknesses, you can target your coaching efforts to particular areas of need. Be honest with them about areas they need to work on and note their progress. This works especially well if carried out as part of the library's performance planning and evaluation process.

Allow librarians to take initiative on assignments that will lead to growth, both personally and professionally.

Encourage them to develop and put their own ideas into practice, or assign projects to each of them that stretch their areas of expertise. Such projects might build skills in new technology; they might highlight the need to enhance communication both within and outside the organization; they will likely involve time and workflow management improvements, as well as the need to balance big-picture and detail-oriented points of view, and will help librarians increase their expertise in supervision issues.

Support their participation in professional activities: associations, conferences, presentations, publications. Provide opportunities for them to present on a topic of their expertise to library staff, encouraging them to get feedback, polish their presentations, and take them to the state library conference level. Give financial support if possible and consider such activities as work time, well worth the investment.

Promote lateral enrichment and movement. It serves everyone well to understand the tasks and challenges of other library operations. There is much to learn throughout a library or library system, in terms of both workflow and the larger issues that affect a whole library. Varied experiences also contribute to librarians being strong candidates for senior management positions. Our job descriptions for librarians and for other classifications are generic. Although this sometimes results in external candidates not being sure about which area of the library they would be working, it allows us, at least theoretically, to move staff laterally and shift areas of responsibility as organizational needs change.

Build librarians' commitment to the library and to each other. This generates trust and supports retention, as librarians envision a professional future for themselves and see enrichment possibilities in their current jobs, even if the opportunity to move up does not come quickly.

Encourage librarians to become a support group for each other. Assign projects for them to work on together, so they coalesce as a team and understand they are making a real contribution as well as learning new skills. Our librarians are working to establish programming for our 18- to 35-year-old patrons, an area of genuine need—which should be

challenging and fun. All such projects give librarians plenty of positive talking points in interviews for future higher-level positions in addition to involving them in the community and allowing them to experiment.

Make them part of a larger library management team, so they have a real say in strategic planning, and put some of their suggestions into practice. We can all benefit from their ideas.

Give new librarians exposure to the next level.

Expose them to details of your job. People sometimes think that, the higher up someone is in an organization, the less actual work they do. When they eventually move up themselves, they are consequently unprepared for the increased workload. Let them know what you are working on, what it involves, how you prioritize and manage your time, and how they might be able to help. It is important for all of us to have a sense of what the next job up entails. Give them the opportunity to try out the job in an acting role if the situation arises.

Discuss middle management issues with librarians. Most senior-level library jobs demand political skills, and although there is no substitute for trial and error this is an excellent discussion topic that helps prepare new librarians. Guide them to connect with the library's greater community by reading local media, minutes of city council meetings, construction project updates, and so on. Let them know how to communicate through the chain of command, including who to approach about what, within and outside the library hierarchy, and how to do so graciously.

Train them for that next job. We are currently beginning an in-house management training program. After a brief survey of our librarians, we separated this program into three training phases according to their expressed needs: (1) efficiency, workflow management, management challenges, implementing change, contributing to the profession, library laws; (2) time management, performance management, budgeting, the library and its community, staff development, systems thinking, doing well and moving up, and handling emergencies; and (3) creating effective teams, marketing library services, troubleshooting technical problems, communication skills, decision making.

The format will be collegial. Rather than having managers be teachers and the librarians students, we will all take turns teaching and learning from each other. This in itself will help develop expertise, presentation skills, self-confidence, a sense of commitment, and systems thinking.

Make it clear that their own professional development, and that of those they supervise, is their responsibility.

Although you can offer much support, staff should be constantly challenging themselves to step outside their comfort zones, offering to present a program even though they don't like public speaking, or serving on a technology planning committee when they prefer to present children's storytimes. With encouragement and a library atmosphere that treats making mistakes as a learning opportunity, they will continue to grow and shine.

Ask them to consider how best to identify and take advantage of the skills and talents of those they supervise. They should think about who on their staff might eventually be able to step into their own frontline supervisory position, since that is the first step into management. They should encourage growth in their staff by delegating some of their own tasks and coaching how to perform them well, allowing for differences in style. Discuss how to identify those tasks that are appropriate to delegate and those that are better to retain. Be certain they are informed about any formal or informal educa-tional opportunities and any financial assistance available.

Invite them to contribute to your own professional development. Be open yourself to new ideas and procedures, and reward creativity. New librarians bring many ideas for new directions, both from their more recent library school experiences and from being part of a younger generation. Be a risk taker and open to change because this in itself is an opportunity for revitalization of the library. It is up to us to recognize it, celebrate it, and move toward implementing some of these new ideas.

IT'S UP TO YOU AS MIDDLE MANAGER

As a middle manager, be aware that at all times you are a role model for new librarians. This isn't to say you need to be serious all the time. The best role models are those who enjoy their jobs, and a job is hard to enjoy without a sense of humor. Keep an eye out for talent, pay attention to developing it, and thrive in your own middle management job. As turnover takes place, your library will have a ready and enthusiastic pool of capable applicants for management positions.

32

BUILDING STRONG MIDDLE MANAGER/ PARALIBRARIAN RELATIONSHIPS

Middle Managers as Mentors

ALLISON SLOAN

EVERYONE OCCASIONALLY NEEDS A NUDGE. MAYBE YOU ARE THE MIDDLE MANager who can encourage and guide a paralibrarian staffer to cultivate his or her potential and contributions to the library. Your paralibrarians may be proficient at their job, and as a manager you notice they seem ready to learn a new skill set. Maybe system changes warrant a review of workflow that takes advantage of a staff person's special abilities.

As mentors, middle managers have the opportunity to foster the professional experiences of paralibrarians. This creates job satisfaction and empowers people to achieve their full potential. Visionary middle managers who take the lead to build a strong paralibrarian team enhance their own work experience and expand their place in the library community. Middle managers create success in their own careers as they discover the rewards of mentoring paralibrarian staff.

In the best circumstances, mentoring is a mutual and rewarding relationship that results in growth and success for both parties. For example, when middle managers encourage their staff to explore how other libraries handle similar work, they benefit when an enthusiastic paralibrarian brings back a new idea. Something as simple as a new labeling project allows a staff member to contribute to workflow success, which brings a sense of job satisfaction that can spread to coworkers.

Paths to growth in a library career develop from many different directions. Volunteerism, committee participation, and learning and leadership opportunities are a few of the areas a mentor taps into. Sometimes the mentee is eager and runs with an idea. Other times, the mentor is not only supporting the effort but hand holding and even giving a push to help a hesitant beginner overcome barriers.

Initiative and volunteerism can open doors. By encouraging a staff member to sign on for a project or cross-train in another library department, a manager provides a chance to highlight abilities beyond the basic routine of the job. Middle managers have an opportunity to help paralibrarians find paths to broaden their experience and develop new skills. For example, circulation technicians are some of the first people patrons meet as they enter the library. They offer to direct patrons to the appropriate help desk, check out books, settle overdue fines, and much more. It's an entry-level library position that requires tact and communication skills, computer savvy, and calm under pressure. Initially, the job is plenty challenging and every day brings something new to the library. Then the training period ends, and the technician becomes comfortable with the pace of the job.

With proficiency, a circulation technician might occasionally offer some minor readers' advisory, though she may not even be familiar with the term or realize that she is doing anything more than talking about favorite books. It is at this point that an insightful middle manager detects this interest, nurtures it, and guides the technician toward professional growth.

It was at a similar juncture in my early library work that an "all staff" e-mail from a middle manager soliciting help to design and create displays caught my attention. That was the light bulb moment that opened up the idea of volunteering for projects outside my department and what became an introduction to the work of every department in the library.

Soon I volunteered to cover an hour at the children's room desk while staff were in a meeting. That was challenging beyond what I could have imagined. Next, I came in for an all-day staff shelf-reading project on a Sunday when the building was closed.

Throughout these forays into volunteering, the key was the approval of my department head, the middle manager who supported my requests to take on volunteer projects. Sometimes it was within my regular schedule, or additional paid time. Sometimes it was on my own time. Often a word from my middle manager pointed out an interesting opportunity I may have overlooked. More important, it was support from my middle manager that allowed me to explore areas outside my comfort zone. When the director asked for volunteers to learn a new circulation software system and help train staff, my manager offered me the opportunity to represent our division.

Working on the circulation system project allowed me to network with staff from other library departments and libraries as well as regional and consortium offices. These are the doors that open with the initiative to volunteer and the support of a middle manager. In my case, it led to a promotion to the technical services department, where I discovered that my new middle manager was a colleague, role model, and mentor.

As a new middle manager, this paralibrarian department head had come up through the ranks. He was excited to take a fresh look at workflow and apply his vision of how best to serve patrons. As he worked toward his MLS degree, he was mentored by the library director. It was a natural progression to learn from his advisor how to be a mentor and then take an active role in guiding my paralibrarian career. He introduced me to some new ideas about what was possible if you tapped into your skills and strengths. Together, we opened doors into paralibrarianship as a career. His job goals included coaching me to look for ways to grow my library experience. Soon, my job goals included participating in the library community to advocate career development of other paralibrarians. In essence, my boss served as a middle manager mentor and guided me to become a mentor myself. With his encouragement, my confidence and experience grew and my job expanded. Gradually, with seniority and experience, I also assumed some responsibilities as a middle manager.

My middle manager had recommended that I apply for a vacant seat on the local cultural council as a community member and representative of the library. When I became chairperson of this committee, it offered me opportunities to develop my personal cultural mission to network and build partnerships among the council, businesses, municipal government, schools, and the library. The council already supported a teen author visit each year, and soon it began holding meetings at the library, participating in a library open house and the town-wide fair. This is a good example of the value of mentoring coming full circle. My middle manager prepared me for leadership, which ultimately allowed the library to benefit from my advocacy.

A good middle manager identifies training that adds value to a paralibrarian's skill set, which later can lay the foundation for broader opportunities. A casual suggestion convinced me I would benefit from a workshop on reference basics. I enrolled in a series of state certification courses that taught reference interview techniques, cataloging, collection development, and library administration. With that accomplished, he suggested that I apply to participate in a library leadership program. Talk about eye-opening and confidence-building opportunities! Suddenly it made sense to become a paralibrarian member of the Massachusetts Library Association, the state's organization for professional library employees. As a consequence, I began to grasp the big picture and focus of libraries in my state.

This is a clear example of successful mentors. The top was guiding the middle, which enabled the middle to facilitate a library staff member to contribute and finally become a mentor for other paralibrarians. This trickle-down effect is key to empowering paralibrarians to think and perform in resourceful and self-directed ways.

When you empower those you supervise, new opportunities, challenges, more involvement, and recognition accrue naturally to your mentee. You have helped a paralibrarian to the head of the class. Now people are calling on her because she has been given the chance to expand her information base and share ideas. Suddenly, there are blogs that need perspective; newsletter articles on a topic she knows something about; conference programs with eager listeners. Annual review time offers middle managers the occasion to recognize a paralibrarian's accomplishments with praise for meeting goals. It also provides a vehicle to reinforce middle management's plans to nudge the staff person to reach further and, as a result, enhance the library and her library career.

A talented mentor allows the capable paralibrarian's job description to expand from ordering, inputting, processing, and weeding to include blogging, conference programming, and committee work. One of the indispensable qualities of your staff person may be his attention to detail when it comes to ordering paperbacks. In your role as mentor, you recognize that his understanding of paperbacks, genres, and formats has developed into a genuine passion for readers' advisory. You recommend that he reply to an e-mail seeking panelists for a program to discuss science-fiction writers.

Ideally, a middle manager mentor enhances opportunities by authorizing planning time and training to encourage a paralibrarian to explore new paths. Increased opportunities may require additional funding. The middle manager mentor may seek his own mentor for guidance to add a new budget line or pursue grant funding to cover the cost of sending staff to a conference or training.

But, when tough times hit, how does the middle manager keep things challenging and developing for their paralibrarian staff? Middle managers must continue to model a positive attitude and teamwork. They can address poor morale and limiting attitudes by responding with positive energy and exploring options. For example, the Paralibrarian Committee in my state developed low-cost, empowering programs at the annual conference, of which library middle managers can avail themselves. One such program is the Book Cart Drill Team, which features creative performance teams that dance, spin, and twirl while pushing book carts. These drill teams are valuable as team builders to boost morale as well as for publicity, marketing, and branding. When library management participates on these teams, it fosters equality by setting an example of partnership and respect.

Mentoring and creative ideas can promote job satisfaction without costing a lot of money. In my library, a paralibrarian responsible for processing and inputting magazines demonstrated initiative by designing a new and improved labeling system for the shelves with an in-house label maker and sticky magnets. In parallel, middle managers can serve as visionaries and enablers to introduce and nudge paralibrarians into broader opportunities and challenges of careers in libraries.

33

MOVING UP THE RANKS AND BACK AGAIN

Lessons Learned as an Interim Library Director

ELISABETH TAPPEINER

'VE MANAGED A SMALL TECHNICAL SERVICES UNIT IN A COMMUNITY COLLEGE library for the past seven years. I enjoy the mixture of hands-on work and the flexibility and problem-solving skills required in an area where technology and shifting priorities demand learning new skills and refining workflows. Also, I believe my experience as a rank-and-file librarian in several areas of technical services helps me connect with students, staff, and librarians who report to me.

When my library director asked me to take over her role temporarily three years ago while she assumed administrative responsibilities on a college-wide level, I believed these same principles would apply. I had management experience and the benefit of knowing our library from a ground-level perspective. I knew that managing a library would be more complex and would cover areas, such as access services, where my knowledge was minimal. I acknowledged that gaps in my experience would present the greatest difficulties for me. Nevertheless, the greatest challenges during my two and a half years as interim library director related to the lack of clarity inherent in being a temporary manager, which limited my ability to make decisions and build a strong team.

Every interim situation is different, but I hope that an overview of what experts in the field have to say, as well as wisdom gleaned from my own experience, will help any prospective temporary manager navigate these murky waters.

STEPPING INTO THE UNKNOWN

Before she assumed her role as an interim senior administrator of the college, my library director and I had a chat about what my new title should be: acting chief librarian or interim chief librarian. We preferred "interim," which to us conveyed an air of legitimacy, over "acting," which sounded tentative and unserious. The conversation probably lasted only five minutes, but it touched upon essential questions that turned out to define my experience as an "interim" library director.

During my term as interim library director, the fluidity of my roles and the terms of my employment presented overarching challenges. For example, most of the time I never fully assumed the role of director of the library—rather, it was shared between me and the absent director, whose values and priorities influenced every decision I made.

In her excellent book *Becoming a Manager*, essential reading for any new manager, Linda Hill describes one of the fundamental paradoxes of moving into management. Many are promoted to management because they are effective and competent in their functional roles. But successful management requires you to essentially abandon this role and become a "generalist and agenda-setter" and "a network builder [who] gets things done through others" (Hill 2003, 6). This shift requires emotional intelligence, flexibility, and a high tolerance for failure.

For interim managers, the effort required to master these essential skills is significant and might at times seem overwhelming, especially given the temporary nature of the position. I can confirm from experience that, if you continue to perform a significant portion of your previous functions, you will not have the time or energy to manage effectively. In retrospect, I should have worked out a plan with my supervisor before she left to delegate my technical services duties to others. Finally, although I accepted the job not to advance in management permanently but out of a sense of service and curiosity, I needed to do a better job negotiating the terms of my new position. I initially committed to serve six months to a year, and I ended up serving two and a half years. The experience would have been better for me and the entire library staff if we had planned for several possible scenarios.

Points to Consider before Accepting an "Interim" Position

- Make sure you clearly understand the responsibilities you are being asked to undertake—obtain a job description in writing.

- Treat your interim position as you would any new job—make sure you fully understand the terms of employment before you accept an offer, with a starting and end date in writing. Request a plan in writing for renegotiating terms of employment if your interim term turns out to be longer than originally anticipated.

- Delegate your "old" responsibilities as much as possible *before* the interim period begins. Don't attempt to do two full-time jobs for any significant period of time, because you won't do either of them well.

- Request regular meetings with superiors. Keep channels of communication open.

- Be aware of your own motivations before stepping into an interim position. Is it to support the library in a time of need, or to advance your career, or both? Be aware that, if management is not your chosen career path, it will be your focus during your tenure as interim manager. Your other interests and skills will, by necessity, become a secondary priority.

- Every workplace comes with long-standing challenges: limited resources, unique personalities, bureaucracy. Once you become a library director, even interim, these challenges take on a new, magnified dimension.

- Most important: If you really don't want to do it, just say no.

WHAT IS AN INTERIM MANAGER?

I recently looked up *interim* and *acting* in the *Oxford English Dictionary* as they relate to temporary leadership and discovered that the corporate world also prefers *interim* to *acting*. In August 2001, *OED* added this "draft" definition for a business context:

> *interim manager n.*: a person who assumes control temporarily, *esp.* one who takes temporary executive control of a business or other financial concern; a temporary or caretaker manager.

The established definition of *acting* in the context of employment evokes ambiguous relationships and roles:

> *acting, adj.*: Of a person: doing a job nominally shared with another or others who may not have an active role; (also) temporarily doing the job or duties of another. Chiefly preceding a title of office or occupation.

The *OED* definition of *acting*, which evokes a lack of clear boundaries, definitely comes closer to describing my own experience as interim director of my library.

Like the *OED*, the literature of business management and higher education administration fails to define the phenomenon of temporary management clearly. In her study on the dynamics of short-term leadership among business executives, Katherine W. Farquhar describes acting managers as placeholders or caretakers who "emerge through the chain of succession as an immediate response to a leadership vacancy." In contrast, interim leaders tend to serve for longer periods and are often expected to "perform major repairs and make substantial progress toward readying the organization for new leadership" (Farquhar 1995, 54). In my own experience, I started out functioning as a "placeholder." The position was presented to me and the rest of library staff as limited in scope and duration. I was tasked with "keeping the ship afloat" during a limited period of transition.

However, as conditions within the college changed and my term of service was extended twice, I became the de facto library director while the "real" director became more deeply immersed in the upper levels of administration. The lesson learned is that during a period of transition there is really no way to tell how long the interim experience may last, and it may be best to empower and support an interim manager from the start.

The literature of business administration defines temporary leadership narrowly as a short-term period of transition between two permanent executives. But in many institutions, interim or discontinuous management is commonly associated with short-term assignments outside the institution.

In their study on the frequent use of interim leadership in higher educational settings, Erica McWilliam and her colleagues use the term *stopgap resourcing* to describe the practice of using internal resources to fill in until the incumbent returns or a permanent replacement is appointed. A situation with a clear endpoint, such as a sabbatical or parental leave, simplifies interim leadership. Nevertheless, many interim managers, myself included, sign on without knowing when the term will end. Erica McWilliam and colleagues argue that after about a year the idea of interim no longer applies: "One year seems to be the point at which distinctions between 'acting' and 'real' begin to blur, the point at which it is possible to speak of an 'acting' appointment as something other than 'discontinuous management'" (McWilliam et al. 2008, 302).

In my own experience, I noticed a shift after completing a year as interim director. I became more confident and less afraid to make changes. At the same time, I felt increasing impatience as this "interim" situation was beginning to feel permanent.

Uncertainty about duration is inherent in many interim situations, but interim managers are further constrained in decision making by the contingent nature of their roles. The notions of managerial responsibility and authority, which are difficult for all new managers, are especially problematic for interim managers. My decisions as interim manager were influenced by two latent beliefs: that the "real" manager of the library was present on campus and involved in every major decision; and that eventually I would return to the ranks and the people

I was supervising would be my peers again. I experienced the weight of responsibility while feeling that my authority was extremely limited.

McWilliam and colleagues describe interim managers as standing in for the real, but not real: in a position but also "ready to vacate it" (2008, 301). Despite the fact that I never felt like the real director of the library, I knew that my decisions affected the economic lives and daily well-being of everyone from veterans on the verge of retirement to students in their first paying jobs. Douglas Hall, who served as interim dean of his business school, describes it this way: "When it is happening, the interim period does not *feel* interim or temporary. It feels (and is) very real" (1995, 85).

The information landscape is evolving constantly, and a possible consequence of long-term interim leadership is a failure to respond adequately to developments in the field. During the period I served as interim director, many libraries were putting in place strategies to address the increasing popularity of e-readers and the development of mobile technologies in libraries. As interim director, I was very hesitant to make long-term plans for and commit resources to these emerging technologies, in part because my faculty did not agree about their place in libraries. Although we did develop pilot programs, I was unable to motivate reluctant participants to implement real and lasting change.

This situation illustrates a common myth about management in general for new managers: rather than feeling empowered, they tend to feel "hemmed in by interdependencies" (Hill 2007, 51). These interdependencies are heightened for interim managers who rely on their colleagues for support, and who know in the near future that they will be peers once again.

MANAGING YOUR WAY THROUGH CHANGE

Although a hard-and-fast definition of interim management remains elusive, researchers agree that the period between two leaders typically constitutes a critical transition in the life of an organization. And regardless of precipitating circumstances, an interim period is commonly referred to as a crisis. It does not serve any organization to have a disempowered caretaker leader during a period of crisis. Farquhar (1995, 53) optimistically calls an interim period a "strategic window" during a time of change and transition. It is easy to miss these opportunities to reorganize and reevaluate priorities, because during most transitions the emphasis is on completing essential tasks.

In his discussion of his own experience as an acting dean, Hall makes the case that any major change in personnel demands engagement and change: "The acting period presents itself as a crisis which can facilitate major changes [and] suggests a much more active role for the acting leader than the terms acting or interim might indicate" (1995, 84). He contends that success during an interim period demands constructive involvement from all levels of an organization, not just from the temporarily empowered manger. Not only is an interim period a time of rapid change, but with constructive support the tenure of an interim manager can lead to growth and positive change.

As is typical with any change in leadership, the transition from permanent to interim director of my library constituted a period of adjustment for everyone. We were reluctant to let go of past relationships with the director, and we shared the expectation that all would return to normal again soon. The transfer of power was tentative and half-hearted on both sides.

In retrospect, I believe that in holding onto the past I missed opportunities not only to strengthen my management skills but also to effect positive change in my library. These missed opportunities come as no surprise; periods of interim leadership typically begin without adequate planning because either they are precipitated by sudden events or nobody believes they will last long. The players are not thinking about "strategic windows," merely trying to find workable and temporary solutions to unexpected changes.

AN OPPORTUNITY TO DEVELOP PROFESSIONALLY

As is often the case with challenging experiences, the term of an interim manager provides a shift in perspective that proves invaluable in the long run—whether you end up permanently in the interim position or return to your old position. The most valuable lessons I learned related to skills needed to work effectively with people.

Probably the simplest lesson is the power of asking for what you want. You are much more likely to get what you want if you make your needs known—not in a pushy or confrontational manner, but simply and directly. As a manager, I was directly involved in allocating all kinds of resources, from vacation days to funds for supplies to professional advice. The people most likely to get what they wanted were those who asked—obvious perhaps, but a lesson I had never fully understood before I controlled library resources.

A more difficult experience was learning how to shift from developing relationships with like-minded colleagues to building a strong team. I have always enjoyed productive relationships with a number of colleagues, which is probably one of the reasons I was asked to serve as interim director. Once you are managing a complex organization, though, you need to focus not just on relationships you find personally or professionally satisfying but on building a strong and productive team. "The new manager must figure out how to harness the power of a team. Simply focusing on one-to-one relationships with members of the team can undermine that process" (Hill 2003, 54). This takes skills in negotiation and consensus building and can be extremely demanding. Still, it's worth the effort. Even after the interim term is over, team-building skills will improve the quality of your work life and make you a more effective professional. The truth is that you can't always choose who you have on your team.

Tips for a Successful "Interim" Experience

- Your best allies are fellow librarians and library workers. Everyone has a stake in the library running well, and they are your best source of good advice and support.

- Team building, rather than one-to-one relationship building, should be a management priority.

- Seek out mentors; find experienced and trusted managers within and beyond your institution.

- Take advantage of the opportunity to meet new people and establish professional relationships outside your usual sphere of activity.

- Don't expect perfection from yourself or anyone else. There is nothing wrong with not knowing how to do something.

- Use this change in perspective to reflect on your career goals. Do you want to manage at this level? Do you see other roles that look interesting to you as possible future directions for your own career?

- Document your decisions and maintain good records to pass along to your successor, possibly your new supervisor.

- Choose an initiative or project you feel strongly about and implement it. Make your mark in a way that benefits the library beyond your interim term.

- If there is a change in leadership at higher levels, make sure the new administration is aware of your status as interim.

- Maintain your sense of humor. You are going to make lots of mistakes, but you'll feel better if you can laugh about them.

NOT QUITE BACK TO WHERE I STARTED

Interim managers are the ultimate "middle managers." They are often managing in the middle of an institutional hierarchy and are, by definition, managing between "permanent" terms of leadership. Their responsibilities are difficult to define, and their arrival is frequently precipitated by a sudden change or crisis.

Although my experience as an interim library director brought daily challenges and headaches, it was a time of tremendous personal and professional growth. It provided an opportunity to learn a great deal about my institution and work with people across the college on projects that were well beyond my usual scope of activity.

Finally, and most important, I came to appreciate even more the strengths, skills, and generosity of my colleagues in the library.

REFERENCES

Farquhar, Katherine W. 1995. "Not Just Understudies: The Dynamics of Short-Term Leadership." *Human Resource Management* 34 (1): 51–70.

Hall, Douglas T. 1995. "Unplanned Executive Transitions and the Dance of the Subidentities." *Human Resource Management* 34 (1): 71–92.

Hill, Linda A. 2003. *Becoming a Manager: How New Managers Master the Challenges of Leadership.* Boston: Harvard Business School Press.

———. 2007. "Becoming the Boss." *Harvard Business Review* 85 (1): 48–56.

McWilliam, Erica, Ruth Bridgstock, Alan Lawson, Terry Evans, and Peter Taylor. 2008 "Who's Dean Today? Acting and Interim Management as Paradoxes of the Contemporary University." *Journal of Higher Education Policy and Management* 30 (3): 297–307.

34

WORKING WITH THE PLATEAUED EMPLOYEE

JANET BUTLER MUNCH

LIBRARY MIDDLE MANAGERS ARE CENTRAL TO THE SUPERVISION, GUIDANCE, AND support of librarians working in their divisions. They know the strengths and capabilities of those reporting to them and are in the best position to observe their daily work closely. Inevitably, every middle manager needs to recognize the signs of plateauing, either in themselves or in those reporting to them. Even for competent, productive employees, plateauing may take the form of diminished enthusiasm for one's job, feelings of stagnation—being in a rut with no options—or even frustration with oneself.

There are only a limited number of positions one can aspire to in the library's upper hierarchical pyramid. This reality can leave staff with a sense of having nowhere to go. Even with a mastery of their daily work, librarians performing the same job for several years can grow bored with the routines. Sameness and lack of challenges can sap one's motivation and zest for work. The resulting plateauing can be a wake-up call that change or serious reflection is needed. Embracing the plateauing experience gives one the opportunity to pause, destress, and think about what one wants in one's professional life and how those decisions would impact one's work/life balance issues. Plateauing is essentially a stage in one's growth or development, not an endpoint in itself.

In an uncertain economy, it is in the best interest of libraries to invest in their most valuable resource—the people they employ. Libraries can ill afford to ignore the challenges of plateauing and necessity of sensitizing supervisors to employees' needs for continual development and sense of importance to the team. If librarians are to feel invested and engaged in their positions, then they need to recognize that what they do is significant. They also should have some autonomy to carry out their duties successfully.

ROLE OF THE MIDDLE MANAGER

Middle managers can do a great deal to mitigate some of the less positive aspects of plateauing of professionals. They interact with upper management and peers who manage other individual library units. Consequently, they have a broad view of overall library operations, enabling them to put the work of individuals reporting to them into a wider organizational context. Middle managers are the organizational linchpin in communicating the needs and concerns of their library unit upward and in interpreting the concerns of management back to the unit.

The culture of the individual library unit is strongly influenced by the supervising middle manager. This individual must be a good professional role model, capable of inspiring others and charting the goals of the unit. The middle manager must guard against judging others too quickly, making assumptions, or marginalizing individual employees. When it is recognized that all can contribute, the unit thrives in a climate of inclusion. With the middle manager's guidance, differing styles can be reconciled and accommodated.

Does the middle manager empower employees to do their jobs or are they demotivated through micromanagement? Librarians want to engage with their work, have some autonomy, and feel the intrinsic reward of knowing they are trusted to do their best. Does the middle manager encourage staff to experiment, take risks, or undertake new library initiatives? Is their good work appreciated or given recognition?

The middle manager needs to listen to unit librarians to determine root causes of problems. If the workload is rising in response to lost positions, can employee frustration be redirected into positive outcomes like job restructuring or reconsideration of overly ambitious or less valuable goals? Are there unit or cross-unit projects that would foster learning, build new skills, tap employee creativity, or provide individuals with more visibility? If more training is needed to clear career obstacles, what possibilities are available within the library or through cooperating institutions? Can the quality of work life be improved through options like flextime or telecommuting? Good middle manager supervisors need to know their organization's resources or be willing to explore such possibilities with upper administration in the interest of their employees.

Finally, does the supervising middle manager trivialize or seriously embrace her role in helping to encourage employee development? Does the middle manager convey her availability to meet with or strategize with those who may be struggling with their plateaued state? Are employees encouraged to think through their career goals and needs?

Other employees may be content in their plateaued state and be either unwilling or unable to assume new opportunities because of personal concerns (e.g., eldercare, health) or other commitments (volunteer work). In reports on the changing nature of the workforce, the New York–based Families and Work Institute found that fewer employees are aspiring to positions of responsibility, family and work balance are receiving greater priority, and there is less of a willingness to make the kinds

of sacrifices in personal lives than has been the case in the past. Employees also object to the stress and negative spillover caused by communication technologies, blurring the boundaries between work and nonwork hours (Knowledge@Wharton 2007). The dilemma for middle managers will increasingly be this: How will individual needs for greater work-life balance be validated and accommodated in the workplace?

Observations for Plateaued Employees

- Plateaued employees are encouraged to work with their middle manager supervisors. It is in the interest of the supervisor and the work unit to help employees understand their situations and provide support.

- Employees need to understand that plateauing is hardly an unusual situation and in fact should be anticipated at one or more points in one's career. Others have dealt with the same phenomenon.

- Plateauing presents an opportunity to stop and take stock. Stepping away from the library for a few hours or even a short vacation could put work in perspective and provide time to consider what one wants and needs.

- One can remain in a plateaued state—moving neither backward nor forward—but must ask whether staying in place and avoiding challenge promotes personal satisfaction.

- Does desire for security outweigh the possible pain of the plateaued state?

- One does not have to change jobs to grow and revitalize one's career. Working smarter or faster can be a personal challenge with its own satisfactions.

- Librarianship requires continual learning and a curious state of mind. This mandate in itself can be stimulating, and working with other energetic, committed professionals can create a synergistic environment.

- When the upward climb in the library is no longer possible or even desired, a lateral move or assumption of related duties could provide the opportunity to learn new things or further develop skills.

- It takes a certain courage to take on new challenges, but will anyone die or go bankrupt if you try something new or take a risk at work?

- Recognize that everything may not go as desired and there may be disappointments along the way. By making an effort, though, you always learn new lessons and grow.

- Replace passivity or inertia with positive action. Read the professional literature. Subscribe to electronic bulletin boards of interest. Be open to diverse experiences, meet and collaborate with others—even outside librarianship.

- Adopt a "can-do" attitude. Move out of your comfort zone. Volunteer for committee work, take a leadership position, make a presentation, write a grant, prepare a manuscript for submission.

- Join a professional association. Attend conferences. Get to know other colleagues and visit their libraries.

- Marrying the job or defining yourself in terms of your work is unhealthy. You are a lot more than your job.

- Supportive family, friends, and outside interests bring balance to one's life and help promote personal resilience in the work environment.

- Ultimately, every employee must define what success means to them and take responsibility for their own attitudes and career development.

WHEN TO MOVE ON

Sometimes people who think they have plateaued are simply in the wrong job. Life conditions may force them to stay in place. It is not easy to pick up and move when children are still in school, elderly parents need care, the housing market is weak, or one has strong community ties. Moving to a new locale, where one has no friends or family, can be a frightening prospect for many. For others, personal situations may allow greater flexibility, and the opportunity to move on may be irresistible. Before changing positions, however, it could be helpful to talk with one's supervisor and clarify options. Nevertheless, it is the employee who must squarely confront the hard questions:

- Is your current job the wrong fit for you?

- Do you feel out of sync with your current library's culture or mission?

- Are there insufficient opportunities to use your skill set where you are?

- Are you unhappy and no longer want to work where you are now?

CONCLUSIONS

Whether one is still relatively new to librarianship or has been a practitioner in the field for many years, it is important to remain adaptable to change and open to learning. Just as libraries are constantly evolving, librarians must continuously redefine themselves to meet the needs of their users and their own career goals. Plateaued employees choose their attitudes toward work and need to make constructive, self-enhancing decisions if they are to feel fulfilled and retain possibilities for mobility. They need to be willing to stretch and rediscover a sense of commitment to their work, even if it means assuming different responsibilities or changing positions.

It may take time to arrive at decisions on how to proceed, but a balanced work and personal life can help plateaued librarians put their situation into context. Discussions with the middle manager and other colleagues can help plateaued employees remember why they entered our service profession in the first place. Librarians need to think about the many ways their work touches the lives of users. They may not always be aware of the extent of their influence or learn the direct impact of their work. Librarians can find intrinsic satisfaction in helping people address their immediate information needs and knowing their efforts promote lifelong learning and facilitate engagement with community resources. Successful human interactions with patrons remotivate librarians to give the best of themselves as they represent their libraries. Self-realization of the value of their service to others ultimately drives librarians' commitment to their work and profession.

REFERENCE

Knowledge@Wharton. 2007. "Plateauing: Redefining Success at Work." In Wharton on Managing Your Career. *The Work/Life Balance* 1: 4–9. http://executiveeducation.wharton.upenn.edu/resources/upload/career-management-work-life-balance.pdf.

35

TAKING RISKS AND LETTING GO, CREATING AND COACHING TEAMS

An Interview with John Lubans

J OHN LUBANS JR. WRITES AND TEACHES ABOUT LIBRARY LEADERSHIP AND TEAM-work. He is author of *Leading from the Middle and Other Contrarian Essays on Library Leadership* (Libraries Unlimited, 2010) and is well known in the library community for his seminal work in the area of bibliographic instruction. His career includes senior administrative posts at large research libraries, most recently as deputy university librarian. He was also visiting professor at the School of Library and Information Sciences at North Carolina Central University for twenty years. We sat down with John to discuss teamwork, team building, and the challenges of leading team-based efforts from the middle.

From your book, *Leading From the Middle,* it seems like teams and teamwork in libraries are subjects central to your thinking. How did that become something you're a believer in?

I've always felt that way, though I started off as a pretty traditional manager in the sense of "I'm the supervisor, I'm the boss, I have to give you direction." A major event in my career occurred at Duke when I was made head of technical services and given goals to eliminate backlogs and make a 15 percent reduction in the staffing budget. I struggled deciding whether to take the position, but then realized why the director asked me: I wasn't an expert. I wasn't going to try, solo, to fix the department's problems.

On my first day, I went in and said, "I know very little about what you do. I need your help. Here are things we have to do." In a matter of a day or two, they came back to me with a four- or five-page list of ideas they'd had for many years that had been ignored and put aside because they hadn't come from "the boss." From that point on, I realized that asking for help from the people with whom I worked wasn't a bad idea.

How would you translate this into other middle management situations, where you have the responsibility to have certain deliverables and a time line by which to deliver them, but you don't want to be a micromanager or dominate the group? What are the virtues of not dominating?

The benefit of teams is that everyone is allowed—indeed, expected—to have an opinion. People are allowed to speak up, and they often have wonderful insights. There is a moment of silence when the boss is not talking that allows people to feel they have permission to say something. But people's natural inclination is to never be first, to always hold back. When the boss lets go, it can really invite very interesting ideas from people who would normally be reluctant to say anything. It comes with practice, though. And it's not always going to work out. If you're not able to let go, there's no way you're going to have a really effective team.

As a middle manager who's trying to create teams and trying to let go a little bit by not giving orders, that in itself is a risk. But there are other kinds of risk: good risks and bad risks, and things that are going to keep you challenged.

You're taking a chance. If your organization allows you to experiment and take those kinds of chances, there are always risks because you might fail. But are you held unreasonably responsible by your boss, or does your boss understand that you're trying something out? If you have a motivated group of professionals who have been stymied and repressed, and you're just turning them loose, that could look like a risk.

But it's less of a risk than trying to work with a mix of people, some of whom are very content with the way things are and some of whom who really want to do things differently. There's a greater risk there for failure. If you turn people loose who already have good ideas, failure is less likely. Of course, you can have real failure when you're too idealistic and think any group can be turned loose. It's not the case. They may lack skills; they may lack support; they may lack confidence. It may take much longer, or it may never happen because they're quite content carrying out directions, doing the job—they're happy with it. There are people like that, and they often do a good job. You don't fire them. In libraries we're given a set of employees; we inherit them. It's not like you're coming in with a new group, each person handpicked by you.

There is a tendency nowadays to look for and hire collaborators, people with a collaborative spirit that's genuine, and then build on those people. But if you've got an "old guard," and they don't want to change and don't see any reason to change, and they're doing the job fairly well, then maybe they need to be left alone.

Those who don't want to be a part of the team probably shouldn't be part of the team?

They probably shouldn't. Most people in a library, including support staff, are smart people, but they often have a long history of people telling them what to do. But if you're genuine about letting go and are expecting them to come forward and offer ideas, and they see that they will be safe, not slammed or ridiculed, some will come forward.

But if this doesn't work, it's best to focus on groups that want to be a team, that want to try out what this means, rather than mandate "Everyone is going to do this." A library I observed tried this latter approach in their cataloging division and didn't do it terribly well. They didn't define the leadership and other roles, just took turns leading the department, and many weren't happy. Their productivity was the same. If you're not going to set higher goals and achieve something more, then what's the point?

I'm not saying people have to work longer or harder—just that we can learn from our mistakes and become more productive through teams.

Do you find that characteristic of teams—that they can help each other learn?

Yes, effective teams do this. Effective teams can achieve greater productivity because the group intelligence is greater than the individual. Team members can learn from each other by buying into a goal that they set mutually. Gail Goestenkors, former women's basketball coach at Duke University, started out by setting the goals for her team, like a boss would set goals for employees. She stopped doing that. The goals the team set themselves were higher. My experience is that team goals are always higher than I would set. That's letting go.

Of course, there are poorly functioning teams that set a lower goal. You have to train all participants about what it means to be part of a team, what constitutes an effective team. I have found that we underestimate the amount of time and training teams require to become effective. But there's a resistance to training and the investment it takes.

And it's an investment on every member of the team's part?

Yes. But if the group doesn't want it, then it's probably not going to happen. Some of my teams that worked really well were kind of accidental. As I look back, I realize what they had, and I can compare those elements to team research findings. There was commitment to achieving something great, and everyone was working. There was a greater understanding of what they were about. There was more than one individual telling them how to do it.

The team approach seems to require a lot of nurturing.

Nurturing, and also intervention. If things aren't working, you have to intervene. I've had teams who really believed I'd given them permission to go off by themselves and never talked to me. These kinds of teams tend to do far less than they're able to do.

One of the benefits of teams is that they have a manager who's not working that closely with them who can give an objective viewpoint. We often fail to define empowerment for teams. What does it mean to be empowered? Your manager still has a role.

So, when you create a team, you have to be very clear about what the roles and responsibilities of the team members are, what the objectives are?

And that they report to somebody, that there is accountability—they aren't dictated to, but there is accountability. And if they're clever and want to get things done, then they should be including you, at least informing you, so you can offer insights and support. Sometimes there can be a lack of respect for the supervisor who is not doing the actual work: "How could someone like a boss know to do anything better or differently?" There becomes a disdain for somebody outside the group. And that's a mistake.

So, you can create a team, and they can go rogue in some way?

Yes. And that's when you have to intervene. There is the fundamental question, how do we rejuvenate and keep teams highly effective? There also has to be the organi-

zational structure to sustain it, and you have to have the skills to intervene with a team that is floundering. Just saying that you're available if people have issues is not enough. No one will ask you. How does someone feel comfortable enough to ask a boss or supervisor to intervene? That's difficult.

You have to actively check in with the team?

Yes. But it can be strange if you try to sit in on the team's work. You can become the elephant in the room. That's not checking in.

You've written about how the Orpheus Ensemble is constantly challenging itself with new pieces, more ambitious pieces that demand the performers continue to grow. How do you do that in the workplace?

We need to step back, reflect, and ask ourselves, "Where have we been? Where are we? Where do we want to be and how do we get there? What are we dreaming about?" Or when we finish a project, we ask ourselves, "How did it go? How could it have been better?" That's where we learn. And that's also the trigger for the next phase, because there's always work to be done. If there's pressure of a reduced budget, you have to talk about that and figure it out. "What are we going to do next?" is a very difficult question to ask when you're successful. That's where the manager has a role to push that question. Staff can do a great job and then fall into a slump. The manager has to have almost a counseling role.

Counsel other people to stay refreshed and engaged?

Yes, or simply find out what's going on. Particularly when you've reached a plateau, or when you have dysfunctional team members, you have to be able to explore it. You have to take action. Sometimes it can be someone else on the team who can do this. It doesn't always have to be you.

WHAT IS A TEAM?

A team is a small number of people of complementary skills who are committed to a common purpose, set of performance goals, and approach for which they hold themselves mutually accountable

—Katzenbach and Smith,
"The Discipline of Teams"

Since their seminal *Harvard Business Review* article on teams and teamwork, "The Discipline of Teams" appeared (vol. 71, no. 2), Jon R. Katzenbach and Douglas K. Smith have gone on to produce numerous books on the subject as team-based work has become more and more ubiquitous in businesses including libraries. Having a clear sense of what a team is and how it best functions is essential for middle management success.

According to Katzenbach and Smith, there are three general kinds of teams:

Teams that recommend things—"task forces, project groups, and audit, quality, and safety groups asked to study and solve particular problems."

Teams that make or do things—"frontline" teams responsible for core products and services or for developing new products or services.

Teams that run things—teams that are "in charge of" others or "oversee some business, ongoing program, or significant functional activity."

Each kind of team has its own needs and challenges. Katzenbach and Smith provide advice for managers on how to guide such teams toward success. But whatever kind of teams they are, Katzenbach and Smith suggest that all successful ones have "shared leadership roles," "individual and mutual accountability," "specific team purpose that the team itself delivers," and "collective work products." They must also "[encourage] open-ended discussion and active problem solving meetings," "measure performance directly by assessing collective work-products," and "[discuss, decide, and do] real work together."

In other words, teams translate for themselves "broad directives" from above into team-defined performance objectives, then hold themselves accountable for working together to meet them. To do this effectively, teams must be made up of individuals—usually between two and twenty-five people—who possess the kind of skills and talents needed for self-directed, collaborative work:

Technical or functional expertise—practical or intellectual skills that equip team members to perform the concrete work required to fulfill the directive.

Problem-solving and decision-making skills—cognitive skills that allow team members to make smart "decisions about how to proceed" as the work progresses and becomes more complex.

Interpersonal skills—communication skills that allow team members to resolve conflicts constructively, a willingness for "risk taking," being able to offer "helpful criticism, " being able to look at situations objectively, being able to give others "the benefit of the doubt," and a willingness to "recognize the interests and achievements of others."

Teams have to have members with a balance of both practical and interpersonal skills—technical ability and emotional intelligence. Teams of poor communicators with technical prowess and teams of good communicators without practical know-how are both likely to fail.

Based on their extensive observation of teams, Katzenbach and Smith note several things successful teams do characteristically:

- Establish urgency, demanding performance standards and direction
- Select members for skill and potential, not personality
- Pay particular attention to first meetings and actions
- Set some clear rules of behavior
- Set and seize upon a few immediate performance-oriented tasks and goals
- Challenge themselves regularly with fresh facts and information
- Spend lots of time together
- Exploit the power of positive feedback, recognition, and reward

It seems like teams can have a life cycle in some way where there's an energy, a spirit, a direction that can evaporate.

One reason for that is that we avoid being honest with each other—the so-called storming phase of group development—we don't talk about our concerns with each other. Storming is very difficult. Most teams I've observed skip that step. We may be comfortable, but we really don't trust each other. We trust each other so far. Or if we're lucky, as I've been at times, everybody feels good about each other, they're friendly, they seem to have *simpatico.* Then it's okay, but that's accidental.

It does seem accidental. Can you create that kind of vibe? Or is it just something that is or isn't in some sense? If you're developing a team and there isn't that feeling of trust and honesty, can it be generated or created?

It can happen, but you have to be paying a lot of attention to everything, and there has to be a lot of hand holding and clarification, there may be hurt feelings, there has to be an openness. Once that happens, you may achieve something, but if you hold back—if you can't be honest with each other—then I don't see how a team can be effective. You may get the job done, but you could've done it differently and a whole lot better.

What are the barriers to honesty incommunication? Why do we put up that defense? Why do we take offense?

We avoid conflict. We don't want to hurt people's feelings. But I think there's something more sinister than that. We don't really want to expose ourselves, we don't want to be blamed for someone's hurt feelings. And so we accommodate, we compromise, we postpone, and we hope for the best instead of articulating our differences.

Candor takes practice. The skilled manager does not avoid, and our tendency is to avoid.

If you are middle management and team building, if there are conflicts or problems or stalls, you have to make it clear and verbalize everything?

Yes, you have demonstrate it. If I look at myself, I would be more verbal than I was as an assistant director. I figured, "It's obvious. We've got to do this." It's not obvious when you're in teams. A big lesson. What's obvious to you is not necessarily obvious to others.

And you can't just sit there. If you have two people who despise each other, you have to address that eventually, and if you don't address it, you have a dysfunctional team and you've failed to do your job. I see this as a very important role for the manager. You have to go out and become more of a coach.

So, you're not just creating a team, you're coaching the team?

You should be seen as a coach, and you should be respected. The best coaches are respected by the team, and their input is valued. This is true of the best teams made up of the best people. Again, in libraries we inherit a mixed bag, so there may be other agendas that people have. They may resent managers. But if you can put together some good strong people, then the manager's role really is coaching. But in an effective way. It's not just cheerleading, although it's a lot of fun to be a cheerleader. There are some losses, after all—you can't win every game. What do you do with the losses?

I've studied leaders like Simone Young, the conductor. She's very much in the tradition, but she's seen as more of a consulting kind of conductor. While she's directing a rehearsal, she's fully in charge, yet she's very open to hearing from the musicians, and she creates an atmosphere where if things don't go right, that's okay because rehearsal is about "hearing it again," as she says. It's an opportunity to get better, not to condemn someone. I have also seen her—during a rehearsal of a new contemporary orchestral piece—apologize to the group when she has screwed up. Imagine that! Her doing that sets the tone and makes a positive difference in how the musicians behave in the rehearsal.

Is the music better? Yes, I think it is.

ANNE C. BARNHART became head of instructional services at the University of West Georgia in 2009. Previously she was librarian for Latin American and Iberian Studies, Chicana/o Studies, and Religious Studies at the University of California-Santa Barbara. Anne received her MS in Library and Information Sciences from the University of Illinois at Urbana-Champaign, where she currently teaches an online collection development class. She earned her MA in both religious studies and Latin American and Caribbean studies from Indiana University.

ROBERT BARR is a branch manager for Johnson County (Kansas) Library, supervising its largest branch, with twenty-seven staff members and a highly circulating collection. He enjoys the psychology behind performance management and is doing his best to contribute to a fun, fair, and enjoyable workplace.

JOE C. CLARK is a librarian with nearly a decade of middle management experience in academic libraries. He served as head of library media and the slide library at University of Maryland–Baltimore County for seven years, supervising three staff and many students. He is now head of the Performing Arts Library at Kent State University, where he supervises both professional and paraprofessional staff.

KRISTINE CONDIC has been reference coordinator for five years at Kresge Library, Oakland University, Rochester, Michigan. She has served as electronic resources coordinator for more than twenty years and as a reference librarian for almost thirty years. She holds a second master's degree in training and development.

CEES-JAN DE JONG is access services coordinator at the University of Alberta, responsible for interlibrary loan, circulation, stacks maintenance, shelving, and the book and record depository. Before arriving at Alberta in 2009, he worked as access and reference services coordinator at the University of Winnipeg. CJ has a BA in psychology from the University of Calgary and received his MLIS from the University of Alberta in 2005. Currently managing a staff of more than thirty people, he has numerous opportunities to apply management skills he has picked up over the years.

ROBIN L. EWING is access services coordinator and associate professor at St. Cloud State University in Minnesota. She earned her MLIS at the University of Oklahoma in 2001. Her research interests include information literacy assessment, Web 2.0, and leadership.

AMANDA LEA FOLK has been a librarian since 2006, after receiving her MLIS from the University of Pittsburgh. In addition to serving as a collection development librarian, she has been a middle manager at both public and academic libraries. She is currently reference/public services librarian at the University of Pittsburgh–Greensburg, a position that allows her happily to manage from the middle.

JEFFREY A. FRANKS, associate professor and head of reference at Bierce Library, University of Akron, since 1995, obtained his MLS from Kent State University. His publications have appeared in *Library Management Tips That Work* (ALA), *E-JASL*, *Reference Librarian*, *Journal of Educational Media*, and *Library Science*. Jeffrey's publications reflect his acute interest in library management practices, innovative reference models, and learning commons development at the University of Akron.

CURT FRIEHS has worked in academic and public library settings. He has presented at ALA's Reference Research Forum, Library and Information Technology Association Annual Forum, and local library conferences. In addition, he wrote a monthly newspaper column for the *Wyandotte Daily News*. He has written for *Journal of Business and Finance Librarianship* as well as *Journal of Web Librarianship*. His research interests primarily focus on finding creative and pragmatic solutions to common library issues.

BERNADINE GOLDMAN is assistant library manager in the Los Alamos County Library System, New Mexico. She earned her MLS degree at the University of British Columbia and Master of Public Administration at the University of New Mexico. In a long career in public and academic libraries, she has served as head cataloger, interlibrary loan librarian, children's librarian, branch manager, and reference and information services manager before accepting her current position in 2007.

KEITH PHELAN GORMAN is assistant head of special collections and university archives, University Libraries, University of North Carolina–Greensboro. He has supervised students, volunteers, paraprofessionals, curators, and librarians in a number of different library, academic, and museum settings. Keith's current research interests lie in special collections engagement, blended librarians and instruction, and the role of archives in shaping a community's shared memory. He received a PhD in history from the University of Wisconsin–Madison. After ten years of teaching, Keith obtained an MLS from Simmons College in 2004.

SAMANTHA SCHMEHL HINES received her MS in Library and Information Science from the University of Illinois at Urbana-Champaign in 2003. She has worked as a cataloger for the National Czech and Slovak Museum and Library in Cedar Rapids, Iowa, and as a reference librarian at Kirkwood Community College in Iowa City. In 2004 she was hired by the Mansfield Library at the University of Montana–Missoula and is currently distance education coordinator and social science librarian. She is author of *Productivity for Librarians* (Chados, 2010).

GAYLE HORNADAY received her MLS from the University of Illinois at Urbana-Champaign in 1977. She has been a public librarian for more than thirty years, working as a reference librarian in Winnemucca, Nevada, and Findlay, Ohio, as well as in the Milwaukee area. Since 1994 she has been employed at the Henderson Libraries in Nevada, where she has served as assistant director since 1996.

LOUIS HOWLEY is a librarian at the Cholla Library of the Phoenix Public Library. He received his BA in philosophy from Arizona State University and MLS from the University of Arizona. He has served as secretary and chair of the Library Technology Interest Group of Arizona Library Association and as secretary of the Arizona Chapter of the Special Libraries Association. For nineteen years Louis has written the column "On the PL Road" for the Arizona Library Association Newsletter and has visited more than 180 libraries in the state for the column.

NANCY J. KRESS is head of the Access and Delivery Services Department at the University of Nevada–Las Vegas. She is responsible for services and management associated with borrowing, lending, and storing library materials. Her research includes business process and lean principles applied to library operations and middle management. She holds an MLIS from the University of Illinois and Certificate in Process Management and Improvement from the University of Chicago Graham School.

MELISSA LANING has a BA in sociology from Boston University and received her MSLS from the University of Michigan. She has held various positions at the University of Louisville Libraries over the past three decades and currently serves as associate dean for assessment, personnel, and research. She previously held library positions at George Washington University's Gelman Library and at Xavier University in Cincinnati.

JOHN LUBANS JR. writes and teaches about library leadership and teamwork. He is author of *Leading from the Middle and Other Contrarian Essays on Library Leadership* (Libraries Unlimited, 2010). His career includes senior administrative posts at large research libraries, most recently as deputy university librarian. For two decades he was visiting professor at the School of Library and Information Sciences at North Carolina Central University. He holds master's degrees in library science from the University of Michigan and in public administration from the University of Houston.

DOROTHY A. MAYS is head of public services at Olin Library, Rollins College. She is liaison to the Crummer Graduate School of Business.

JANET BUTLER MUNCH is associate professor and special collections librarian at Lehman College, City University of New York. She holds a BA in history from Mercy College, MLS from Pratt Institute, and DLS from

Columbia University. She has sustained a long interest in staff development issues for librarians and chaired the Professional Development Committee of the Library Association of the City University of New York.

NEAL NIXON currently serves as director of Kornhauser Health Sciences Library of the University of Louisville, where he has worked for nearly thirty years in various capacities. He has also been an adjunct faculty member in the library schools of both Indiana University and the University of Kentucky. Neal has a BA in communications from the University of Kentucky, MA in telecommunications from Michigan State University, and MALS from the University of Kentucky.

ELIZABETH O'BRIEN received her MBA from Schulich School of Business at York University in Toronto in 2009. She has been a middle manager at the CNIB Library for the Blind and later at the University of Toronto's Scarborough Library. Currently Elizabeth is Scarborough Library's coordinator of library systems, which includes IT coordination, evaluation and assessment activities, and project management.

BARBARA PETERSOHN has more than twenty years' experience working in different types of libraries and has managed public services staff in all these settings. For the past ten years she has supervised an extended public service point for Georgia State University, where she recently assumed the position of digital projects manager. In addition to her MLS, she earned an MSIT in instructional design and technology. Barbara has published articles on teaching the research process, peer review for librarians, and use of educational technologies in library instruction. She served on the Instruction section's Research and Scholarship Committee of ACRL and is currently chair of Georgia Library Association's Scholarship Committee.

KATHRYN BOCK PLUNKETT is digital information literacy librarian at Southeastern Oklahoma State University in Durant. She serves as chair of the MPLA Communications Committee and recently participated in the MPLA Leadership Institute and Oklahoma Library Association's Gold Leadership Institute. She was named OLA's Outstanding New Librarian for 2010.

MARIE L. RADFORD is associate professor and chair of the Department of Information and Library Studies at Rutgers University School of Communication and Information. Her PhD is from Rutgers University and MSIS from Syracuse University. Her latest books include *Leading the Reference Renaissance* (Neal-Schuman, 2012); *Reference Renaissance: Current and Future Trends*, co-

edited with R. D. Lankes (Neal-Schuman, 2010); and *Conducting the Reference Interview* (Neal-Schuman, 2009), coauthored with C. S. Ross and K. Nilsen. Her research interests are interpersonal communication aspects of information services (both traditional and virtual), evaluation of e-services, academic libraries, nonverbal communication, cultural studies, and media stereotypes of librarians.

JENNIFER ROWLEY is professor in information and communications in the Department of Information and Communications, Manchester Metropolitan University, UK. Her extensive research and publication activities cover information management, knowledge management, e-business, and related disciplines. Key books include *Being an Information Innovator* (Facet, 2011); *Leadership: The Challenge for the Information Profession* (with S. Roberts, Facet, 2008); *Organizing Knowledge*, 4th ed. (with R. J. Hartley, Ashgate, 2008); *E-Business: Principles and Practice* (Palgrave, 2002); and *Information Marketing*, 2nd ed. (Ashgate, 2006). She is editor of *Journal of Further and Higher Education.*

MAUREEN DIANA SASSO is director of the Information Services Division of Gumberg Library at Duquesne University, where she manages the public service departments. She cochairs the Information Literacy Steering Committee and coordinated the team that developed the required core freshman research course. She is a past president of the Western Pennsylvania/ West Virginia Chapter of ACRL.

DEBBIE SCHACHTER is director of learning resources at Douglas College in British Columbia, Canada. She was recently elected chapter cabinet-chair of the Special Libraries Association and is a member of the OCLC Global Council. Debbie has experience managing and supervising staff in special, nonprofit, public, and academic library environments. She writes a regular column on library management in SLA's *Information Outlook.*

ALLISON SLOAN has worked as senior library associate at Reading Public Library in Massachusetts for more than twenty years. Honored by *Library Journal* as Paralibrarian of the Year (2010), she serves as chairperson of the Massachusetts Library Association's Paralibrarian section. Allison has a BA from Boston University.

SALLY DECKER SMITH spent her entire thirty-year career in public libraries, more than half in middle management. She is currently enjoying a second career as a public library consultant in the area of staff development.

NICOLE SUMP-CRETHAR is assistant professor in digital library services at Oklahoma State University. She currently serves as chair of the Information Technology Roundtable of the Oklahoma Library Association. She was previously information technology librarian at Oro Valley Public Library in Arizona.

ELISABETH TAPPEINER is assistant professor and collection development librarian at Hostos Community College, City University of New York. She was interim library director for more than two years.

LIZA WEISBROD has been microforms and government documents librarian and music librarian at Auburn University for five years. She holds an MSLIS from the University of Illinois at Urbana-Champaign, BM from the University of Missouri–Columbia, and MM from the University of Notre Dame. She has worked in both reference and technical services and served in various supervisory capacities along the way.

JOE M. WILLIAMS is head of access services, University Libraries at the University of North Carolina–Greensboro. He received his MSLS in 2000 from the University of North Carolina–Chapel Hill. Joe has managed students, paraprofessionals, professional librarians, and IT staff in several academic libraries and public services positions. His current interests include planning and assessment of learning spaces, public services design, new technologies, scholarly communication and collaboration, and strategic planning.

W

Wagner, Rodd, 27
Walter, Scott, 137
wants versus needs, 39
Weber, Max, 41–42
Weisbrod, Liza, 97–100
Wentling, Rose Mary, 16
Williams, Joe M., 135–140
willpower, procrastination and, 67–69
Wilson, Ian, 139
Winning with Difficult People (Bell and Smith), 28
Wood, Elizabeth J., 42

Work Breakdown Structure, 18
work environment
    behavior engineering model on, 88–90
    books on, 136
    ensuring positive, 80–81
    entrepreneurial leaders and, 131
    procrastination and, 68–69
work roles and skills, 8–9, 155–157
    See also specific roles and skills
work samples (performance improvement toolkit), 90–91
workflow charts, 19

"Workforce Issues in Library and Information Science" (Marshall et al.), 136
Working for You Isn't Working for Me (Crowley and Elster), 107

Y

Yang, Jixia, 105
Yates, Martin, 31
Young, Simone, 163

You may also be interested in

LIBRARY MANAGEMENT TIPS THAT WORK

Carol Smallwood

There's no shortage of library management books out there—but how many of them actually tackle the little details of day-to-day management, the hard-to-categorize things that slip through the cracks of a larger handbook? *Library Management Tips that Work* does exactly that, addressing dozens of such issues facing library managers.

ISBN: 978-0-8389-1121-1
208 PAGES / 6" x 9"

SMALL PUBLIC LIBRARY MANAGEMENT

JANE PEARLMUTTER & PAUL NELSON

ISBN: 978-0-8389-1085-6

BUILD A GREAT TEAM
One Year to Success

CATHERINE HAKALA-AUSPERK

ISBN: 978-0-8389-1170-9

THE CHALLENGE OF LIBRARY MANAGEMENT

WYOMA VANDUINKERKEN & PIXEY ANNE MOSLEY

ISBN: 978-0-8389-1102-0

BE A GREAT BOSS
One Year to Success

CATHERINE HAKALA-AUSPERK

ISBN: 978-0-8389-1068-9

GETTING STARTED WITH EVALUATION

PETER HERNON, ROBERT E. DUGAN, & JOSEPH R. MATTHEWS

ISBN: 978-0-8389-1195-2

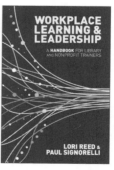

WORKPLACE LEARNING & LEADERSHIP

LORI REED & PAUL SIGNORELLI

ISBN: 978-0-8389-1082-5

Order today at **alastore.ala.org** or **866-746-7252!**

ALA Store purchases fund advocacy, awareness, and accreditation programs for library professionals worldwide.